The Singular Stiperstones

Tom Wall

Published in Great Britain by

Tom Wall, 18 Kempton, Lydbury North, Shropshire SY7 0JG
walltom@hotmail.co.uk

Copyright © Tom Wall

The author asserts the moral right to
be identified as the author of this work

ISBN 978-1-909644-17-5

Front page photo courtesy of Gordon Dickins

*Illustration on opposite page by Anne Gilbert
from the 'Ecological Flora of the Shropshire Region'*

Printed by Orphans Press Ltd, Leominster

2014

The Singular Stiperstones

Landscape, reminiscence, literature and wildlife

Tom Wall

Dedicated to the people of The Stiperstones
on whose kindness, reminiscences and photographs
I have so freely drawn

Contents

Acknowledgements

The Stiperstones has inspired a whole shelf of literature – novels, children's books, memoirs, reminiscences, travelogues, descriptive and academic studies and mining history. It is this literature that provides the running theme for my narrative, and I owe a major debt to all those on whose writings and reminiscences I have drawn. Three sources in particular require immediate acknowledgement: the novels of Mary Webb, principally *The Golden Arrow* (1916) and *Gone to Earth* (1917); the compilations of oral reminiscence entitled *Never on a Sunday: memories of the Stiperstones mining communities* (2000) and *Once Upon a Hill: the lost communities of the Stiperstones* (2011); and the memoirs of George Evans, Bill Francis, Jeanette Merry and Iris Muriel Jones. Without these three sources *The Singular Stiperstones* would have been a meagre offering.

I am grateful for permissions to make extensive use of these and other publications. These have come from Shropshire Mines Trust for *Never on a Sunday*; Natural England for *Once Upon a Hill*; the family of the late George Evans for *A Voice from the Hills*; Vince Jones for *Stiperstones Child*; Peter Francis for *Hasty Pudding and Kettle Broth*; Eleanor Welham for *The Rock*; Wynford Wyke for *Walk With Me*; the Estate of the late Michael Powell for *Million Dollar Movie*; the Estate of the late Malcolm Saville for various of his books; Justin Coldwell for *A Tale of Two Houses*; Val Littlehales for *Mild Cedric*; and Gladys Mary Coles for *The Flower of Light: a biography of Mary Webb*, including an extract from the diary of Sarah Alice Scott. Richard Grenville Clark, artistic and literary executor of the late Frederick Carter, kindly gave permission for his work to be reproduced; Shropshire Caving and Mining Club extended permission for the reproduction of drawings by the late Malcolm Newton; Natural England permitted the use of unpublished information about The Stiperstones National Nature Reserve; and James Lawson and David Pannett generously shared unpublished writings with me.

I am grateful to numerous photographers, artists and their families for allowing me to use their work. Many have allowed me to use their images free of charge; their generosity is acknowledged by the words 'courtesy of' in the attributions. I am particularly indebted to Gordon Dickins, Paul Glendell, Nigel Jones, John Mason, Ben Osborne, John Robinson and Dan Wrench who provided a range of royalty-free images for me to choose from.

Historic images taken by unknown photographers have been kindly and readily lent by many from the local community; their names appear alongside their photos. Margaret Lock gave permission to use images collected by her late husband, Ken; some of these have been copied from his surviving collection, others from existing publications. Eleanor Welham provided photos of her great aunts, Jeanette and Dolly Merry, and of their cottage at The Rock. One at least of these was taken by the late A P (Peter) Wallace and good fortune led me to his photo albums dating from the 1950s to the 1970s; they are now in the care of his daughter, Jillian Wallace, and I am very grateful to her, and her sister, Jennifer Wallace, for allowing me to use them. And it is pleasing to be able to include photos taken by the late Charles Sinker, for which I am indebted to his daughter, Rebecca.

The staff of Shropshire Archives (a remarkable institution) have been endlessly helpful, as have various librarians, most notably those of the former English Nature (in particular Jean Batty and Morag Daines) and of Shropshire Council. Nick Southwick, Jane Price and Kelvin Lake have responded patiently, helpfully and promptly to multiple queries. Simon Cooter, my successor as Senior Site Manager on The Stiperstones, has kindly hosted many forays into files and records at the National Nature Reserve office.

I am much indebted to a range of experts who have read chapters, given encouragement, pointed out errors and suggested improvements: Peter Toghill, Michael Rosenbaum and Andrew Jenkinson (geology); David Pannett (geology and land use history); Ivor Brown (mining and tourism); Michael Shaw and Steve Holding (mining); Andy Cuckson (mining and transport); the late Jennifer Westwood (lore and legend); Gladys Mary Coles and Susan Higginbotham (Mary Webb); Mark O'Hanlon (Malcolm Saville and Magdalene Weale); Richard Grenville Clark (Frederick Carter); Philip Oswald, Ian Trueman, Sue Townsend, Will Prestwood, Sarah Whild, Pete Boardman, Nigel Jones and Simon Cooter (wildlife); and Hugh Hannaford (archaeology). I owe special 'thankyous' to Cassy Clayton, Jane Price and Isobel James who read and commented on the entire text. But in all cases I take responsibility for any residual errors of fact or interpretation. I have striven for accuracy but if readers notice any mistakes I do hope they will put me right.

Peter Francis has done much over the years to root out some of the well-concealed truths and legends of the area and I have made extensive use of his writings, published and unpublished. I am greatly indebted to him for his spade-work, help, suggestions, pointers and encouragement, and for sharing his knowledge so generously with me.

I owe thanks to many others for their help in a variety of ways, and I regret that because I have taken so long (more than 10 years) to complete my text they may by now have forgotten the assistance they rendered. Nevertheless my thanks go to Albyn Austin; Margaret Austin; Richard Beaumond; Duncan and John Bennett; Suzanne Bosman; Steve Brown; the late Peggy Chidley; the Cook family; Steve Crook (Powell & Pressburger Appreciation Society); Joan Daniels; Mike Dennis (Stiperstones Brass); Gordon Dickins; David Evans; Noel Evans; Pat Evans; Brian Faulkner; the late Jack Foley; Bob Fowke and Steve Edwards (YouCaxton); the late Margaret Gelling; Sarah Gibson, John Hughes and Jan McKelvey (Shropshire Wildlife Trust); Emily Green (National Coal Mining Museum); Aidan Hart; Doris Hewitt; Chris Hogarth; Simon Holloway; Peter Howell; Julia Ionides; Sandra Johnson; Caroline Jones; Brenda Jones; Kevin Lane and The Industrial Railway Society; Mark Lawley; Muriel Lewis;

ACKNOWLEDGEMENTS

Verna Lewis; Ken Lucas; Cameron Moffett (English Heritage); Andrew Morrison (British Geological Survey); Linda Pearson; George Peterken; David Poynton; Will Prestwood; Margaret Price; Derek and Jean Rowson; Seabury Salmon; Helen Sample; Hilary Saville; Barney Rolfe-Smith; Brian Janes and Ross Shimmon of The Colonel Stephens Railway Museum and The Colonel Stephens Society; Shropshire Caving and Mining Club; Shropshire Family History Society; Shropshire Mines Trust; Father Silouan; Rebecca and Mark Sinker; Paul Stamper; Ken Stott; John Thompson; Amanda Tomkins (Scenesetters); Sal Tonge; Linda Tonkin (Black Country Geological Society); John Tucker; Chris Walker; Elizabeth Wall; Sophie Watson (Clwyd-Powys Archaeological Trust); Frances and John Williams (Music at Leasowes Bank) and Moyra Stewart Wyllie.

Finally, and most importantly, Gisèle Wall has contributed endless hard work, patience, help, encouragement and drive; she has scanned and meticulously clarified images, taken photos, drawn figures, provided IT support, done the indexing, designed and laid out the text, and maintained the momentum needed to complete the project. Without her, *The Singular Stiperstones* would be no more than a plurality of drafts.

'The hill': an introduction

There is not, perhaps, a more singular feature in the physical geography of England than the Stiper Stones.

Roderick Murchison *The Silurian System* (1839)

The Man Stone

An imposing pillar of rock juts up from beside the high point of The Stiperstones. This statuesque, faintly humanoid monolith must surely be why the immediately adjacent tor is named Manstone Rock. The tor caps the five-mile-long ridge of The Stiperstones, the most distinctive wild skyline in Shropshire. It is a landscape which, in the opinion of the celebrated nineteenth century geologist Sir Roderick Murchison, has a physical geography unsurpassed perhaps in its singularity by any other in England. The Man Stone is the figurehead for this remarkable ridge and its extraordinary surroundings, a place to which the eye is drawn from miles around and to which, over the millennia, successive generations have turned in pursuit of survival and enrichment, mystery and science, life and literature, beauty and wildlife, exercise and pleasure. These various pursuits have added new

The Man Stone

This photograph, taken by Michael Martin, was the winning entry in a competition held in 2007 to mark the 25th anniversary of the declaration of The Stiperstones National Nature Reserve.

layers of singularity to The Stiperstones; they are explored in the chapters that follow.

Wild though this place is, mining lured a numerous community to its flanks, bringing man and the environment together in a way that makes man central to its story. But it is a story that starts before mining commenced. The grazing and berry crops of The Stiperstones have been exploited since, it is assumed, the Bronze Age, when the ridge was chosen too as a place to bury the dead. Iron Age people found a fine site here for a hill-fort. Miners from Roman times onwards have dug in search of its minerals. Edric, a Saxon warrior, was doubtless attracted by its wildness, and this may also appeal to the Devil and to Shropshire's ghosts and its witches who coven here. Over the last two centuries geologists have investigated its rocks and topography, naturalists its wildlife and, more recently, mine historians its adits and shafts. Meanwhile, writers of fiction and travel books have found inspiration in its spectacular landscape and its overlays of human history, legend and natural history, and in recent years local people have committed their memories to tape and to print. The writings and witness of this diverse and numerous company have inspired this book.

Writers and narrators

The Singular Stiperstones seeks to be a well-informed guide to some of the more important aspects of this exceptional place but it does not pretend to be an exhaustive account and it offers little in the way of original research, seeking instead to bring diverse observations together in an original way. It is a personal account and a discursive one, an exploration of topics that have aroused my curiosity over the years and which may, I hope, be of interest to others. It explores some obscure upland by-ways and, perhaps, a few cul-de-sacs too. But it is about people as much as place, seeking to honour through their writings and narrations those who have by word and deed made The Stiperstones what it is – a place where questing man and a demanding environment have come together, creating, within quite a narrow compass, a multitude of small but interesting narratives.

Successive generations of hill-folk and miners have left their mark on this landscape. In the words of Ellis Peters (see Chapter 6) it 'retains the impress of all those departed generations of labour and activity, pulsating in its present silence and loneliness'. The landscape, the human 'impress' and the folk-lore engender the *genius loci* of The Stiperstones, its 'spirit of place'. Writers have drawn on this spirit, have framed their readership's perceptions of the place and have left in turn their own indefinable trace. None more so than Mary Webb (see Chapter 5), who expresses something of this ongoing process in *The Golden Arrow*: 'The personality of a man reacting upon the spirit of a place produces something which is neither the man nor the place ... This third entity, born of the union, becomes a power and a haunting presence – non-human, non-material'. I hope that this book will convey something of all of these elements: the landscape together with its wildlife, the folk-lore, 'the impress' of generations of labour and activity, the indefinable traces left by writers and narrators and the 'haunting presence' of the place.

At the core of *The Singular Stiperstones* are the words of these writers and narrators. I have chosen the word 'narrators' for those from the local community who have committed their reminiscences to tape, parts of which have appeared in the local oral history publications *Never on a Sunday* and *Once Upon a Hill*. To this rich store of recollection can be added memoirs contributed by three local individuals, Bill Francis, George Evans and Muriel Jones (née Smith) and some poetry too. Through the words of these writers and narrators, across more than a century and a half of publication, this book explores some of the principal facets of this genuinely iconic Shropshire landscape. In doing so, fact is used to shed light on fiction, and vice versa.

For many of those on whose experiences and words I draw, The Stiperstones has been a home and a work place, for others it has been a research site, a holiday retreat or somewhere visited in passing, and a number have used it as a dramatic backdrop for fictional events. Their perceptions, both fictional and factual, provide the framework for this book. Amongst them are a number of people of some renown, either within the local community, or more widely, and their importance to the story of The Stiperstones is acknowledged by outlining their personal histories.

Extensive use is made of the reminiscences of older residents. Many are still with us but sadly some have passed on. I have decided to treat all of their narrations in the present tense rather than jumping from present to past and back again. I hope that this will not cause offence to the bereaved and that they will feel that the memory of those who have died lives on through their recollections.

Alongside the literary storehouse of The Stiperstones there is a photographic one. A relatively numerous local population and a photogenic landscape have helped create an important resource which I have drawn on repeatedly to enrich my text. Many of these photos are historic and have not previously been published, so I have captioned them at length in order to put their interest and significance on record.

The text touches on the everyday, but the esoteric too, and whilst some of the more obscure points are referenced in endnotes, to acknowledge the source of every piece of information would have involved a plethora of notes and a more academic approach. I have however aimed to include all my sources in the extensive bibliography, both as acknowledgement of my indebtedness to others and as an aid to those who wish to investigate particular topics more fully.

'The hill'

The Stiperstones is a topographic feature as shown on the map to be found inside the back cover of this book. A heather-clad ridge, it runs from southwest to northeast and is capped by a series of major rock outcrops of a type referred to

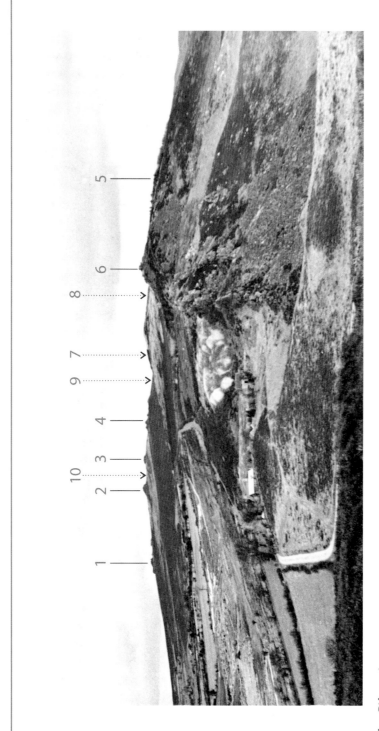

The Stiperstones

Taken in 1954 from Black Rhadley Hill looking northeast, this photo shows, on the far horizon, from left to right, the Devil's Chair (1), Manstone Rock (the highest point) (2), Saddle Rock (3) and Cranberry Rock (4) (a group of outcrops). Closer to, on the right hand side of the ridge, the conifers of Big Wood (5) are just discernible against the horizon – it was the only conifer plantation then visible from this point. To the left of the plantation, high ground obscures Nipstone Rock, while closer to, The Rock (6), stands above Rock Cottage, the holiday home of Miss Merry (see Chapter 9), but the cottage is hidden from view. In the centre of the photo are pale mounds of mine spoil (7) to the right of which stands another tor, which does not have a name (8). Immediately below the spoil is a cottage (now gone) (9) and to the left, Rock Farm (10), once the home of Bill Francis (see Chapter 9); it survives, but is no longer a farm. Photo A P Wallace.

by geologists as 'tors'. It is always called '**T**he Stiperstones', and, at the expense of typographical simplicity and elegance, this is the form used throughout this book. But for those that live on its flanks, it is simply 'the hill'. It looms steeply above them, blocking the view, but from its summit vast panoramas are opened across Shropshire and neighbouring counties, and deep into Wales, where Cader Idris sits hunched on the horizon and on clear days the pinnacle of Snowdon can be picked out pointing skywards.

The ridge of the hill is cleft on its western flank by a series of steep-sided 'beaches' or 'dingles': Tankerville Hollow, Perkins Beach, Mytton Beach, Black Hole, Crowsnest Dingle and Snailbeach. Ellis Peters draws out the contrast between ridge and 'beach': 'While the long crest stands open and jagged against the sky, the side valleys give shelter to abundant tree cover in a complex of beautiful and almost secret places laced with little racing brooks'. By contrast, 'on its eastern flank The Stiperstones declines gradually through a wealth of varied heathland and fields and plantation into the valley of the East Onny'.

Heath and heathland are the words used throughout this book to describe the principal plant community of the hill, in which Common Heather (also known as Ling) is dominant. Some might refer to the habitat as 'moorland', but it lacks the deep, damp, peaty soils that this term normally suggests. Soils on The Stiperstones are generally shallow, and although the hill rises to nearly 1,800 feet and experiences some of the extremes of the uplands, the plant and animal life of The Stiperstones have affinities with heathland (normally a lowland habitat) as well as with moorland.

We think of heathland as a dry-ground habitat and The Stiperstones is not quite as wet a place as it may seem to the many who have come away from it rain-soaked and wind-swept. Noel Evans of Tankerville has been taking daily weather readings for more than 25 years. His weather station, known to the Met Office as 'Pennerley', is part of the official national network of recording locations. Here, over the 20 years 1987-2006, Noel recorded an annual average of 920.8mm (36¼ inches) of rain. His station stands at 1,171 feet above sea level, and although this is a good way up the flank of the hill, rainfall will be greater 585 or so feet higher up, at the summit. Nevertheless, when the Pennerley average is compared to the Met Office's average for Wales of 57½ inches, it seems that The Stiperstones lies in something of a rain-shadow.

Boundaries

Black Rhadley Hill is the southern extremity of the area covered by this book and The Hollies, near Lordshill, the northern. These boundaries truncate the geology, but respect long usage, as explained in 1839 by Roderick Murchison:

> 'Although the Heathmont [Heath Mynd], west of Linley, constitutes geologically the south-western termination of this ridge of quartz rock, and Pontesbury the north-eastern extremity, thus giving the range a length of ten miles, the central or lofty portion for about four miles [actually five] is alone known in the country under the name of the Stiper Stones.'

And what about the western and eastern boundaries of the area? On the west side the boundary is taken to be the road running north from Black Rhadley Hill through The Bog and the village of Stiperstones, to Snailbeach. On the east side it follows the paths, tracks and roads that run northeast from Black Rhadley Hill via Great Wood House to The Knolls, passing then below the former Gatten Plantation and along the eastern side of The Paddock through to Upper Vessons. These boundaries encompass the ridge of The Stiperstones, but they are, of course, artificial, and from time to time, particularly when the story is a good one, they are surreptitiously stretched.

The area enclosed within these boundaries, as shown on the map inserted within the back cover, amounts to some 2,800 acres. It encompasses all of The Stiperstones and The Hollies Site of Special Scientific Interest (1,453 acres), which, in turn, embraces The Stiperstones National Nature Reserve (1,174 acres), and all but 4 acres of the 17 acre Pennerley Meadows Site of Special Scientific Interest, 2 acres of which is included within the National Nature Reserve. These sometimes confusing designations are of real importance, but they can get in the way of an appreciation of the wider Stiperstones landscape as both a visually and ecologically coherent unit.

The integrity of this unit, the central five-mile stretch of the ridge, has been compromised over the last half century by land-use change. Agriculture and forestry overran the ridge at The Knolls, splitting the area in two, with most of the southern half of The Stiperstones being literally lost to view behind a shroud of conifers. Out of sight has meant out of mind, and until recent years, many of the studies of the site's geology and wildlife have overlooked the land south of The Knolls, despite it being an integral part of the ridge. This oversight has been compounded by the understandable adoption of the name 'The Stiperstones' for the National Nature Reserve, which runs only from The Knolls northwards.

The *Back to purple* project (see Chapter 10) is seeking to redress the situation on the ground, restoring the whole of the ridge to heathland. This book shares its objective by treating the whole of the ridge from Black Rhadley through to The Hollies as The Stiperstones, as did Murchison, and as have successive generations of cartographers, who have repeatedly inscribed the name all the way along the spine of the hill.

The tors: 'rugged cyclopean ruins' …

The tors of The Stiperstones are its dominant and most dramatic feature. Murchison described them as 'broken and serrated edges … they stand out on the crest of the ridge at short intervals, like rugged cyclopean ruins, some of the principal of which are about 50 or 60 feet high and about 120 or 130 feet in width'.

There is no tor as such on 'Black Rhadley Hill' but there are some cliff-like exposures just southwest of its summit. Moving northeast, at the former Rock Farm and 'The Rock' are two outcrops from which chaotic masses of stone run down steep slopes, creating some of the most impressive rock scenery

The highest tors

Above: An etching from Murchison's *Silurian System* (1939). The artist, T Webster, was standing beside Scattered Rocks, looking southwest towards, from right to left, the Devil's Chair, followed by two un-named outcrops, and lastly, Manstone Rock, the highest point of the ridge.

Below: The same view in a photo of August 2008, courtesy of Andrew Allott, who took it for his book *The Marches* (2011).

Black Rhadley Hill

Rock outcrop at the southwestern extremity of Black Rhadley. This photo of 1960 was taken by A P Wallace looking across the valley of the River West Onny to Corndon.

Nipstone Rock

This photo of 1954 by A P Wallace includes his wife, Olive, and their daughters Jennifer (on the left) and Jillian. The dog's name is Trudi and the head of the Nipstone Pig is evident in the outline of the right hand half of the rock; it is looking to the right.

Cranberry Rock

This profile explains the alternative name of Lion Rock. The lion couchant looks to the right. Photo, 2013, Gisèle Wall.

of the whole hill. From there, continuing northeast, the ridge runs on via a modest exposure to 'Nipstone Rock', and then through un-named outcrops to 'Cranberry Rock', a good place for finding the red berries of the 'dwarf-shrub' locally referred to as Cranberry but which botanists call Cowberry *Vaccinium vitis-idaea*. 'Cranberry Rock' is sometimes called 'Lion Rock', and when viewed from the side, one can pick out the profile of a lion lying down with its head pointing to the southwest.

The Ordnance Survey records no name for the next three tors. The first is a low and jagged crest. The second is not a tor, properly speaking, but a photogenic pile of boulders; the angularity of the most upstanding one gives the group as a whole the local name 'Diamond Rock'. The third is sometimes called 'Saddle Rock' as, in profile, it forms the pommel of a saddle which runs to 'Manstone Rock'. As already indicated, this latter tor is taken to derive its name from the detached pillar jutting up like an Easter Island statue at its northern end, but

Diamond Rock

Looking towards Cranberry Rock with Heath Mynd beyond. Photo, circa 2002, courtesy of Gordon Dickins.

Manstone Rock

The Man Stone is on the left and the Ordnance Survey triangulation pillar on the summit. Photo, 2013, Gisèle Wall.

The Devil's Chair

'The Chair loomed over them … like a fist flourished in the face.' (Mary Webb *The Golden Arrow*). A painting by Pat Evans of Tankerville, reproduced courtesy of the artist.

the name 'Pinnacle Rock' is sometimes used too, presumably because of the man-made triangulation pillar on the summit of the tor, marking the highest point of The Stiperstones, 536 metres (1,759 feet) above sea level.[1]

Running on northeast, two imposing but anonymous tors on the east side of the ridge-path, are followed shortly, on the west side, by the 'Devil's Chair', a long and narrow outcrop terminating in a wide, grassy, chair-like depression with two arm-rests, large enough to seat a devil of gargantuan proportions. Why the Chair should have the Devil's name on it is the matter of legend, but, as Ellis Peters remarks, when it comes to the naming of eye-catching outcrops, 'the Devil is always liable to take a hand, claiming all the best landmarks as well as all the best tunes'.[2]

Beyond the 'Devil's Chair' lies 'Scattered Rocks', an apt name for a discontinuous series of low exposures. They are followed by 'Shepherd's Rock' which was doubtless used in the past by graziers as a lookout from which to survey their flocks, or indeed to guard them, as an earlier name is the 'Wolfestone'.[3] A run of smaller tors follows, sometimes referred to collectively as 'Habberley

Rocks', the biggest of which is an impressive feature; from here, paths lead on eventually to the village of that name.

... and 'watching monsters'

Descriptions of the tors are legion, to be found in factual accounts going back to William Camden's *Britannia* (1586-1607): 'great heapes of stone and little rockes ... that rise thicke together'.[4] Archdeacon Joseph Plymley (1803) observes the 'bare and ragged summits, resembling the ruins of walls and castles'. Walter White (1860) sees them as 'the bare spines of some fossil monster, huger than imagination ever dreamt of'. G H Morton (1869) writes of 'a succession of projecting crags which stand out in towering grandeur'. For A G Bradley (1905) they are 'uncanny monoliths'. Magdalene Weale (1935) remembers 'that gaunt range ... virile and hard with the hardness of immense age, and crowned with its strange outcrops of black quartzite like so many ruined fortresses'. S P B Mais (1939) describes the 'black quartzite crags rising along the ridge of the Stiperstones like the fin of a fish'. For H W Timperley (1947) it is 'the sombre crag-notched spine of the Stiperstones ... harsh and often saturnine ... like a barren and jagged wilderness on the edge of the world', while for Jeanette Merry (1979) 'these ancient Stiperstones rocks jut out like watching monsters keeping guard over the slopes below'. In a poem of 1983 Allister Fraser evokes 'these castled stones' which 'protrude through Shropshire soil like shattered bones'. Ellis Peters (1999) refers to 'the antediluvian lizard-length of The Stiperstones' and Jim Perrin (2003) to 'the long ridge ... capped and crested ... by shattered tors of quartzite'.

The 'cyclopean ruins' have also figured in fiction (see Chapters 5 and 6). For D H Lawrence, in his novella *St Mawr* (1925), the ridge is 'one of those places where the spirit of aboriginal England still lingers, the old savage England' and Malcolm Saville in *Seven White Gates* (1944), a children's adventure story, describes 'the great bulk of the Stiperstones crowned with the black, sinister quartzite rocks'. Mary Webb, in her novel *The Golden Arrow* (1916), focuses on the most celebrated of these rocks, the Devil's Chair:

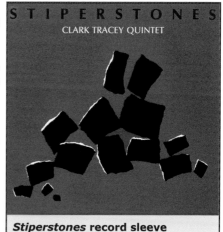

STIPERSTONES
CLARK TRACEY QUINTET

***Stiperstones* record sleeve**

Designed by Fiona Tracey for Steam Records, 1987; reproduced courtesy of Clark Tracey.

> 'Nothing ever altered its look. Dawn quickened over it in pearl and emerald; summer sent the armies of heather to its very foot; snow rested there as doves nest in cliffs. It remained inviolable, taciturn, evil. It glowered darkly on the dawn; it came through the snow like jagged bones through flesh; before its hardness even the venturesome cranberries were discouraged.'

The Devil's Chair has inspired music too, thanks to an annual festival held at Leasowes

Bank, a hill-top former farm a mile and half to the east of The Stiperstones from where the tors etch a jagged horizon.[5] In 1987 'Music at Leasowes Bank' commissioned a jazz suite from two up-and-coming young composers, Clark Tracey and Steve Melling; their composition, *Stiperstones*, was performed at the Festival that year by the Clark Tracey Quintet, and later recorded.[6] Some of the jagged-ness of the tors reverberates in the six vigorous movements of the suite, each named after one of the outcrops. And the music certainly rocks.

But not everyone responds positively to The Stiperstones. Alice Scott visited in July 1877 on a geological society outing from Worcestershire. The twenty-five year old's diary entry is dismissive:

> 'We were finally deposited at the foot of some hills which we climbed and were enveloped in mist. When we reached the top however, the object of the day was achieved, ie to look at some rocks called the Stiperstones. We walked some way through heather and then met the carriages which took us to the station. We were very wet and having had nothing to interest us, felt anything but pleasant when we arrived back at 11pm.'

Three years later Alice Scott married George Meredith; their first child was Mary Webb. The failure of The Stiperstones to enthuse the mother of the author was first revealed by Gladys Mary Coles in *The Flower of Light*, her biography of Mary Webb.[7]

Why the name 'Stiperstones'?

The Rev C H Hartshorne, drawing on research for his *Salopia Antiqua*, told Murchison that the name Stiper Stones 'had its origin in the Icelandic "steypa" (*fusio metallorum*), a term singularly well applied to the fused and altered rocks of the metalliferous tract'.

Richard Morgan (1997), a place name expert, does not include this possibility in his discussion of the derivation, and it would not fit with any of the old names that he lists. These start with *Tenfrestanes* (dating from 1190, and perhaps lacking an initial *S* due to French influence), and include *Stenufretames* (1226) and *Steyfrestanes* (1300). It is not until 1594 that he first finds *Stiperstones*, in William Camden's *Britannia*. The Old English words *stīpere,* meaning 'a prop or post', or *stīpele,* 'a tower', might appear to be plausible precursors but Morgan doubts a derivation directly from either, because although these words pre-date the medieval names for the place, the medieval names are clearly not derived from them. He speculates however that Stiperstones could stem from a personal name, *Stænfriþ*, with the Old English *stīpere* somehow exerting an influence and accounting for the development of the name into *Stiperstones.*

Murchison splits the name in two – 'Stiper' and 'Stones' – as if they are adjective and noun. Today the two are joined and it is always rendered as 'Stiperstones'. It is the name given to the ridge, and as such it is a singular noun. But the name also conveys plurality, seeming, whatever its derivation, to be referring to the 'tors' or 'stones' that punctuate the skyline, or the stripes of stones that calibrate its flanks.

Unlike 'Stiperstones', most of the place-names that crop up in this book seem to have straightforward derivations. 'Shepherd's Rock', 'The Hollies' or 'Crowsnest' are cases in point, although in matters of etymology things are sometimes less straightforward than they might at first appear, indeed I've been told that on one old map 'Crowsnest' appears as 'Grousenest'. Amongst other more puzzling names is 'beach'. All of the 'beaches' lie on the west side of The Stiperstones: Perkins Beach, Mytton Beach, Snailbeach and, a mile to the northwest, Wagbeach. The first two are steep-sided valleys and the other two refer to valley locations as well, but none is served by a significant watercourse. These names have parallels on the east side of The Long Mynd, where 'batch' recurs frequently in the names of the more abrupt valleys such as Nut Batch, Minton Batch and Small Batch. The Anglo-Saxon 'bœc', denoting a valley with a small stream, the north-country word 'beck,' and the German word 'bach', also meaning a brook or stream, may well be related to 'beach' and 'batch'.[8] 'Dingle', as in Crowsnest Dingle, is synonymous with 'beach' and interchangeable with it, so that some will say Mytton (or Myttons) Beach, others Mytton Dingle (indeed

Perkins Beach

Looking across the top of Perkins Beach towards the Devil's Chair. There is mine spoil in the foreground, and a sheep grazes the remnants of grassland carved out of the hill by the occupants of this former hill settlement; it is now 'going back to the hill'. Photo, July 2009, courtesy of Dan Wrench.

both are used in this text), and although the frequently heard Perkins Beach Dingle rolls easily off the tongue, it is tautological.

Another puzzling question about the 'beaches' is how they were formed. This and other geological enigmas are explored in the next chapter.

Chapter 1

'The singular Stiperstones': geology and landscape

'There ben a drove of stwone-tappers gon up to the Cheir this mornin',
a man working in the little barytes mine told me.
'Stone-tappers?' I queried, 'what are they?'
'They ben gon up to tap the stwones,'
he replied with a smile full of indulgence for a harmless pastime.

Magdalene Weale *Through the Highlands of Shropshire on Horseback* (1935)

Sir Roderick Impey Murchison

The Stiperstones excels as a geological phenomenon even in a county celebrated for its geology, and it is much visited by 'stwone-tappers'. Sir Roderick Impey Murchison (1792-1871) of whom mention has already been made, was amongst the first of a series of celebrated geologists drawn to this extraordinary place;[1] perhaps he had a hammer in hand in order to tap its stones.

Murchison confessed to having 'led in mischief' rather than application when at school. He was groomed for a career in the army, serving during the Peninsular War before resigning and marrying in 1815. The years up to 1824 he later described as his 'fox-hunting period', but thereafter, with strong support from his wife, 'who saved him from becoming a mere

Sir Roderick Impey Murchison in some of his regalia

He is sporting three of the many medals awarded to him (some, according to the *Dictionary of National Biography*, thanks to assiduous lobbying). From right to left, the medals appear to be the Order of the Bath, the Peninsula Medal and, round his neck, the Order of the Polar Star. Mezzotint by William Walker after a painting by W H Pickersgill, 1851, by permission of the Geological Society of London.

idler', he devoted his considerable energies to the pursuit of geology. He had wealth and social position, and the manner and bearing to go with them. Indeed he seems to have been somewhat over-bearing and gained an unfortunate reputation for giving inadequate credit to his co-workers and helpers. His contemporary, Dr Henry Bull, the Herefordshire polymath, once referred to him as '... that Old Grumpy conceited Sir Rodk Murchison'.[2]

Murchison travelled widely in Britain and Europe, but his principal area of study in the 1830s was Shropshire and surrounding counties. He was drawn to the county, as many geologists have been since, because of its geological diversity. As today's best-known interpreter of Shropshire geology, Peter Toghill, points out, 'of the 12 geological periods recognised, 10 are represented in Shropshire ... this is remarkable when one considers that in an area like Snowdonia only three geological periods are represented'.[3]

Murchison's particular strength was in discerning the sequence of rocks, and it was said that he could read the geology of an area with remarkable rapidity. His reading of the landscape of Shropshire and nearby counties led, in 1839, to the publication of his magisterial work *The Silurian System* which he revised several times and re-published in 1854 in a more compact form under the title *Siluria*.

Quartzite, flagstone and shale

The rocks of The Stiperstones were attributed by Murchison to what he called the Silurian period. He took the name from the tribe known as the Silures which may at one time have inhabited the Marches, and it was adopted by him as 'expressive of the deposits which lie between the old red sandstone [rocks of the Devonian period] and the slaty rocks of Wales [of the earlier Cambrian period]'.[4] The latter rocks were given their name by Murchison's sometime collaborator, sometime rival, the Reverend Professor Adam Sedgwick, and the name was used by Murchison to embrace the rocks of The Long Mynd (now attributed to the Pre-Cambrian). However, it was later found that there was some overlap between the upper part of the Cambrian of Sedgwick and the lower part of the Silurian of Murchison, and in 1887, Professor Lapworth, yet another geologist of note, proposed the name Ordovician for the overlapping sequence, naming the rocks after the Ordovices, a tribe which inhabited North Wales. So the

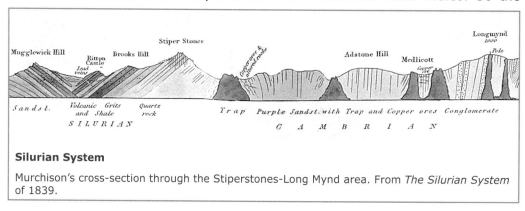

Silurian System

Murchison's cross-section through the Stiperstones-Long Mynd area. From *The Silurian System* of 1839.

sequencing became Cambrian (oldest), followed by the Ordovician, the Silurian and the Devonian.

Today the Stiperstones Quartzite is attributed, following Lapworth, to the Ordovician period (495-443 million years ago) and it forms part of what is known as the 'Shelve Inlier', an 'inlier' being an area where old rocks are surrounded by younger ones. The Shelve Inlier is an irregular area running to 43 square miles, centred approximately on the settlement of Shelve, which lies two miles west of The Stiperstones. To the south and west of the 'inlier' are rocks of the Silurian period and to the north are the Upper Coal Measures of the Carboniferous. All of these rocks were laid down more recently than the rocks of the Ordovician, but to the east lie Pre-Cambrian rocks. These are older than the rocks of the 'inlier' – a fact seemingly overlooked by those who first applied the term to the area.

This is a 'classic' geological locality, one that forms a standard or model of its kind – a 'type area'. So Shelve, described aptly enough by W T Dean, a twentieth century geologist, as 'an otherwise obscure hamlet', appears in the geological text books and is known to students of the subject across the world. Andrew Allott, author of the 'New Naturalist' volume entitled *The Marches* describes the landscape of the inlier as 'splendidly scruffy and disreputable but also wild and romantic' and deserving of a name more resonant than the 'prosaic' Shelve Inlier. He proposes 'Ordovicia', but for now the otherwise obscure hamlet retains its international renown.

The Stiperstones Quartzite was laid down in shallow water, possibly as a beach, and it lay on the southern margin of what geologists call the 'Iapetus Ocean'. Along with the rest of what is now southern Britain, it was then 65° south of the equator. There followed an extraordinary transglobal drift, a journey of 7,500 miles lasting some 500 million years at an average rate of just short of one inch a year. This imperceptible creep over unimaginable aeons of time eventually brought 'Shropshire' north from the Antarctic Circle through the tropics and across the equator to its latitude today, 52° north.

But to return to the beach, Peter Toghill explains how its sand and pebbles were bonded by a quartz cement to form a white quartz sandstone, technically described as a quartz arenite. He points out that the term quartzite is in fact a misnomer, because Stiperstones Quartzite is simply a very hard sandstone, whereas quartzite is a term normally reserved for sandstones which have been metamorphosed by heat and pressure. Wrekin Quartzite is a similar misnomer, but because these historic names are so well entrenched in the literature, geologists have chosen not to correct them.

The Stiperstones Quartzite is some 150-280 metres thick; above it and to a depth of up to 1,000 metres lie the Mytton Flags, and then 240 metres of Hope Shales; to the east lie the Shineton Shales. The flags are muddier and weaker than the quartzite and were laid down in deeper water; the Hope Shales are made up of very fine particles deposited at still greater depth. It is the Mytton

Aerial view from Windy Corner

Looking northeast along the northern two thirds of the ridge, October 1977. Much of the area from Manstone Rock to near the Devil's Chair is showing white where plants and soils have been burned off and lichens seared from the stones by the summer fire of 1976; the Devil's Chair itself stands just beyond the area of damage. The pale line of a firebreak bulldozed by the Forestry Commission snakes up from left to right across the ridge, just short of the Chair; it emerges again from the right hand edge of the photo having been driven along the west and south boundary of the Gatten Plantation. Near the bottom of the photo a path winds up through the heather from Windy Corner to Cranberry Rock. Below Windy Corner is some recently cultivated ground with areas of dark peaty-looking soils and surviving fragments of heathland to their left, since erased. The white blob in the grassland towards the bottom left is the cottage formerly occupied by Bert Johnson (see *Once Upon a Hill* page 15), it too has been erased. This is one of a series of now historic aerial photos taken by Will Prestwood (Shropshire Wildlife Trust) and Chris Walker and Colin Hayes (Nature Conservancy Council). Reproduced courtesy of Natural England.

Flags which harbour the mineral veins which are of such importance in the history of The Stiperstones.

Earth movements at the end of the Ordovician period, referred to by Peter Toghill as 'the Shelveian event', creased the rocks, including the Stiperstones Quartzite, into quite tight folds, tilting the former beach up at a sharp angle, 80 degrees in places, so that it poked skywards forming the ridge of the hill. The ridge is visible for miles around, including from Attingham Park, the stately home which lies some 13 miles away, southeast of Shrewsbury. From 1751 to 1818 the Hills of Attingham owned the Gatten Estate which embraced the eastern flank of The Stiperstones. Richard Pugh, who had been Bailiff and Gamekeeper on the Estate, is recorded in 1840 as remembering 'the southeast or Gatten side of the Great Rocks [the name then applied to the Devil's Chair and its now nameless companions] being whitewashed as an object of family property to be plainer seen from Attingham'.[5]

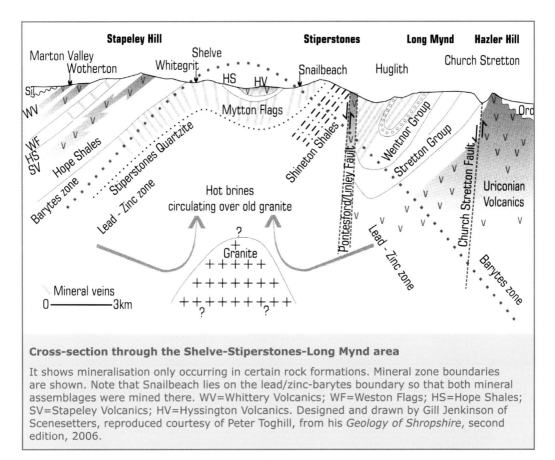

Cross-section through the Shelve-Stiperstones-Long Mynd area

It shows mineralisation only occurring in certain rock formations. Mineral zone boundaries are shown. Note that Snailbeach lies on the lead/zinc-barytes boundary so that both mineral assemblages were mined there. WV=Whittery Volcanics; WF=Weston Flags; HS=Hope Shales; SV=Stapeley Volcanics; HV=Hyssington Volcanics. Designed and drawn by Gill Jenkinson of Scenesetters, reproduced courtesy of Peter Toghill, from his *Geology of Shropshire*, second edition, 2006.

Setting aside this temporary whitening, many of the descriptions of the quartzite tors stress their blackness. They may indeed appear black against the light, and from a distance, but they are in fact grey, and then only because of a surface film of lichens. As H W Timperley points out, 'if the weather-stains and the lichen were cleaned from [the] rocks … how the hill-top would dazzle in the sunlight!'. This is because the Stiperstones Quartzite is actually whitish in colour and includes sparkling crystals, described by Murchison as 'numerous small white facets of quartz crystals, presenting a vivid contrast to the dull brown heath over which they are strewn'. The point was not lost on Mary Webb. In *The Golden Arrow*, John Arden tells Stephen Southernwood, who can't see beyond the blackness of the Devil's Chair, that 'if you only look you can see all colours in that black rock, all colours and sparkling white'.

Stephen, immature, overwrought, and cowed by circumstance and landscape, attempts to 'knock the old Chair to blazes' with dynamite, but makes 'little more difference … than a woodpecker makes to a tree on which he hammers'. So he fantasises about reducing the unyielding quartzite of the Chair to powder in the rock crusher at the 'Lostwithin Spar Mine'. Its hardness and integrity would have defeated him. They make cutting and splitting impractical too, and because of this, and its haphazard angularity, with few stones offering straight faces

The Paddock House

This well-built house is constructed of what were, no doubt, carefully selected but still irregular blocks of Stiperstones Quartzite; they contrast with the regularity of the brick-work. The photo shows Thomas and Elizabeth Edwards in front of their home with three of their seven children, Bert, George and Mabel.[6] Photo, circa 1907, courtesy of Verna Lewis, Mabel's daughter-in-law.

Joe Roberts's cottage

This cottage, built of Mytton Flags, stands in Crowsnest Dingle. Photo, 2009, courtesy of Gordon Dickins.

and good cornerstones being a rarity, Stiperstones Quartzite is a troublesome building material. It is this awkwardness in the stone that must explain why, despite The Stiperstones being such a stony place, there are few dry-stone walls, boundaries being delineated instead by stone-faced banks incorporating a pronounced batter and much soil. And why, on the populous west flank of the hill, most cottages are built not with Stiperstones Quartzite but with the rather more amenable Mytton Flags.

The Stiperstones Quartzite, referred to locally as Stiper Stone, has however been used as the base for many miles of local roads, and in *Never on a Sunday* Henry Jones recalls that it was also taken to Shawbury, Sleap and Cosford airfields: 'For a couple of years there was a team of men with sledge hammers breaking the stone … to about six inches in size … they worked all along the ridge … The first bed of each runway was six inch stone'. Piles of stones, most obviously at Nipstone Rock, still provide evidence of stone breaking. Here, and elsewhere along the ridge, the stone for breaking was simply picked off the surface, but it was quarried near Pontesbury, at Polesgate and the Nills (where Mary Webb lived in 1916 while writing *Gone to Earth*). Here a mechanical rock crusher was used, but it is said locally that the quarrying of the Stiperstones Quartzite was eventually abandoned because, due to the hardness of the stone, the cost of replacing the teeth of the crusher outweighed the value of the stone that was produced.

Periglacial features

The tors

Allister Fraser, in his poem 'On The Stiperstones' describes the tors as 'These brooding crags, born in the remorseless grind/Of ice …', and they were indeed shaped by ice, despite standing proud of the ice sheet. The consensus is that the tors took on their present outline during the Devensian (Last) Glaciation, which peaked 18,000 years ago. At that time The Stiperstones was close to, but not over-topped, by the ice sheet, which reached the Strettons, six miles to the east, and the Rea Valley, three miles to the west. Climatic conditions were nevertheless extremely severe, with the hill locked in the vice of permafrost. This worked on moisture trapped in the joints of the quartzite, expanding it by 10% as it froze, thereby jacking out piece after piece of rock. Gradually, over millennia, this process wore away the less resistant areas, particularly where the rocks were most closely jointed, leaving the less jointed rock-masses upstanding and surviving as the tors. The process was prolonged and remorseless and although they strike us today as very impressive features, the tors are merely the occasional and severely eroded remnants of the pre-glacial landscape. It has been suggested that the original surface has been lowered by up to 18 metres,[7] and even in the area from Cranberry Rock to Shepherd's Rock, where the tors are of most frequent incidence, they now occupy only some 15% of the line of the ridge.[8]

Rocks along the ridge encased in ice

Photo, 1998, courtesy of Gordon Dickins.

Having been shaped in the vicinity of, but not by, glacial action, the tors are referred to as 'periglacial' features ('peri' meaning near or adjacent). Other periglacial features of The Stiperstones are the beaches, stone stripes and rock platforms. The elements continue of course to weather these features (generally imperceptibly, although occasionally a larger block may fall away from the tors), but the major processes by which the landscape was formed are no longer active. They can only be inferred from observations of what remains *in situ* and comparisons with other parts of the world where periglacial processes are still active.

Mary Webb perceives the relict, fossilised, nature of the landscape: 'this [the quartzite] wore so slowly that many centuries would do no perceptible work on it … such pieces as sometimes broke off and crashed down the slope were only, compared with the pile, like marbles dropped from a palace window'.[9]

The beaches

How were the 'beaches', the impressive, steep-sided but short valleys of The Stiperstones formed? Malcolm Saville, the children's writer (see Chapter 6), describes 'the almost precipitous walls of Mytton Dingle [Beach] thrusting into the side of The Stiperstones as if the Devil, who has made this mountain his own, had cut a great wedge from it'. Searching for a more prosaic explanation, the geologist G H Morton, a contemporary of Murchison, notes that 'the present rivulets and streams seem to be very inadequate to cause any great change in the valleys along which they flow'. But he also notes the steepness of the gradients, and in glacial times, during periods of thaw, when much larger volumes of water would have flowed down the hillsides, the topography would have given velocity and erosive power to these melt waters.

The Beaches

From left to right: Crowsnest Dingle (largely hidden), Mytton Beach and Perkins Beach. Stiperstones Village is bottom left, and the south facing slope of Tankerville Hollow is bottom right. Photo, October 1977, by Will Prestwood *et al*, reproduced courtesy of Natural England.

On occasion over recent centuries there have been telling reminders of the immense force of flood waters. The 'Shrewsbury Chronicle' reported that on 27 May 1811 there was a violent storm of hail, such that

> 'near the Snailbach [*sic*], hailstones two inches in circumference lay almost a foot deep. About five o'clock in the afternoon, a cloud burst upon the ridge of hills called the Stiperstones, and a torrent of water, with irresistible force, and thundering sound, rushing down the hill side, swept away several cottages belonging to the Snailbach miners.'

Downstream, three people from Minsterley lost their lives and nine from Pontesford. So much water flowed down the Rea Brook that when it reached the English Bridge at Shrewsbury, the Severn is said to have risen four feet in less than ten minutes.

An indication of the erosive power of floodwater can also be gained from the so-called 'Flooded Wires' at the head of Mytton Beach. These are four deep scars running, in parallel, straight down the very steep hillside; they are said to have been carved virtually overnight by storm-water. The date is not known, but local opinion favours the early years of the twentieth century. In *The Golden*

Flooded Wires

Looking across Mytton Beach to the 'wires' which run straight down the slope into Mytton Beach from the saddle of mine spoil at the top of Perkins Beach. The Devil's Chair is just visible in the far distance. Autumn tints are colouring the bracken. Photo, 2013, Gisèle Wall.

Arrow, published in 1916, Mary Webb makes what appear to be two references to them. She describes the hill as having 'as many gashes and fissures as an old tree – one especially, where there had once been a cloud-burst, went almost sheer to the level of the plain'. And she writes of Stephen Southernwood and Deborah Arden gathering Foxgloves from what could well be the recently cut 'Flooded Wires'. Foxgloves erupt on recently disturbed ground, and the young lovers go to where 'the hill was gashed for nearly its whole height, and a tide of foxgloves rolled sheer from top to bottom like arterial blood'.

Stone stripes

Richard Clark, who has studied and written about the periglacial features of The Stiperstones in considerable detail, compares them to landforms occupying much more extensive areas on the Falkland Islands. He describes not just the tors, but also 'stone stripes' and 'rock platforms', and he compares the former, for which The Stiperstones is particularly well-known amongst geologists, with the 'stone-rivers' of the Falklands.

Stone stripes on the western flank of the ridge

Manstone Rock (left) and Saddle Rock (right) show as grey islands amongst paler stone near the centre of this aerial photo taken looking northeast across part of the ridge on 30 March 1955; they are virtually linked by what could be a patch of late-lying snow running across the slope. Numerous stone stripes run down the near side of the ridge; curiously a number seem to be paired, being joined at the top. Beyond the ridge, conifers are dotted across the Gatten Plantation, the residue it seems of a nineteenth century planting felled in the 1930s (the area was left unplanted until the 1960s, see Chapters 9 and 10). Photo from Cambridge University Collection of Aerial Photography (ref P196).

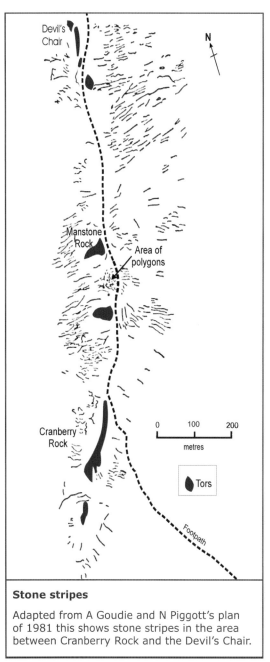

Stone stripes

Adapted from A Goudie and N Piggott's plan of 1981 this shows stone stripes in the area between Cranberry Rock and the Devil's Chair.

It is only in aerial photographs that the sheer number of these stripes becomes apparent. A particularly striking photo (previous page), taken in 1955, shows the bands of pale stone alternating with the darker colours of the heather in the area of Saddle and Manstone Rocks; they pattern the hillside like piano keys.[10] In 1981 A Goudie and N Piggott published a plan based on measurements they had made of the stripes in this central area of the ridge. They found that the stone stripes have mean widths of about 3 metres, as do the intervening strips of vegetated ground, although some stripes are as much as 7-10 metres wide. Most of the stones in the stripes are 0.2 to 0.8 metres in length, but many are bigger, attaining lengths of as much as 2.5 metres. They are heavy and angular, never rounded, and the slopes over which they have spread are shallow, typically inclined at only 7-12 degrees. Today the material is stable – it is made up of large, angular blocks which are going nowhere – yet in the past, they have moved long distances. Although individual stripes can generally only be traced over distances of up to 50-70 metres, material has migrated down-slope as much as 300 metres from its presumed point of origin on the ridge. Goudie and Piggott also found 'stone polygons' on the flatter parts; these have diameters of 7-9 metres, with their centres composed of relatively fine material colonised by plants, and an outer ring of angular boulders.

What forces created this chaos and then imposed a pattern on it? They were clearly elemental and were not applied at random, but they are not easily explained. It is sometimes suggested that the stones simply tumbled down the slopes, when the strings of the apron in which the Devil carried them broke. It

Stone stripes on the eastern flank of the ridge

The Devil's Chair stands just right of centre and beyond it, to the right, lies Stiperstones Village. To the left of the Chair the fires of the 1976 summer have exposed an extensive area of patterned ground (the distance from the ridge down to the top of the Gatten Plantation is about 300 metres). Here fires have burned off the heather and scorched the stone clean of lichens. The patterning continues beyond the reach of the fire below the Chair. A firebreak bulldozed by the Forestry Commission runs along the top edge of the Gatten Plantation and branches off diagonally in the direction of the Devil's Chair. It can also be seen running almost horizontally across the photo from right to left along the top edge of the fire-bleached ground. Photo, October 1977, by Will Prestwood *et al*, reproduced courtesy of Natural England.

is a beguiling notion, but even taken as a metaphor it is inadequate: a random release of a jumble of stones, by whatever means, cannot explain the patterning of the ground. It is difficult to comprehend the forces and processes which, even given a timescale of in excess of 10,000 years, could have distributed so much material relatively evenly over such wide and gentle slopes, and in doing so have sorted it into stripes.

Great depths of snow, melting during periods of warmer weather, could have led to floods of melt-water capable of moving the rocky debris around. However, it is considered that the water bound within the soil was of greater importance in the process. This thawed during the brief summers, but was unable to percolate downwards due to the permanently frozen sub-soil. It is thought that the water-logged ground became a slurry of large and small stones, together with finer material, and this crept down what are quite gentle slopes. It did so very slowly,

27

Vegetated ground between stone stripes

Students from Preston Montford Field Studies Centre taking measurements across stone stripes and the intervening strips of vegetation near Manstone Rock, September 1965. Photo by Charles Sinker, reproduced courtesy of his family.

but bear in mind that as little as one inch of movement per year would amount to 278 yards over a period of 10,000 years.

But how were the stones sorted into stripes? To the layman, explanations for this 'patterned ground' appear at best tentative. Nina Piggott gives an explanation in an article entitled *Witches' stones on Shropshire crags*. During periods of thaw, melt water accumulated in surface cracks and percolated downwards. Intense freezing created wedges of expanding ice which forced the ground between the cracks to heave upwards. This caused larger rock fragments to fall away from the centre and accumulate along the lines of the ice wedges, thereby creating parallel lines on slopes and polygonal shapes on flatter ground.

Richard Clark suggests an explanation based on the development of sub-surface drainage flows which progressively washed away the finer material. The stone stripes are the expression of these sub-surface flows; here all the finer material has been removed, leaving nothing in which heather and other plants can take root. Between the stripes finer material remained in place and here plants can gain a foothold.

Both writers offer these explanations as hypotheses rather than established fact, and their conclusions remain tentative. Neither explanation appears

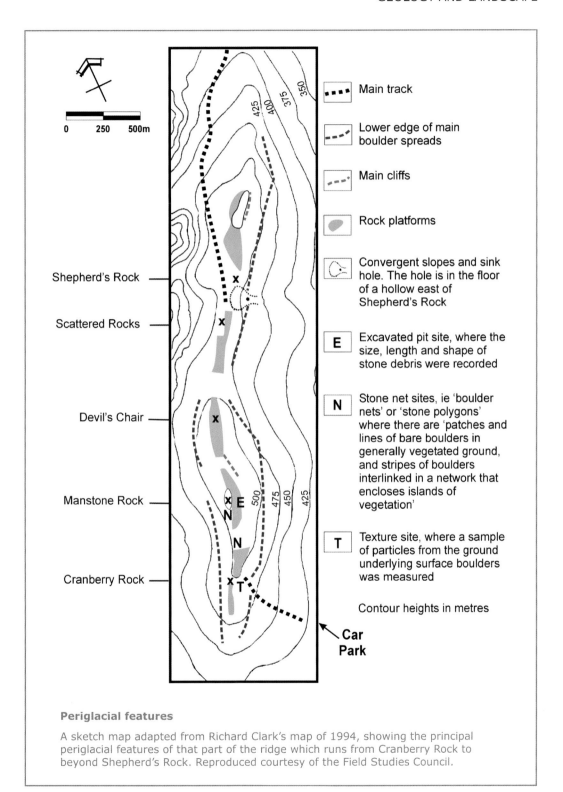

Legend:

- **····** Main track
- **– – –** Lower edge of main boulder spreads
- **–·–·** Main cliffs
- Rock platforms
- Convergent slopes and sink hole. The hole is in the floor of a hollow east of Shepherd's Rock
- **E** Excavated pit site, where the size, length and shape of stone debris were recorded
- **N** Stone net sites, ie 'boulder nets' or 'stone polygons' where there are 'patches and lines of bare boulders in generally vegetated ground, and stripes of boulders interlinked in a network that encloses islands of vegetation'
- **T** Texture site, where a sample of particles from the ground underlying surface boulders was measured

Contour heights in metres

Map labels: Shepherd's Rock, Scattered Rocks, Devil's Chair, Manstone Rock, Cranberry Rock, Car Park

Scale: 0 250 500m

Periglacial features

A sketch map adapted from Richard Clark's map of 1994, showing the principal periglacial features of that part of the ridge which runs from Cranberry Rock to beyond Shepherd's Rock. Reproduced courtesy of the Field Studies Council.

entirely convincing: unremitting and relentless forces were undoubtedly at work over centuries and millennia but how could they have worked in such a discriminating way?

Rock platforms

Richard Clark draws attention to another type of feature well represented on The Stiperstones, 'Crestline Rock Platforms', and includes them in his sketch map of periglacial features. These are bare, near-horizontal platforms some 10-20 metres wide, which at six locations cut across the dominant structures in the central sector of the ridge. Such platforms have been described from various locations in England and elsewhere, including the Falklands, and several theories have been advanced to explain their formation. These theories seek to overcome the difficulty, amongst others, of understanding how the rock which was eroded to form these platforms, was removed across such gently inclined gradients, thereby revealing the platforms themselves.

Clark refers to these platforms as 'cryoplanation surfaces', a term which indicates once more an origin consequent upon frost action in periglacial conditions. But in seeking an explanation for their formation he notes that 'widespread recognition of platforms designated "cryoplanation" has not been accompanied by complete elucidation of formative processes, even in areas of active periglacial activity'. In other words, no one really knows.

Fossils

The study of the relatively recent periglacial landforms of The Stiperstones has been to the fore over the last few decades, but earlier researchers concentrated on much older phenomena. Notable amongst these researchers were the successors to Murchison: Professor C Lapworth and W W Watts (a Shropshire lad who became Professor of Geology at Imperial College, London), who were followed by Professor W F Whittard and his assistants and collaborators, notably Messrs T R Fry, M White and W T Dean. Their principal area of study was the Ordovician rocks of the Shelve Inlier.

During the formation of the rocks of the inlier – rocks which show a continuous geological sequence through much of the Ordovician period – the area lay under the sea. On the sea floor the rocks were laid down as sediments within which were embedded the remains of sea creatures which lived and died in the sea and on the sea bed. These became

Worm burrows

An illustration taken from Murchison's *Siluria*. His explanatory text states that 'the vertical tubes, curved at their base, and their trumpet-shaped openings, are well preserved, and of a size equal to those made by the common Lobworm [= Lugworm] on our coasts … The burrows have two apertures and are connected below by a loop-like tube, as at 'a'.'

the fossils which can be found today and which were the bread and butter of researchers such as Whittard and his assistants. Their efforts concentrated on finding and describing fossil remains so as to identify the species characteristic of the successive layers of rocks, each of which corresponds to a particular time period and particular oceanic conditions.

The Stiperstones Quartzite however provides scant fossil material. Murchison noted worm tubes or burrows, G H Morton states that 'casts of seaweeds, *Crusiana*, have been found', and Peter Toghill refers to rare specimens of the trilobite *Neseuretus*. The Mytton Flags were more productive, yet, as W T Dean says, even these are not obviously fossiliferous, and the casual hunter of fossils will find them unrewarding. It takes an expert to home in on them, one such as Whittard's research assistant Tom Fry, who 'displayed a remarkable aptitude for obtaining faunas from even the most unpromising strata'. In the Mytton Flags he found graptolites (small, floating, colonial organisms, now extinct), gastropods (molluscs) and trilobites.

Ordovician trilobite *Ogygiocarella debuchi*

According to Andrew Allott (2011) this species was misidentified, understandably, as a diminutive flatfish (it is only about 2½ inches long) when first discovered in the 17th century. Photo of specimen number G.10573 courtesy of Shropshire Museums.

Between 1955 and 1966 Whittard published an eight-part monograph on the trilobites of the inlier, to which Dean added a concluding part in 1967 (Whittard having died the previous year). Trilobites were primitive sea creatures with jointed limbs; they ranged in size from an almost microscopic 0.55 millimetres to nearly 1 metre in length, but were typically 3-10 centimetres long. They are amongst our most familiar fossils and more than 3,900 species have been described. They had their widest distribution and greatest diversity in the Cambrian and Ordovician periods (545 to 443 million years ago), but became extinct in the Permian (about 275 million years ago). Whittard and his assistants found some 6,000 trilobites in the Shelve Inlier, identifying 119 species and 8 subspecies, of which 62 species and three subspecies were new to science. Some bear scientific names indicative of the locations in which they were found, including *Myttonia confusa* and *Myttonia multiplex*, *Bergamia matura* and *Bergamia rhodesi* and *Lordshillia confinalis*, denoting the Mytton, Bergam (or Burgam, as it is more generally spelt) and Lordshill areas, all of which lie on the west flank of The Stiperstones.

Mining Geology

The Stiperstones was once at the heart of major mining activity as outlined in the next chapter. For hundreds of years miners burrowed into mineral veins to west and east of The Stiperstones. The veins, which may be anything from less than half an inch to 10-16 feet across, are thought to have been deposited from hot (100° to 500°C) aqueous solutions and vapours rich in dissolved minerals.

The origin of these hydrothermal solutions is debated, but the current theory, as explained by Peter Toghill, is that many originated as mineral-rich brines derived from saline seawater circulating in the earth's crust. These brines might have penetrated as much as three miles below the surface, gaining more minerals on the way, before rising up and being injected as veins into the parent rock, which, in the immediate vicinity of The Stiperstones, is the Mytton Flags; the veins do not extend into the Stiperstones Quartzite (see the geological cross section). The minerals of greatest economic importance over the years have been galena and barytes. The latter occurs to the east of The Stiperstones too, here in Pre-Cambrian rather than Ordovician rocks.

Galena (lead sulphide) is a heavy mineral, blue/grey in colour, cubic in form and with a definite metallic look to it. Barytes or barite (barium sulphate) is a very dense, white, opaque mineral, tabular in shape and remarkably heavy.[11] A number of other minerals occur; the commonest are sphalerite, calcite and quartz. Sphalerite (zinc sulphide) sometimes called blende or zinc blende, has a bronze metallic appearance and is complex in shape. Calcite (calcium carbonate), like barytes, is white, but it is translucent, noticeably light in weight and rhomboid in shape. Quartz (silicone dioxide) is very hard, transparent and pyramidal. Amongst rarer minerals are iron and copper pyrites, witherite and silver. The next chapter outlines the history of the mining of these minerals and touches on the lives of those who owned, managed and worked at the mines.

Chapter 2

'Wold ancient mines': miners and mining

Wold ancient mines they be, and a vast of lead's been took from 'em, time and agen.

Mary Webb *The Golden Arrow* (1916)

Samuel Hughes

MEMOIR

OF THE LATE

SAMUEL HUGHES,

A SHROPSHIRE MINER.

WITH SOME OF HIS

HYMNS, SPIRITUAL SONGS,

AND LETTERS.

―――

"The entrance of thy words giveth light: it giveth understanding unto the simple."

―――

HERTFORD:

1878.

Price 6d. each, paper wrapper, or 5s. a dozen. May be obtained, post free, from the editor, W. Benson, West Street, Hertford.
The profits will be given to the widow and sister of Samuel Hughes.

Samuel Hughes was born at Habberley in 1809. At the age of 12 he was put to work underground at the Snailbeach Mine, where he toiled for much of his life. In 1878, the year of his death, a *Memoir of the late Samuel Hughes, a Shropshire Miner* was published.[1] As far as I know, there is no surviving photograph or portrait of Samuel, and the *Memoir* is the closest we can now get to the man himself. Its seriousness and spirituality tells us much about his character and its title page will have to stand in for his likeness.

The main events of Samuel Hughes's humble life are known to us through the *Memoir*, and this can be said about few of his equally humble contemporaries. His life story is of course unique, but it includes elements common to hundreds of those working at mines around The

Title page of the Memoir of Samuel Hughes

The quotation is from Psalms 119 verse 130.
The Bodleian Libraries, The University of Oxford.

Stiperstones. As such it is used here to shed some light on the unchronicled and forgotten working, social and spiritual lives of nineteenth century miners and their families; it also provides a cue for outlining working practices in the mines. Samuel's story is supplemented with details from the lives of others with connections to the mines. It draws, where possible, on the experience of known individuals in order to personalise what was effectively the occupation of an entire community. In common with the rest of this book, it uses literary sources to complement the narrative.

That this narrative can be written is thanks to the many who have researched the mines, conserved them, written about them, provided a visual record of them through drawings and collections of photographs, and gathered together the reminiscences of those whose lives began before mining ceased. Amongst those on whose work this chapter heavily depends are Martin Allbutt, Fred Brook, Ivor J Brown, Peter Francis, James Lawson, Ken Lock, Malcolm Newton, Adrian Pearce, Jane Price, Michael Shaw, Roger White, the Shropshire Caving and Mining Club and the Shropshire Mines Trust.

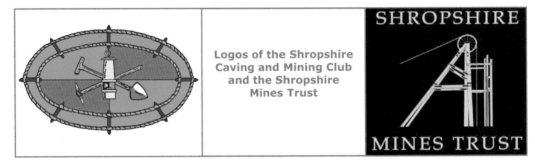

Logos of the Shropshire Caving and Mining Club and the Shropshire Mines Trust

Much of what follows relates to the nineteenth century when numerous mines were operating, but, in the words that the novelist Mary Webb (see Chapter 5) gives to Nancy Corra, the secretive herbalist living amongst the spoil-heaps of 'the Clays',[2] these are 'wold ancient mines'. Some have been exploited since at least Roman times, and it is with the Romans that the story begins.

The Centurion

'Beneath The Stiperstones, clothed in woods of oak and pine, is a small clearing, close to the village now called Snailbeach. This is the entrance to the Roman lead mine, one of the chief causes, it is said, for the Roman settlement in Shropshire … Outside the mine, on this autumn morning [of about 125AD] … stands a young Centurion of the Thracian cohort, hawk nosed and dark of eye, waiting impatiently for the moment when the convoy will be ready to start.'

In this, her essay of 1923, 'The Return of the Romans: a dream of Uriconium',[3] Mary Webb imagines a convoy of lead setting out from Snailbeach under the eagle eye of an imaginary young Centurion. It is on its way to Uriconium, the Roman city more usually referred to as Viroconium, or Wroxeter (the name of the adjacent village), which lies four miles southeast of Shrewsbury.[4] The Stiperstones is clearly visible from Viroconium, standing out on the horizon some

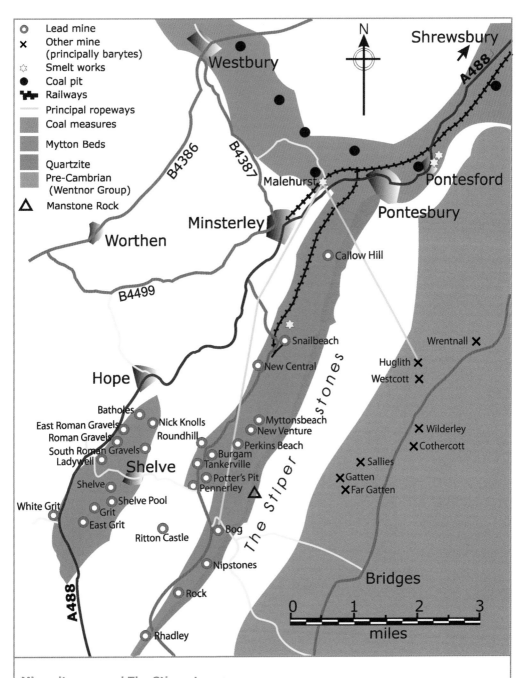

Mine sites around The Stiperstones

A schematic map, adapted from those published by Fred Brook and Martin Allbutt, Ivor Brown and Michael Shaw, showing key rock types and most of the main mine sites and their associated features, including part of the Shrewsbury Coalfield. Most of the lead mines produced other minerals, notably barytes, but quantities, including of lead, were often small.

13 miles to the southwest. Mary Webb was fascinated both by The Stiperstones, where, as she knew, the Romans had mined for lead ore, and by Viroconium, which was being excavated at the time.

It seems that the Romans obtained the ore by the quarrying of outcropping veins. They may well have done so at Snailbeach, but any evidence has long since been obscured by subsequent workings, and their main area of activity may have been at a mine later called 'Roman Gravels', which lies two miles west of The Stiperstones. Michael Shaw, a mining historian, explains that this mine was known as 'Gravels' or 'Shelvefield Gravels' until about 1858 'when romanticism was exploited to sell mine shares and the "Roman" was added'.[5]

It has been suggested that the Romans mined as well as quarried. Roderick Murchison mentions reports that they had reached a depth of more than 100 yards and Fred Brook and Martin Allbutt, twentieth century historians of the

Roman Gravels from the air

The opencast workings visible towards the bottom left of the photo are thought to be of Roman origin. The site of the so-called Old Engine Shaft and the main mine buildings dating from the eighteenth and nineteen centuries are parallel to the road, and New Engine Shaft of the 1870s is at the lower edge of the clearing, upper centre. Photo, 1992, courtesy of Clwyd-Powys Archaeological Trust (ref CPAT 92-MB-0335); description drawn from Michael Shaw's 2009 account of the area's mines.

lead mines, state that in the 1870s miners broke into workings 50 feet below the surface which contained pottery and tools from the Roman period.

Mary Webb's fictional centurion would probably have been overseeing the work of chain-gangs of slaves and prisoners.[6] Amongst their implements may have been 'ancient wooden spades', as shown in 1856 to Thomas Wright, the antiquarian, by the Rev T F More of Linley Hall. Wright attributes the spades to the Roman period, but modern authorities dismiss them as medieval.

Oak spades or shovels of disputed age from mine workings at Shelve

They are about 9 inches wide and have a hole near the centre which slopes back towards the projection at the rear. Apparently the hole was intended for the insertion of a handle which may then have been bound to the projection. Reproduced from Thomas Wright's *Uriconium* of 1872; their current location is unknown.

The lead which the Romans unearthed was presumably smelted in the immediate vicinity of the mines. In his *Miner's Dictionary* of 1747, William Hooson describes ancient smelting sites called 'boles', and Roman techniques may have been similar:

'... above all, upon the Hills, call'd Stiperstones in Shropshire, there they may be found very common, and are very little Places, and they seem to have done their Business by laying a Round row of Stones on the Ground, and placing the Fire in the middle; they picked the Ore on, or near the surface of the Ground on those Hills, and perhaps melted not one hundred Weight in one place.'[7]

The convoy overseen by Mary Webb's centurion will have been carrying 'pigs' of lead; these were moulded bars from which the material for lead goods could later be taken. Roger White, a leading expert on Viroconium, describes three Roman 'pigs' found in Shropshire, one at Snailbeach (in 1796) and the others at Aston and Snead, respectively three miles northwest and two miles north of Bishop's Castle. All have identical inscriptions: IMP[eratoris] HADRIANI AVG[vsti], ie [Property] of the Emperor Hadrian Augustus (Hadrian was Emperor from 117 to 138 AD) and each is marked with a palm branch (a symbol which Roger White says is of unknown significance).[8] The Aston pig (now at Linley Hall) carries the initials 'MINB' and that from Snailbeach 'NSI', thought likely, in each case, to be the initials of the mining official responsible for their production. Each is a real 'lead weight', coming in at

Roman 'pig' of lead

A drawing by Malcolm Newton of the pig of lead from Aston. Courtesy of Shropshire Mines Trust.

around 190lb. Members of the Shropshire Mines Trust cast a replica 'pig' in 2003; it is kept in the 'Miners' Dry' at Snailbeach.[9]

The Romans used lead for water pipes, to line pools, cover roofs, make coffins, and as a constituent of pewter. A little lead shrine to the Goddess Venus found at Viroconium is evidence that lead was used for cultural objects too.[10] But in mining for lead, the Romans were above all perhaps in search of an element which can be refined from some lead ores: silver. Shropshire ores generally have a low silver content but it has been suggested that the deposits on which the Romans concentrated – those lying closest to the surface – may have been silver-rich. So the silver for the imaginary Roman spoon and 'Greystone Treasure' in Malcolm Saville's *Lone Pine Five* (see Chapter 6) could perhaps have been sourced locally.

The Goddess Venus

This diminutive lead shrine (three inches tall) was found at Wroxeter; it is housed in the museum there. The following description is based on that of Glenys Lloyd-Morgan (2000): Venus's right hand touches her left breast and she holds her left hand over her pudenda. At each side of her stands a small child; their presumed identities are Eros, on her left, holding up a circular hand mirror, and on her right, Anteros. Photo English Heritage.

Madoc ap Einion, the John Lawrences and Thomas Lovett: tenants

After the Roman period, it is not until the twelfth century that there is further substantive evidence of mining activity. During the reign of Henry II (1154-1189) activity was significant enough for him to lay down laws specific to the mining of lead in the Stiperstones Forest.[11] In 1181, Hugh Pentulf, Sheriff of Shropshire, received £55 for 'the King's lead' from mines at 'Schelfe' (Shelve). In the same year Madoc ap Einion paid 40 marks for a five-year lease on the same mines, and a year later 110 cart-loads of lead were sent to Gloucester for works at Amesbury Abbey.[12] Much later (1552), a John Clifton is recorded as holding a mine in Hogstow Forest, possibly at Snailbeach. It is probable that throughout this period 'mining' continued to be essentially a quarrying activity, and that it was not until the seventeenth and eighteenth centuries that lengthy tunnels and shafts were dug underground.

Vestiges of the East Roman Gravels Mine in the Hope Valley

The A488 runs in the foreground, the ridge of The Stiperstones forms the horizon. Ken Lock Collection, 1980.

In 1676 and again in 1686 a group of Derbyshire miners took out leases at Snailbeach, and it seems that by 1684 mining was in progress at The Bog.[13] The Grit Mine (near Shelve) was first sunk in 1750, Snailbeach came into its own in the 1780s and, one by one, the other lead mines of the area were sunk. Eventually there were in excess of 50 mine sites, although many were speculative rather than productive ventures.

Amongst the leading families were the Lawrences. They were local to the area and may have been involved as early as 1580, but it was between the 1780s and 1820s that they came to the fore, being involved in all the more important lead mines in Shropshire. At the head of the family was a succession of John Lawrences – Michael Shaw, in his account of the lead, copper and barytes mines of the county, lists four of them. John Lawrence (either I or II, the record is unclear) and his partners established the White Grit Mine company in the 1760s; it was to become the biggest enterprise in the area.[14] By 1783 the workings were deep enough to require a pumping engine to keep them dry, and one was purchased at a price of £900 from the firm of Boulton and Watt in Birmingham; it operated to a depth of 60 yards. But we learn that two years later the engine was sold and John Lawrence (II or III) resorted to taking easily-won ore from mines at Roman Gravels, Batholes, Pennerley and The Bog, working from adits (horizontal excavations into hill-sides) rather than digging deep shafts in which water accumulated. The John Lawrences also set up smelt mills at Malehurst and Pontesbury and controlled four collieries in the Shrewsbury Coalfield.

Meanwhile, the Grit Mine became neglected, and in 1825 the landlord refused to renew the Lawrences' lease, which passed instead to Messrs Lewis and Phillips. They were both involved in the Leigh Tunnel Drainage company which proposed to drive a five-mile long level to drain all the mines in the areas of the Gravels and the Grit. John Lawrence IV contested the granting of leases to the company and took the matter to court. He won four lawsuits but bankrupted himself in so-doing. By 1835 most, indeed possibly all, of the Lawrence possessions had been lost.

While the Lawrences' fortunes foundered, those of Thomas Lovett and his nine partners in the Snailbeach company prospered and Snailbeach became the

To Mining Adventurers are offered the valuable LEASE of the BOG LEAD MINES, Steam Engine, Gins, Boats, &c. the Property of Mr. John Lawrence, jun. a Bankrupt.

BY MR. SMITH,

On Wednesday, the 24th of February, 1830, precisely at Twelve o'Clock, on the Premises, at the Bog Mine, in the County of Salop ;

LOT I.

THE valuable LEASE of those inexhaustible LEAD MINES, called the BOG, extending over a Mining District of upwards of Three Thousand Acres.—The Work is open, and there is a navigable Level for Boats that Drains at One Hundred and Fifteen Yards. And there remains Two Thousand Four Hundred Tons of Ore to be raised, free from Royalty.

LOT II.

In the following or such other Lots as may be agreed upon at the Time of Sale ;

A capital STEAM ENGINE, 42 Inch Cylinder (Double Power), with 2 Wrought Iron Boilers, Steam Pipes, and 55 Yards of 15-Inch Pumps, Working Barrel 14-Inch, with Plates for Pump Rods and Joints, Part of 2 Winches, Pair of large Pit Blocks, Capstan Frame, valuable Capstan Rope about 200 Yards, Timber Hanging Rods with Iron Work for the Engine Pumps, Cast Iron Rails and 2 Rail-way Waggons under Ground, 3 Gins, Ropes, &c. 3 Wood Boats and 1 Iron Boat, with various other Articles.

For further Particulars apply to Mr. J. W. Watson, Attorney ; Mr. Wm. Hazledine ; or the Auctioneer, all of Shrewsbury, if by Letter, Post-paid.

Announcement in the *Salopian Journal* of 20 January 1830

This advertises the auction of the lease of the Bog Mine and associated equipment owned by Mr John Lawrence junior, a Bankrupt. Note that Lot II includes four boats which were presumably used on the Boat Level. Shropshire Archives.

principal mine in the area. The company was formed in 1783 and its business expanded to the point where it employed some 500 workers. The evidence of their extraordinary labours is tangible – mine shafts and adits, a complex and far-reaching network of deep underground workings and, above ground, in Mary Webb's words, huge 'hills of slag, white without purity' — yet we know the life histories of few of the workers involved. An exception is Samuel Hughes, who was mentioned at the start of this chapter; his story touches on many aspects of the life of the mining community.

The 'white hillocks' at Snailbeach, 1992

The octagonal Resting Hill Chimney is visible in the foreground amongst oak trees. A flue ran to here from the smelter which was almost a mile away. Diagonally downhill to the right, but still well within the wood, are the almost hidden, and then unpreserved remains of the Pumping Engine House, and lower down, at the edge of the wood, the Compressor House. The field in the foreground has just been cultivated; prior to this it was unimproved grassland with a scatter of Rowans and numerous Bluebells. Photo, May 1992, courtesy of Clwyd-Powys Archaeological Trust (ref CPAT 92-C-636).

Samuel Hughes: miner

The young Samuel walked to work from Habberley, 1¾ miles to the northeast of Snailbeach. By the standards of the time it was a modest distance, but once at the mine, there was still a lot of leg-work to do. Until the 1870s access within the mines was usually by timber ladderways built into the shafts. In evidence to the Kinnaird Commission, which reported in 1864 on the Condition of Mines in Great Britain, Samuel Hughes's contemporary, Samuel Jones of Snailbeach, stated that it took him 30 minutes to climb down to his workplace each day and an hour to climb back out.[15] Underground, the two Samuels and their like worked to free the mineral from its enveloping rock. They drilled holes (mostly by hand, but from the early 1880s with drills powered by compressed air), filled the holes with explosive and then fired them, thereby loosening the mineral. They loaded it into barrows or wagons, pushed or hauled these along tramways to where the level met the main shaft and then transferred the mineral into 'kibbles' or other containers for winding up to the surface. By the 1870s, the decade of Samuel Hughes's death, the mineworkers of the Stiperstones area were producing some 10% of the country's lead ore.

Some of the miners were referred to as 'tutworkers': they might receive a wage or be paid against a contract for sinking shafts, driving tunnels and hauling materials, at so much per yard or fathom. Others belonged to 'bargain companies': a group of perhaps four to a dozen miners who contracted to extract ore from a specified location for so much per ton. Then there were 'tributers': they won the ore and were paid, according to current market value per ton, on the amount of ore obtained. 'Labourers' received a wage for carrying out a wide range of work both above and below ground. Last but not least were the

Iron kibbles

Kibbles of crushed and sorted ore at the Upper Works, Snailbeach in 1968. Photo by A P Wallace.

A group of miners at Huglith Mine, 1930s

A number are wearing the traditional headgear of the wide-brimmed 'hard hat' onto which is stuck a 'gob of clay' complete with candle. Emily Griffiths Collection.

'craftsmen', such as smiths, carpenters, joiners, stonemasons and engineers, all key employees, particularly when a mine was being developed.[16]

By agreement with the mine company the miners worked between six and eight hours per shift, which included getting to and from the underground workplace, with up to an hour's break for food. The work was gruelling but the hours shorter than we might have assumed. Candles provided the only light. They were lodged on ledges within the mines as well as being fixed with a 'gob of clay' to the hats the miners wore – bowlers hardened with resin. This head gear may have been of some use for getting to and from work sites but can hardly have been practical during active work.

Samuel Hughes: reveller

In later life Samuel Hughes confessed that at about the age of 18, following the death of his father, 'he gave loose to the reins of folly and wickedness; the wake, the fair, the races and sometimes even fights were the objects of his delight'. It may be that the fights were at the local inns. If so, he may have frequented 'The Crown' which stood 1,362 feet above sea level on the western flank of The Stiperstones overlooking Pennerley and The Bog. Licensed 'out of memory' as a 'beer house', 'The Crown' appears to have closed in about 1902, but its ruins can still be found, and its reputation has been handed down. Nearly a hundred years later Les Hotchkiss (born nearby in 1927), reminiscing for *Never on a Sunday*, recalls being told that 'men used to come [to 'The Crown'] from the Bridges for bare knuckle fights'. Henry Jones (born 1930), a Pennerley resident, remembers that 'it was said they could hear for a mile the miners singing in The Crown on a Saturday night … Mrs Chidley [the landlady] used to sweep the beer that had been spilt on the floor out through the door with a broom after they'd gone'.

Other drinking places serving the mining community included 'The Miners' Arms', 'The Stiperstones Inn' and 'The Cross Guns'; all were the property of the mine landlords. 'The Miners' Arms' at The Bog was first licensed in about 1845; it finally closed in the early 1960s and is now a private house, as is 'The Cross Guns' at Crowsnest, which was open from about 1838 to 1934.

Les Hotchkiss remembers 'The Miners' Arms' as 'a rare place in the old days' and Henry Owen (born 1918) recalls that it was 'a wonderful meeting place' where rents were paid and 'three parts of the tenants would get drunk' on rent day. Clifford Lewis (born 1923), himself a peaceable man, describes it as 'a good fighting place', while Jim Booth (born 1928), although acknowledging a degree of hyperbole, recollects that 'every other weekend they used to reckon the ditches down from the Bog pub would be running with blood!'.

Henry Owen remembers it as a place for more peaceful pursuits too: dominoes, quoits and tippet. Tippet was played by teams of four or five sitting opposite each other. The team holding the tippet, a button, would put their hands on the table and their opponents would have to guess in which hand the tippet was held. Les Hotchkiss recalls that there were 'some very good tippet players, they'd study the expressions on people's faces'. But this was an exclusively male pursuit, as was billiards and other games played in the club houses at Crowsnest, Tankerville and The Bog. As Graham France (born 1921) recalls, 'it was men only – no ladies. They would be at home doing the housework. Any woman going to the pub was [considered to be] a slut!'.

According to the 1901 'Returns of Licensed Houses', the original licence for 'The Stiperstones Inn' dates back 'out of memory'; it continues to serve residents and visitors to this day. In 1901 it is recorded as being owned by the Earl of Tankerville, and as having six bedrooms and stabling for 14 horses.[17] Today it is owned by the Sproson family, has two guest bedrooms and stables two race horses owned by former publican John Sproson.[18]

Samuel Hughes: house-builder

Samuel Hughes married at 22 and started a family, but where to live? Mining was expanding and its operations were labour-intensive, leading to high employment and pressure on housing. Snailbeach Mine is said to have employed 550 in 1851 and there were probably in the order of 1,000 working at the Stiperstones mines at that period. It had become a busy area. However, many of the miners were itinerants, and according to the evidence given in 1863 to the Kinnaird Commission by Captain Henwood, 'underground agent' of Snailbeach Mine, 'during the week the miners use cabins and barracks near the shaft and the smelters have bedrooms in the smelting house yard'.[19] Other miners were 'scattered over the hills', but housing was scarce, as were patches of land which were sought after for the grazing of animals and growing of crops to supplement mining wages and sustain growing families.

To find accommodation, the miners moved up the valleys and onto the hill. The highest dwelling on The Stiperstones, known as 'Tin House', was occupied at this time. It is perched, 1,526 feet above sea level, between Perkins Beach and the Devil's Chair; today it is a complete ruin but is still referred to by name as 'Tin House', presumably because at one time corrugated iron ('tin') covered its roof. Others call it 'Mary Webb's Cottage', and although it was never lived in or owned by Mary Webb, it is a good candidate for Stephen Southernwood and Deborah Arden's cottage in *The Golden Arrow*, 'standing wide-eyed facing the Devil's Chair', and this may account for the name.

'Tin House' figures in two maps prepared by David Pannett when, in the 1960s, he was working as a historical geographer at the Field Studies Council's local centre at Preston Montford. They illustrate the uphill spread of dwellings on the eastern fringe of Pennerley as mining expanded, and their abandonment as it contracted.

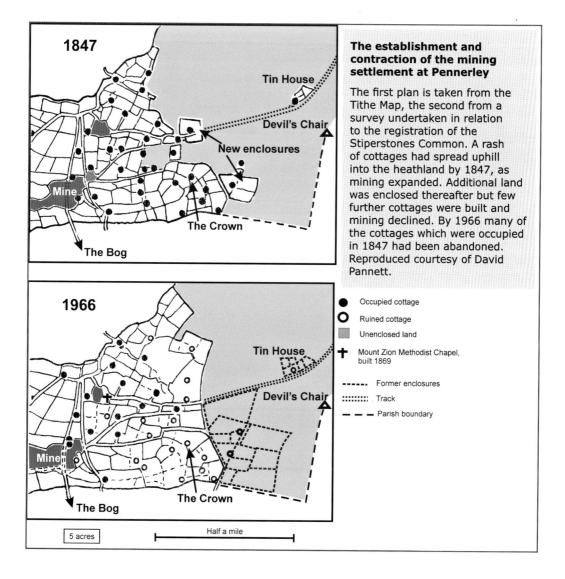

The establishment and contraction of the mining settlement at Pennerley

The first plan is taken from the Tithe Map, the second from a survey undertaken in relation to the registration of the Stiperstones Common. A rash of cottages had spread uphill into the heathland by 1847, as mining expanded. Additional land was enclosed thereafter but few further cottages were built and mining declined. By 1966 many of the cottages which were occupied in 1847 had been abandoned. Reproduced courtesy of David Pannett.

● Occupied cottage

○ Ruined cottage

▪ Unenclosed land

+ Mount Zion Methodist Chapel, built 1869

------ Former enclosures

∷∷∷∷ Track

– – – Parish boundary

In Perkins Beach itself, a hill settlement developed, running up the steep gradient to a point almost as high as 'Mary Webb's Cottage'; presumably its residents worked in the adjacent Perkins Beach and New Venture mines. It is surely to the now long-abandoned cottages of this settlement that Mary Webb refers under a fictional name in *The Golden Arrow*: 'Below Stephen's cottage ... the hamlet of Lostwithin clung to the slope of the hill with frenzied tenacity; the cottages looked like small stones taking part in a huge landslip.'[20]

However, Samuel Hughes found somewhere to live which was closer to his work and at a lower altitude, building a cottage in Crowsnest Dingle. What sort of house did he build? We don't know, but some indications of the housing of this period (the 1830s) come from *A Short History of Perkins Beach Mine*, an anonymous essay, which, though written in 1898, describes the practice of Samuel Hughes's time:

> 'In those days it was customary with the mining population for want of better accommodation to select a site on the mountain, then obtain the assistance of a few of their fellow workmen, some of which would then repair to the adjoining plantations and for a nominal price purchase of [sic] quantity of larch or other small poles ... Meantime the other portion of men would be employed building walls with sods. The first consignment of timber arriving, one or two, considered most expert with axe and saw, would commence forming a roof to the habitation which would be slated with the class of material the walls were built of. And when convenient a scanty coat of straw, generally mixed with heather, may be laid on the top to ensure its being waterproof. The ground floor consisting of the natural subsoil.'[21]

This, then, was the 'Squatter's Cottage', a crude structure of sods and poles 'slated' with a 'thatch' of sods, straw and heather. The *Short History* reports that by next morning the Lord of the Manor or his Agent would arrive to demand a rent, albeit nominal, granting, in most cases, an adjoining allotment as a garden plot. Subsequently:

> 'Many of these structures as time wore on, and with an agreement between the Landlord and the squatter, have been made into convenient dwellings and a cow, sometimes two, have been kept, thereby greatly enhancing the value of what aforetime was nominally a barren mountain.'

Over time then, the original crude structure would presumably have been replaced with stone walls and a roof of thatch, slate or tiles. So, though cramped and basic, the very few so called 'squatters' cottages' that survive today, built of stone, squared timber and tile, are far removed from their antecedents. The process was described to Magdalene Weale in the 1930s by 'old Mrs Pugh' who told her 'the history of her little home':

> 'Hastily and by night her husband built it, first a hovel with a turfed roof and an impoverished chimney. Then they kindled the precious fire which was to give them the right to live; for if by morning smoke was seen issuing from the chimney, "I see smoke!" the neighbours would cry and the word would go round that a newcomer had earned the right to live among them. Then with stones from the Chair a cottage arose, next a patch of wild moorland was reclaimed, and now two

**Number 5
Pennerley**

The man in the centre of this photo of about 1900 is George Betton (1839-1920), to his left stands his wife Harriet (née Jones, 1843-1923), and to his right his daughter, also Harriet (1883-1964), mother of Iris Muriel Jones (née Smith 1920-2009), see Chapter 3. Note the thatch on the near end of the cottage and the engine house of Potter's Pit to the rear. Reproduced courtesy of Vince Jones, son of Iris Muriel.

Number 4 Snailbeach

A former miner's cottage, 2005. This is one of very few such cottages not to have undergone significant extension and modernisation, yet it is still a significant upgrade on the primitive squatter's cottage. Photo courtesy of Kelvin Lake – I A Recordings.

cows graze in fields fenced against the ever-watchful heather eager to come back into its own.'

And why did the Lord of the Manor allow these squatters living space? The explanation is provided in an interview for *Never on a Sunday* with Mr Roger Hulton-Harrop whose family formerly owned mineworkings:

'... you get nothing for nothing. To get the minerals you needed miners and they needed somewhere to live with their families ... The miners needed somewhere to live so that the family [ie ourselves, the landowners] could make a profit from the land.'

Samuel Hughes: believer

One day, when in his mid-twenties (it will have been 1833 or 1834), Samuel Hughes saw people building Lordshill Baptist Chapel; amongst them, gathering stones, was the minister, Edward Evans. Samuel was surprised and thought 'there certainly must be something more in religion than I have ever been aware of'. He heard the first sermon in the new chapel and 'became a regular hearer'. Eventually, after much doubt, soul-searching and torment, he became a member at the little chapel, began to teach in the Sunday school and to speak at the prayer-meetings, becoming a lay preacher. His *Memoir* contains the words he wrote of 37 hymns and spiritual songs.

The words of one song, written by Samuel in 1848, record the death of Mary and Annie, two of his children; they died on the same day. It is clear from *Never on a Sunday* that such tragedies were not exceptional. Diphtheria, scarlet fever, tuberculosis and measles in particular, killed many, especially the young. Emily Griffiths (born 1917) whose eloquence and clear recollections of life on The Stiperstones made her an acknowledged and admired oral historian of the area, draws on her own family's memories of one particular epidemic:

'There was a terrible scourge, they said it was scarlet fever but I should think it was something more virulent than that, probably diphtheria; but every small child in the area died and my grandmother lost her three little boys within a fortnight, there was the five year old, the two and a half year old and the baby, a few weeks old.'

Given the religious persuasions of the community, Samuel Hughes's involvement with the Baptist church is unsurprising. *Never on a Sunday* explains how, in common with many other mining districts, nonconformism took a strong hold from the early years of the nineteenth century. In 1803 Baptists were meeting at a house in Snailbeach; some years later they started using the blacksmith's shop of the Snailbeach Mine, and, after meeting there for 15 years, were in the throes of building their own chapel at Lordshill when seen by Samuel Hughes.

From 1840, attempts were made to hold regular Methodist services in Snailbeach. By 1859 a permanent congregation had been established, and in 1876 the Methodist Chapel was finally built. At the same time other chapels were being established at Pennerley and Perkins Beach, as well as a Meeting House, long-since ruinous, at The Paddock, a settlement on the northeastern fringe of the ridge which was abandoned in the middle years of the twentieth century.

The building, in 1872, of St Luke's Church, on the edge of Snailbeach, was an attempt by the Anglicans to establish a 'mission church', but it had little early success; a note in the register recorded that the Church 'has unfortunately been closed on and off owing to the utter indifference of the people up here'. By contrast, the local chapels grew in strength, probably reaching their peak in the late nineteenth and early twentieth centuries, meeting spiritual and moral needs and providing an important focus for the life of the community. Samuel Hughes's religious devotion was no exception; the mining communities as a whole were devout. Three of the seven miners killed at Snailbeach on 6 March 1895, when the winding rope lowering their cage down Old Shaft broke, were lay preachers.[22]

Stephen Southernwood, foreman at the Lostwithin Mine in Mary Webb's *The Golden Arrow* was a lay preacher too, though his faith proved fickle. Webb's description of the ugly red-brick chapel where Stephen preaches and is first seen by Deborah Arden, appears however to be based on none of The Stiperstones chapels: 'Above the door, with a nervous and pardonable shuffling of responsibility (apparently by the architect) were the words, "This is the Lord's doing"'.[23]

By contrast, the charming chapel and minister's house at 'God's Little Mountain' in Mary Webb's *Gone to Earth* is evidently, both by location and synonymy, though not by architecture, the real Lordshill Chapel. It was the initial building of this chapel that had so moved Samuel Hughes in the 1830s. The land had been provided by the Fifth Earl of Tankerville. Whilst he may well have been swayed by evangelism, the opportunity to get one over on the Marquess of Bath, who owned the neighbouring land, is said to have been persuasive too. Apparently the Marquess was 'high church' and had refused to allow the Baptists to build on his land. They approached the Earl of Tankerville instead, allegedly in the hope that a recent dispute with the Marquess over shooting rights might make him more sympathetic. The outcome was permission to build their chapel just across the stream which separated Tankerville's land from that of the Marquess, indeed the Fifth Earl both preached and sang in the new building.[24]

By Mary Webb's day the chapel had been re-built, and by then 'the graveyard, where stones, flat, erect, and askew took the place of a flower-garden', included the grave of Arthur Wardman, one of the lay preachers killed in the accident of 1895.[25] The chapel and attached dwelling were in due course to be the principal setting for the film version of *Gone to Earth* (see Chapter 5).

In 1994, out of the blue, another chapel with a dwelling attached began to materialise on the edge of The Stiperstones. Brother Aidan Hart, a member of the Orthodox Church, with support from what later became the Stiperstones Trust, a registered charity, purchased and restored a derelict miner's cottage, 1,273 feet above sea level, at the southern end of The Paddock, a deserted settlement on the eastern flank of the hill. Attached to the cottage was a former

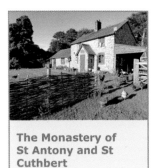

The Monastery of St Antony and St Cuthbert

Photo courtesy of Father Silouan.

cow-byre, which Brother Aidan, who had worked as an iconographer at the Iviron Monastery on Mount Athos in Greece, converted into a diminutive and exquisite church adorned with frescoes and icons; together, the cow-byre and cottage became the Hermitage (now the Monastery) of St Antony and St Cuthbert. Since 2001 the incumbent has been Father Silouan, who began monastic life in 1990 in the monastery of St John the Baptist at Tolleshunt Knights, Essex. In the ancient tradition of Orthodox monasticism he lives a life of prayer, silence, liturgy and work, while welcoming individuals and groups who come to learn, meditate and pray; his writings include *Wisdom Songs* (2011), *Wisdom and Wonder* (2011), and *Wisdom, Prophecy and Prayer* (2013). Aidan Hart still lives locally; he has become internationally known for his work in a variety of iconographic mediums including carving and fresco.

St Cuthbert

Detail from a fresco within the church of the Monastery of St Antony and St Cuthbert. Reproduced courtesy of the artist, Aidan Hart.

Tankerville, Bath and More: landowners

The Earls of Tankerville (of Chillingham Castle, Northumberland), along with the Marquess of Bath (of Longleat, Wiltshire), the Mores (of Linley, near Bishop's Castle) and the Lysters (of Rowton, near Shrewsbury), were the principal mine owners. As landlords they let their mining rights and received in return rents and royalties, an important source of income. It was perhaps not surprising therefore, that with production on the wane, the Seventh Earl of Tankerville stayed in the area for a while in 1906, trying to promote the mines (although the distribution to each householder of framed photographs of himself and his wife, Lady Leonora, in their 1902 Coronation robes suggests that self-promotion was an objective too). The Earl and Lady Leonora associated with evangelists and participated in services in chapels and the open air. Many years later, Margaret Corfield (born 1887), a local resident, recalled that the solos the Earl sang in his 'fine, well-trained baritone voice' delighted local people.[26]

The Seventh Earl of Tankerville was not the only landowner to seek to promote the mines. In his memoir *A Tale of Two Houses* (1978), Sir Jasper More MP (1907-1987) of Linley, recounts with humour and gusto the vain hopes of his impoverished father (T J Mytton More 1872-1947) that the mines, which had been a major asset to his family in the nineteenth century, would rescue the

Lord and Lady Tankerville

They are dressed for the coronation of Edward VII, 1902. Reproduced courtesy of Derek and Jean Rowson.

More family fortunes in the twentieth. Sir Jasper recalls that 'Part I' of his father's annual summer holiday 'Talk' to his sons majored on how remarkable it was that so few people realised the antiquity and importance of the More family. 'Part II' was the 'Whole Sad Story' detailing his father's grievances against family and government. 'Part III' was the extraordinary failure of mining companies to appreciate the great wealth that lay under the turf of the Linley Estate. According to Sir Jasper's father:

'A company was now [c1918] interested in the mines and talking in big figures, but these people never took proper advice and now they had started at the wrong end, not actually on the Linley Estate and everyone who knew anything about it knew that our mines were the most productive and our lead was the best. Incidentally he was having a diviner over in a day or two and I must come and watch him. But there wasn't only lead, there was also barytes and also probably lots of other minerals. And then the timber … And then there was the quarry …

In honour of the diviner we would be taken by motor to the northern end of the estate and would alight on one of the old slag heaps. Maps would be produced and there would be much talk of veins and lodes and faults … The diviner would get his bearings and set out with measured tread while we watched spell bound. Suddenly the metal semicircle would heel over and hit the diviner smartly in the stomach … "There's surely metal here," he would say; and my father's face would glow with satisfaction. After a few more similar performances my father would commission a Report. These Reports, of which my father ordered several in his life and which must have cost him a sizeable sum, were all to the same effect; that the metal was undoubtedly there and that all that was needed was someone with the sense and the money to come and work it.'

Henry Dennis: mine manager

In order for a mining enterprise to get underway the landlords needed to attract tenants, such as the Lawrences and Lovetts; they looked in turn to business partners to provide the necessary capital. But success depended on the employment of capable individuals to direct operations on the ground. The titles of 'Agent', 'Mine Manager' and 'Mine Captain' are those used by mining historians for such individuals. The distinctions between these titles are unclear, but it is clear that men of acknowledged ability served in these roles, notably Arthur Waters from Cornwall (active in the area from the late 1850s until his death in 1887), Stephen Eddy of Skipton, Yorkshire and his son James Ray Eddy (who were involved at Snailbeach from 1857), Enoch Parry (1836-1895) a local man, son of a lead miner,[27] and William Oldfield (1851-1928) from Wrexham. Their qualities included energy and experience and a high degree of engineering, commercial and management skills. Henry Dennis (1825-1906), who took over from J R Eddy at Snailbeach in 1871, is another notable example. He is described by mine historians Martin Allbutt and Fred Brook as 'a veritable dynamo of initiative and drive' and he was undoubtedly a man of great ability.

Henry Dennis (1825-1906)

Wrexham County Borough Museum.

Henry Dennis was born at Bodmin, Cornwall, where he worked for the Cornwall Railway Company. In 1850 he came to Wales, where he set up in Ruabon in 1857 as an independent surveyor and mining engineer; he went on to become a major figure in the industries of North Wales and Shropshire. It is said that the various enterprises under his control employed over 10,000 people, but he still found time to become well-known as a breeder of Shropshire sheep.[28] During his working life he had:

'Surveyed the Glynn Valley Tramway and the Snailbeach District Railway, sunk various collieries, worked his own Legacy Colliery from 1870 to 1875, built gas and water works near Ruabon, founded the present-day brick and tile firm of Dennis Ruabon, operated lead mines at Llangynog and, with his son, conceived the famous Gresford colliery sunk in 1908.'[29]

The cigar he smoked (accompanied by black coffee) while dealing with his correspondence before an 8.30am breakfast, would not be recommended by his doctor today, but his personal recipe for a long and energetic life would be: 'I have always been an early riser. I took plenty of exercise and I invariably got up from the table when I could eat more'.[30]

Engaged initially as general manager of the Snailbeach Mine Company Limited, Henry Dennis, along with Thomas Heaton Lovett and John Jones, was to head this company, which took over the Snailbeach Mine in 1885.

From 1871 onwards Henry Dennis carried out extensive modernisation of the mine and its services, including setting up the Snailbeach District Railway (see Chapter 3). Other innovations included the Compressor House which supplied compressed air to winches and drills operating underground. Such mechanisation was a factor in the reduction of the work force from 500 in 1851 to 130 in 1878, but by the end of the nineteenth century the mine still struggled to be competitive against lead now being imported from open-cast workings in Spain and Australia.

A particular problem, addressed by Henry Dennis through the construction in 1872 of the 'New' Reservoir at Snailbeach, was the provision of water. The element that was such a nuisance below ground was nevertheless, in the words of Ivor Brown, 'an essential commodity for all working mines ... needed often as a source of power, for dressing ore and for the steam engine boilers ... on a mine surface there was rarely sufficient of it.' At Snailbeach, a gathering system of ditches and culverts brought water to the reservoir from three-quarters of a mile away at the north end of the Stiperstones ridge, where a channel was dug to bring the water from east to west against the lie of the land. Smaller reservoirs may be seen at all the significant mine sites; a number of them are now important for wildlife (see Chapter 7). Ultimately however this and other costly modernisation works at the Snailbeach Mine failed to make it profitable.

George Lerry, who wrote an account of Henry Dennis's life, describes him as 'a typical Victorian coalmaster – a keen man of business and a hard worker'; he was also an initiator and manager of many diverse enterprises, an innovator and a moderniser. A remarkable man, and, I suspect, a hard man too. The hanging of huge paintings of Napoleon on his sons' bedroom walls was doubtless didactic, and a tribute from one masterful character to another. It is a detail that is not endearing.

John Hewitt: a mining casualty

By the time that Henry Dennis became manager of Snailbeach Mine, Samuel Hughes had moved on. We learn from the *Memoir* of his life that 'when [his] health and strength began to fail, he removed to the mining district near St Asaph in North Wales, where the prospect of lighter and more profitable employment was held out to him; and afterwards to the coal district near Mold'. He returned however to end his days in his cottage in Crowsnest Dingle.

But amongst the many who did work under Henry Dennis were members of the Hewitt family. In a photograph of about 1890 we see John Hewitt sitting sightless, his eyes covered by a bandage, the consequence of a mining accident in 1883 involving a drilling machine.

Compressed air drilling machines had been introduced to Snailbeach Mine by Henry Dennis in 1881, and by 1882 four such machines were in use. Long steel drills were used to make holes into which dynamite was introduced and fired, preparing the way for extraction of the minerals.[31] On 15 May 1883 remnants of dynamite in a previously drilled shot-hole exploded when a new hole was being

The Hewitt family, about 1890

Back row, left to right: Albert (born 1864), Mary (1869), Margaret (1871), Alice (1875) and Alfred (1878). Middle row: Rosanna (1886), their father John (1835 or 1840-1903, blinded in a mining accident in 1883, wears a bandage across his face), Eliza (1882), their mother Margaret, née Wardman (1845-1916) and Thomas (1884). Winnifred (1888) is at the front. The Hewitt family bible lists four other children: John (1866-1882), another boy 'no name died when three days old', and Elizabeth and Charlotte, whose dates were 'not to hand' when the bible was inscribed. Reproduced courtesy of Peggy Chidley, one of Alfred's daughters.

Alfred Hewitt as a young man

In this extract from a family photo he looks about 20, suggesting a date of around 1898. Reproduced courtesy of Peggy Chidley.

drilled alongside. John Odgers, 'the foreman of boring machines', was killed and three other miners were seriously injured including John Hewitt; his eyes were so badly damaged that thereafter he always wore a bandage across his face.[32]

Alfred Hewitt: lead mine worker

John Hewitt's son Alfred (1878-1974) lived into his mid-90s, earning the title 'the last true Shropshire lead mine worker', but, marked by the accident to his father, he always refused to work underground. He worked on the surface plant at the mine, and also as a servant in the mine manager's house, and it was on his way there on 6 March 1895 that Alfred saw men stretching out the remnants of the broken rope that had caused the loss of seven lives when the cage it was lowering crashed to the bottom of the mine.[33]

Alfred Hewitt in his eightieth year

He is standing beside the headframe of Black Tom Shaft at Snailbeach in 1957; it subsequently collapsed but a replica was erected in 2012. Reproduced courtesy of two of Alfred's grandsons, Vivian and Vincent Chidley.

In later life Alfred Hewitt provided mine historians with much information about the workings of the mine. He had many conversations with Ken Lock, and at the age of 91 he explained to Ivor Brown the operation of the Resting Hill Pumping Engine on which he worked from the mid 1890s until the closure of the Snailbeach lead mine in 1911. The engine, referred to by Alfred, for reasons now unknown, as 'Lady Mary Deborah', pumped water out of the mine.[34] This was generally a requirement because, as mining progressed and shafts deepened, excess water became a problem. Previously, drainage levels had been dug to evacuate water, but where the topography did not lend itself to this solution, horse-driven pumps brought water to the surface. Water wheels were used too, and even man-operated capstans. But in the late eighteenth century steam engines, notably those manufactured by Boulton and Watt in Birmingham, were introduced, and nine are recorded at local mines by 1800. They were used for pumping and for 'winding' too – carrying the miners up and down the shafts and bringing the mineral ore to the surface. From the 1830s the 'Cornish type' of pumping engine was introduced to keep the mines dry; these were more powerful and cheaper to operate but could not

The engine house and chimney at Watson's Shaft, Tankerville Mine, 1980

Examples of Malcolm Newton's extensive series of drawings of the old mine workings grace many publications about Shropshire's mines. His 'signature' was of two birds in flight, here he placed them between the two structures. Courtesy of Shropshire Mines Trust.

be used for winding. The steam engines were housed in massive stone engine-houses which numbered a dozen by 1850, each with a chimney alongside. Fred Brook and Martin Allbutt describe how, by the 1870s, the western flank of The Stiperstones was 'a landscape dotted with the smoking chimney stacks of Cornish pumping engines and with the wooden headgear above the many shafts'.

Once it reached the surface the ore passed through a variety of processes on the nearby 'dressing floors'. First the ore was washed and large pieces were broken down to a manageable size by hand. It then passed though a 'crusher'. It is to the discordant noises emanating from this machine that Mary Webb alludes in *The Golden Arrow*:

> 'From the yard at the spar mine came weird, plaintive sounds, as the rock-crusher ground the body of the mountain to fragments. These sounds were so wild and eerie that they might have been the forlorn music of fairy players sitting, shadowy and huge, in the dim rock-foundations, fiddling madly of nameless terror, fluting of unreachable beauties and rocky immortalities, harping on their own heartstrings to the deaf ears of men.'

The ore was then moved to the smelter. The first to be built locally was at Malehurst, near Pontesbury, in about 1778; it was adjacent to the Malehurst Colliery.[35] Others followed, and the fine hexagonal chimney of the Snailbeach smelter of 1885 still stands, proudly overtopping the oakwood of Resting Hill. Ore from the other mines was carried to Malehurst or to the railhead at Minsterley

Snailbeach Mine in the 1890s

In this view looking southeast from Snailbeach Coppice, the Ore House, where the dressed ore was stored, is bottom right and Resting Hill Chimney, top left. The chimney belches smoke drawn up the long underground flue from the Smelt House which lies well out of view behind and below the artist. Just below the chimney stands the Engine Shaft Pumping House from which the massive, pivoting beam projects, moving the rods which worked the pumps deep in the mine below. Down the slope, amongst fields, stands the Count House where the miners were paid. Mounds of spoil rise to the right of the Ore House and immediately above it the twin gable-ends of the Locomotive Shed stand on the edge of the congested heart of the mine. A painting commissioned by the late Ken Lock, probably in about 1980, from Arthur Hunt, a Shrewsbury artist. Reproduced courtesy of Margaret Lock, Ken's wife.

from where it was taken on for smelting elsewhere, including North Wales. Coal was carted in the opposite direction, being carried up to the mines either from the railhead, or the Pontesbury coalfield.[36]

The busy-ness of it all is captured by Thomas Poole, a diarist, in his entry of 28 June 1836 describing the Snailbeach Mine:

> 'A scene of great activity and industry is presented in these mines to the casual visitor, the working of the ... pumps, the kibble going up and down the shaft constantly, the miners signal rapper, the smiths and carpentry shops, railways, breaking of ore, packing and washing it and finally weighing it by the agents into the carts or wagons which convey it to the smelting house at Pontesbury. It is strangely contrasted by the stillness which pervades the night; as the workmen live at some distance nothing is heard but the heavy straining and heaving of the engine.'[37]

For many years Snailbeach was indeed a busy place, but levels of activity fluctuated and were eventually to tail away. Alfred Hewitt's life encompassed the wane of lead mining, followed by the peak and decline of barytes mining and ultimately by the cessation of the mining of either mineral at Snailbeach. He was just 33 in 1911 when the Snailbeach Cornish Engine ceased working and the lead mine closed. Alfred married at this time, so it was particularly fortunate that he found employment at Black Tom Shaft, right by his home in Snailbeach, where barytes was being extracted. Later he worked at the Huglith Barytes Mine (near Habberley) before finishing his years of full-time employment at the County Council quarry at Callow Hill (near Minsterley).

It is for lead that the Stiperstones mines are best known, but latterly barytes and calcite were of greatest importance; small quantities of zinc, witherite and silver were produced too. Michael Shaw refers to Shropshire as 'a major player' in barytes production, often contributing between a quarter and a third to national production, most of it from the Stiperstones area. Major extraction did not start until the 1850s but by the 1890s barytes had become the most important mineral mined locally.

Barytes (barium sulphate) has many uses, notably as an inert filler in paint and paper production, as an aid to grading coal in coal washing plants and for barium meals. George Evans (born 1908) remembers lugging lorry loads to Liverpool's many paint mills and says that it was hauled as far as Tunbridge Wells to the Imperial Gramophone Record Company, apparently for mixing with resin for the making of records. Extraction of worthwhile quantities ended in 1948 with the closure of the Sallies and Gatten mines on the eastern flank of The Stiperstones but in 1957 Perkin's Level at Snailbeach was reopened so that several tons could be extracted for use as a shield following an incident at Windscale Nuclear Power Station. This was a one-off, but the recovery of barytes from the spoil heaps at Snailbeach continued until at least 1965.[38]

In a search for barytes underground, the last shaft in the area was sunk at Pennerley in 1956. Though honoured by a photo in the *Express and Star*, the search proved abortive. But activity continued at Burgam: worked, off and on, since at least the 1860s, planning permission was granted in 1957 for the winning of barytes but in fact, small quantities of lead were found and extracted. The last lead mine in the county, it finally closed in 1962.[39]

Last shaft sunk

Clifford Lewis (centre), William Wootton (seated) and Mr Chambers, representing the owner J L Burden (Jackfield Mines Ltd), at Pennerley, 1956. Photo courtesy of the *Express and Star,* Wolverhampton, and Verna Lewis, Clifford's wife.

George Betton (1839-1920)

Band Master of the Stiperstones Silver Band, drawn at the Ring O' Bells public house, Chester. This is the George Betton shown previously outside his home, Number 5 Pennerley. Reproduced courtesy of his great grandson Vince Jones.

And what did the miners do outside working hours? Alfred Hewitt took part in activities which were common to many of his fellows. As a boy he walked three times each Sunday to Lordshill Baptist Chapel for Sunday School and services; he was a member of the congregation throughout his life. He sang in the chapel choir and it is said that his tenor voice can be heard in the baptismal scene in the film of Mary Webb's *Gone to Earth* (see Chapter 5). And he was a member of the Snailbeach Brass Band in which he played the cornet.

Bands featured in both religious and mining events in the area. One such event was the opening of the Snailbeach smelter in 1862.[40] This was too early for the participation of Alfred Hewitt, but it seems likely that George Betton (1839-1920) was there. A small-holder and miner living at Pennerley, by 1870 George Betton was Band Master of the Stiperstones Silver Band. It may be that he figures too in the earliest known photograph of what is assumed to be the Snailbeach Brass Band, taken, it is thought, in the 1890s.[41] The photo

Snailbeach Brass Band, circa 1890s

The top photo is the much damaged original; the bottom photo is the much re-worked version used in other publications. Joseph Rowson (1849-1915) holds the drum, to his right stands his son Arthur, to his left his brother Job, on whose left stands Matthew Rowson (thought not to be a close relation). The names of the other two are not known. Note how, in the re-worked version, the lower legs and feet of Arthur Rowson have been duplicated, appearing also as those of the individual on the left of the group who could conceivably be George Betton. Remarkably Joseph and his wife Susannah (1854-1930) had 21 children. Reproduced courtesy of Sue Hartshorn, one of their granddaughters.

is badly damaged and versions published hitherto are reconstructions. In the original, much of the face of the musician on the far left has been lost, but his stance recalls that of George Betton shown in the photograph of No 5 Pennerley on page 55. This is speculation, but it is known that the drum is in the hands of Joseph Rowson, and that his brother Job and son Arthur are in the group as well.[42]

Jack Hewitt and Elijah Parry: barytes miners

Alfred and his wife Jane had four children. His one son, Jack (1915-1991), worked first at the Burgam Mine and then in the Huglith Barytes Mine. Unlike his father, Jack worked underground, where he ran similar risks to those of his grandfather, John, including that of suffering from silicosis through dust inhalation. This condition became prevalent from the 1880s onwards with the introduction of the compressed air drill which blew dust out of the shot holes into the miners' faces. It became known as 'the widow maker'.

Silicosis caused the premature and agonising death of many miners. The dangers were obvious, but, as W Reid Chappell observed in *The Shropshire of Mary Webb* (1930) 'The mine meant comparative wealth, even on the chance of a shortened life', and there was almost no alternative employment. Dorothy Trow (born 1915) recalls the death of her father, Elijah Parry, in 1933 at the age of 45: 'It was no age, but when you saw him suffering you wished for the Lord to take him, he was gasping for his breath all the time'. In the light of tragic cases such as this, and the example of his grandfather, it is little wonder that Jack Hewitt soon found employment away from the mines.

Elijah Parry

Reproduced courtesy of his granddaughter Phyllis Jones.

Joe Roberts: scavenging pebble-dash

Jack Hewitt (who, incidentally, like his father, played the cornet) provides a link with the final phase of mining activity at Snailbeach through his marriage to Doris, daughter of Joseph (Joe) Roberts (1894-1988) (who played the euphonium). Joe's father, William (c1862-c1935), had started work on the mineral dressing floors at Snailbeach at the age of 13. After one year's service he was promoted to the position of clerk in the Snailbeach Lead Mining Company's office, later becoming secretary; he served the company for 37 years in all, up until its liquidation in 1912. Joe himself was to become manager for the Gravel Trading Company, which during the inter-war years worked the spoil heaps for barytes, while the upper parts of the Snailbeach Mine were worked by the Halvans Company. From 1944 this work was taken over by the Snailbeach

The Roberts family and their rabbits

Joe and Florrie Roberts with their children Doris and George at their cottage in Crowsnest Dingle, circa 1928. Reproduced courtesy of Doris Hewitt (née Roberts).

Barytes Company which was 'to all intents and purposes, a one man enterprise in which Mr J Roberts … cleaned out what was left in the upper levels'.[43]

Joe Roberts persevered with underground working up until 1955. He had acquired the mine site (but not the mineral rights) from the Marquess of Bath, and was the principal character in these, the last years of the Snailbeach Mine. The imprecision of the deeds of conveyance led inevitably to various disputes in which Joe Roberts was notably assertive. In a dispute with the Snailbeach District Railways he cut off the water supply to the locomotive shed and removed two rails, trapping two of the three locomotives inside. The terms of a subsequent injunction obliged him to release them.

After 1955 Joe Roberts concentrated on working the spoil heaps, notably for the translucent white rhomboids of calcite used as 'pebble-dash' in decorative finishes on rendered house fronts. The salvaging of material previously regarded as waste was to continue at Snailbeach into the 1970s.[44] Similar activity had gone on elsewhere, and in the early days it was all hand work. George Evans remembers that 'spar', as it was called, was salvaged from spoil heaps at the Oven Pipe (Tankerville Mine), Round Hill, the East Roman Gravels and Pennerley, as well as at Snailbeach: 'You had to turn the tip over, pick out the lump spar, put it in a bucket, carry it up to the top and put it in a ruck – a heap – and you were paid for it by the square yard'.

During Joe Roberts' lifetime the Stiperstones mines mutated from profitable production to inexorable decline to neglected relic to historical curiosity to valued heritage. When Joe Roberts was born, the mines were still active, but by the 1930s Magdalene Weale was labelling this 'the land of dereliction', a landscape in which 'the ruined mine-shafts look utterly forlorn … [and] grey mounds and decayed workings dot the country in mournful profusion'. Her contemporary, W Reid Chappell, described 'the road to Pennerley' as being 'strewn with the black, mocking mouths of disused mine shafts, broken rusty machinery, derelict tin sheds, set in the cold glitter of the abandoned barytes'. But in Joe Roberts' later years this wasteland was beginning to excite the interest of mine historians, and by the time of his death, in 1988, concerted efforts were being made to conserve the mining remains. This was one of the reasons why Shropshire County Council acquired the Snailbeach Mine from his estate in 1990.

Ivor Brown and Ken Lock: salvaging heritage

That we know something of the mines, mine managers and mine workers of The Stiperstones is thanks in particular to those historians who, starting in the 1950s, had the foresight to salvage memories, photos, artefacts and archives, at a time when they were too recent to be properly cherished, when it was difficult to see beyond the scars, ruins and waste heaps to the industrial and community history lying beneath. These enthusiasts safeguarded and researched the history which has since informed the conservation of a significant part of the mining heritage.

Ivor Brown is perhaps the most industrious of the historians of the Stiperstones mines, and he is notably well qualified. He was born in 1937 into a family of miners who had worked at the Madeley Wood Company's collieries (south of Telford) since at least 1780; Ivor himself worked there from 1952 to 1962. Mining soon became more than just his job. He remembers visiting the mines of the Snailbeach area for the first time in 1957 on a scooter. He gave a 'helping hand' at Burgam, near Tankerville, the area's last working metal mine, and at Lordshill Mine (part of Snailbeach Mine) too, but more often spent time gleaning what information he could from the old mine workers, particularly Alfred Hewitt. In 1962 he became a mining lecturer, and in 1977 a mining engineer for Telford Development Corporation. Ivor Brown has published well over 300 notes, articles and papers including a number about the Stiperstones

Ivor Brown giving a 'helping hand' at Burgam Mine, 1959

He reports that 'timber cut locally was used for support, and candles were kept burning at intervals along the adits … there was no machinery, no safety wear and no real urgency, a great contrast to working in a colliery' (Brown 2001). Reproduced courtesy of Ivor Brown.

Ken Lock at the entrance to the Day Level, Snailbeach, 2008

Photo courtesy of Nick Southwick.

mines, as well as *The Mines of Shropshire* (1976) and *West Shropshire Mining Fields* (2001), which provide an unrivalled pictorial record of the mines of the area, supplemented by his own authoritative annotations. In writing this chapter I have drawn extensively on his publications.

Anyone who takes a look at photo credits in books about the mines of Shropshire, including those by Ivor Brown, will soon be familiar with the name Ken Lock. His collection of historic photographs was extensive, and he shared them very generously with others, as well as using them in his own lectures and occasional articles. His knowledge of the Shrewsbury Coalfield and the mines of south Shropshire was encyclopaedic and this too he shared readily. It was acquired through investigations on site, researches in the county archives and conversations with the old miners. Without his timely enquiries much information would have been lost, indeed his quick intervention appears to have been instrumental in saving mine buildings at Snailbeach from destruction. Peggy Chidley (born 1917), daughter of Alfred Hewitt, recounts that, outraged by the destruction of the Halvans Engine House she alerted Ken Lock, whose representations to the County Council led to an immediate embargo on further demolition work. The photo reproduced here shows Ken Lock alongside the replica plaque erected in 2008 at the entrance to the Day Level at Snailbeach, he died later that year at the age of 79. The original plaque had been removed for safe keeping in the 1960s but had subsequently been lost, Ken paid for the replacement which was cast by the Ironbridge Museum Foundry.

Halvans Engine House, 1963

Erected in about 1900 it provided power for separating minerals in the adjacent spoil heaps. One of the most photogenic of the old mine buildings, its destruction (in 1985) precipitated action to preserve other mine structures. Photo by Charles Sinker, reproduced courtesy of his family.

Encouraged by Ivor Brown, Ken Lock and others, notably David Adams, founder member and current president of the Shropshire Caving and Mining Club (SCMC), a new generation of researchers has explored and documented what survives above and below ground, and has done much to safeguard and make accessible the oral, written and physical remains. Shropshire Mining Club (now the SCMC) and others made representations in 1979 at the public examination of Shropshire County Council's proposed reclamation policies. These representations helped make due regard for the industrial heritage an element of policy in land reclamation such as that carried out by the Council at the Bog Mine in the 1980s. This was doubtless a helpful trial-run prior to the much more demanding work carried out at Snailbeach Mine in the 1990s by the Council and English Heritage. Subsequently, Shropshire Mines Trust has taken over management of the Snailbeach Mine site which is now said to have 'the best set of preserved lead mine buildings in Britain'.[45] It is a remarkable and ongoing example of the conservation and interpretation of the industrial heritage, much of it achieved through the knowledge, enthusiasm and hard work of volunteers. The Trust has done important work at the Tankerville Mine too, and this, like Snailbeach, is open to visitors who can now appreciate something of the grind and grandeur of this remarkable phase of the Stiperstones story.

Chapter 3

'Tushing and lugging': transport by road, rail and you name it

Everything was done in those days with a horse and cart or pushbike.

George Evans (1992)

George Evans

This photo was taken in about 1939 at Brockton, Worthen, when George was driving for Bernie Bunce. This bus looks like a Tilling-Stevens. Reproduced courtesy of the Evans family.

George Evans (1908-1993) was born near the New Venture Mine in Perkins Beach but lived mostly at the Black Hole (between the village of Stiperstones and Crowsnest). Right from his early years he was involved in transport, and during his working life the horse was replaced by the internal combustion engine. In the words of Jack Foley, he was 'one of the last generation of horse-drawn carters and one of the first generation of professional motor vehicle drivers'. George Evans's experiences provide a running theme for an exploration of Stiperstones transport in all its many forms.

Jack Foley's words appeared in a 'Salute to George' following his death at the end of 1993. The 'Salute' was published in the *Snailbeach District News* of which Jack was the founding editor, producing the first issue in June 1987; like many subsequent ones it was copied on an old 'Roneo' duplicating machine.[1] From the start the *News* was a free local newsletter delivered monthly by hand to all the residents of Snailbeach and immediately adjacent areas, with copies being sent further afield, even overseas, to former residents. In the words of the opening issue 'the Newsletter hopes to acquaint us with ourselves, so to speak' and more than twenty-five years and several editors later it continues to do so. It has grown in size, sophistication, coverage and distribution, but remains free, surviving on goodwill, faithful volunteer editors and distributors, voluntary contributions and local advertisers.

Many of the early editions of the *News* carried the reminiscences of older residents, including, between 1990 and 1994, those of George Evans. His recollections appeared in 45 instalments under the title 'Recalling the past', the last shortly after his death; they were subsequently collated and privately published as *A Voice from the Hills*.[2]

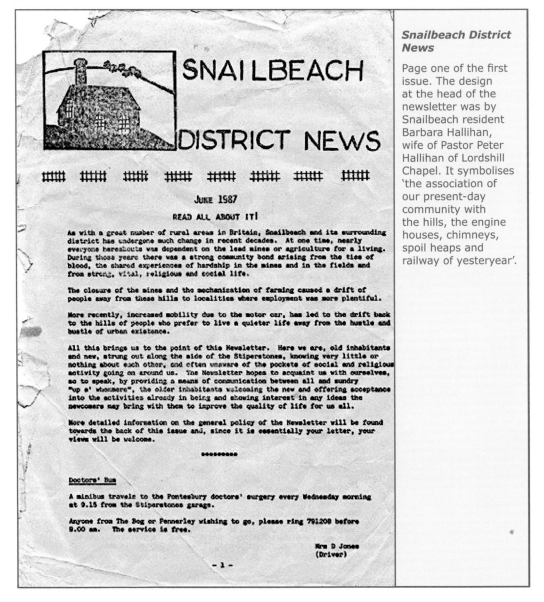

Snailbeach District News

Page one of the first issue. The design at the head of the newsletter was by Snailbeach resident Barbara Hallihan, wife of Pastor Peter Hallihan of Lordshill Chapel. It symbolises 'the association of our present-day community with the hills, the engine houses, chimneys, spoil heaps and railway of yesteryear'.

George Evans's reminiscences start with the words 'As a boy I remember going to Shrewsbury by train [from Minsterley] with my mother and aunt', but from there on he concentrates on horse and cart, push-bike, traction engine, lorry and bus. It is a fascinating account, full of historical interest, and it is entertaining too, with many of George's best stories told against himself – 'So that was one of the first damn silly things I did [ploughing the ground behind his house for oats and potatoes] ... and it's been like that ever since really' – mixed with tricks for keeping temperamental engines running and accounts of village life in the first half of the twentieth century.

Yoke, 'car' and stretcher

To George Evans's recollections can be added those gathered for *Never on a Sunday* and those of Iris Muriel Jones (née Smith) (1920-2009). Born in a cottage next to the Potter's Pit shaft at Pennerley (see page 47),[3] Muriel Jones's recollections, entitled *Stiperstones Child*, cover the years up to 1935 when she went into service.

Like almost all of her contemporaries Muriel Jones remembers the daily task of fetching water:

> 'There was of course no piped water to our house, so one of our chores was to help dad fetch water from a spout just along from the Post Office [at Pennerley] ... Us girls would try to get home without too much spillage, while dad carried two large galvanised pails slung across his shoulders on a wooden yoke.'

Muriel Smith

Muriel, whose married name was Jones, aged 10. Reproduced courtesy of her son Vince Jones.

Marcia Addy carrying water

Marcia is carrying water from Scott Level to 23 Snailbeach in about 1951; an uphill haul of 200 or more paces. Evacuated from Manchester to the home of Esmer and Bert Davies, she returned to holiday there most summers during post-War school holidays. Reproduced courtesy of Marcia Fletcher (née Addy).

George Evans's early recollections include the so-called 'car', a device commonly used to move minerals down hill-sides:

> 'At the Ventor mine,[4] they brought the material out of the level in a tram, which they pushed on lines which they had laid on the floor of the tunnel ... it was then re-loaded into a horsedrawn car, as they called it ... The car that the horse pulled down the hill had heavy iron runners like a sledge. It weighed about half a ton empty and when loaded they would put a ton or more in it.'

Henry Jones (born 1930) remembers watching an old shire horse called Jack 'tushing' (dragging) an empty car back up the hill:

> 'It was really hard tushing it up – like he'd walk forty yards and he'd stop and pant, he'd walk another forty yards and have a puff. A fella called Jack Evans owned this horse. He farmed at the Green Farm near the school and us kids was always fascinated to watch him with his horse up and down the track they had worn in the hill.'

Jack, Jack and car

Jack Evans leading his horse Jack downhill with a loaded car, 1943. This drawing, done from memory by Cliff Lewis many years later when visiting his daughter in Australia, relates to Burgam Mine where Cliff worked in the early 1940s. Reproduced courtesy of Verna Lewis, his wife.

Les Hotchkiss (born 1927) recalls the 'lugging' (hauling) of stone too:

> 'My father had a horse and an old sledge, 'cars' we used to call them. They would be filled up [with stone from the ridge] and brought down to where the Devil's Chair car park is now.[5] Men would break the stone ... and a horse and cart would lug it out onto the Bog road.'

Underground there was much 'lugging' done by the miners, and above ground there was much of it done by one and all, including the carting of hay from the fields. Most of the hay was carried by horse and cart, but Doris Hewitt (born 1916) and others remember an alternative method too: 'At Lordshill I remember making cocks of hay and the horses would lug them on drays, while at Crowsnest we used two poles – it was a much smaller scale'. Mary Webb includes an account of this in *The Golden Arrow*: 'On the day that it [the hay] was ready to be "lugged" Joe came home early. A twill sheet on two poles reminiscent of an ambulance stretcher, was piled with hay and carried by Joe and John as carefully as if it really were an invalid'.

Shanks's pony and some old pram

There was a lot of such lugging and leg work in the past. George Evans recalls that 'it was nothing to walk over the hill to and from school or work – everyone did'. Such 'functional walking' has virtually ceased, but 'recreational walking' has become increasingly popular. Functional walking, notably to and fro across the hill, originated from a scatter of homes and work places; as a result, maps

Stretchering hay

Carrying hay at Snailbeach in about 1930. Mary Rowson stands in front of the stretcher which is carried by her mother Alice (left), and aunt, Joysie Evans. Reproduced courtesy of Mary Challinor (née Rowson).

show a more extensive network of paths than those in use today. There may be more walkers nowadays, but there are fewer paths.

In *Never on a Sunday* Phyllis Jones (born 1936) recalls the post round that her mother did on foot from Snailbeach Post Office: 'Lower Works … Upper Works … [both at Snailbeach] Lordshill, to the Vessons, over to The Hollies, up to Blakemoorflat then right over the back of the hill and back down Perkins Beach Dingle, finish the Dingles and walk back home'. Elsie Rowson (born 1924) recalls that the complete round, which she walked for a decade or so up until the late 1960s, was 11 miles and 6 furlongs, and on occasion she had to carry two ten pound electrical batteries all the way to Gittinshay – 'by the time you got there it [the post bag] would be pulling your neck out'.

George Evans recounts that, on flatter ground, if you had something to transport 'you'd see people, women sometimes or young boys, going with some old thing they'd rigged up with wheels on, some old pram perhaps, to the station to fetch a half hundredweight or a hundredweight of coal … and at the same time you would see horses with drays around there collecting and carting the milk'.

Horse-drawn transport

Before the days of motorised transport, travel to and from Minsterley Station to catch the train to Shrewsbury would have been on foot or in some form of light horse-drawn two-wheeled carriage or trap. There were a number of operators using such traps which, according to Stanley Evans (born circa 1907), writing in the *Snailbeach District News*, might take as many as 16 passengers. George Evans remembers that though still a school-boy, he used a horse and trap to run fitters and clerks employed at the Bog Mine to and from the station when they went home at weekends.

Horses provided the essential motive force for the transport of minerals, timber and a variety of goods. George Evans's grandfather, father and uncle hauled

Edwin Davies and his 'carrier cart'

Edwin Davies (circa 1853-1933) of Snailbeach carried passengers to and from Minsterley Station. He was the uncle of another Edwin (Neddy) Davies (see Chapter 10). Reproduced courtesy of Nina Pinches, whose husband, Tom, was grandson of the Edwin Davies in the photograph.

minerals from the Bog Mine, and later from the New Venture Mine in Perkins Beach, to Minsterley, and Johnny Butler (born 1920) and Della Pugh (born 1916) recall watching horse-drawn timber carriages, with four horses in a team, hauling timber, following the felling in 1925 of trees between Crowsnest and Granham's Moor.

The coal man, Jimmy Gittings, with his old grey horse and open cart, is remembered by Muriel Jones. Though 'a small, round-faced man with white hair and jovial be-whiskered face' he was 'a man possessed' as he drove the poor horse 'straining up our lane, staggering under the weight of a full load of coal … almost on its knees on many occasions … and in the end it was'. She remembers groceries being brought up from Pontesbury on M P Jones's yellow carts pulled by exhausted horses (Pennerley is 800 feet higher than Pontesbury), except in the frequently snow-bound winters, when her father and others had to push the deliveries in wheelbarrows up the last mile, including 300 feet of ascent, from Stiperstones Village.

Emily Griffiths (born 1917) recalls that even when motorised transport was available, there was one circumstance at least when horse-drawn transport was still a requirement. Her father had stewardship of the local Home Office explosives magazine and used to take explosives over the hill to Huglith Mine with a pony and trap 'because you were not allowed to transport high explosives except in a specially constructed vehicle – not a mechanically powered vehicle with sparks and petrol involved'.

Dennis the engineer

Trains first reached Pontesbury and Minsterley in 1861 following the opening of a branchline from Hanwood; they carried both passengers and freight. This was still some way from the lead and barytes mines of The Stiperstones, but brought rail transport within reasonable reach and stimulated proposals for a rail link to the mines themselves, as an alternative to carrying the minerals in horse-drawn wagons.

In 1873 the Snailbeach District Railways Company was incorporated by Act of Parliament; it was authorised to consist of two railways of 2 foot 4 inch gauge.[6] Railway No 1, a matter of 3 miles, 2 furlongs, 5.44 chains in length, was to run from a junction just west of Pontesbury Station, the penultimate stop on the branchline, to Crowsnest. The engineer for the railway was Henry Dennis (1825-1906), the manager of Snailbeach Mine; it was built by Elias Griffith of Chirk, and it operated in one way or another for some 80 years. The railway's history was researched in the 1940s by the late Eric S Tonks, one time President of the Industrial Railway Society, and it is on his work that this account largely depends.

This first instalment of the Snailbeach District Railways (SDR) opened for freight traffic in July 1877; officially, at least, it never carried any passengers. It ran uphill at an uninterrupted gradient from Pontesbury to Crowsnest and was well suited to the transport back downhill to Pontesbury, largely by gravity, of the heavy minerals from the mines. Here there were transhipment sidings allowing freight to be moved from the narrow gauge of the SDR to the standard gauge of the main line and vice versa. The railway included a branch serving a smelting works, and another which climbed into the heart of the surface works of the Snailbeach Mine, as well as serving the railway's engine shed. The basic layout is shown on the plan reproduced here.

At the Shrewsbury Smithfield Sale on 4 September 1877, two months after the opening of the railway, one lot was '10 carthorses, powerful, upstanding, seasoned, of good ages, 17 hands high etc, for sale in consequence of the completion of the Snailbeach District Railway which will render haulage by road unnecessary'.

Railway No 2 was to be a continuation of the line, working its way across Crowsnest Dingle then along a shelf cut into the hillside round Mytton Beach and Perkins Beach, terminating near Tankerville Mine. Bridges 65 feet and 46 feet high were planned to carry the rail line across Crowsnest Dingle and Perkins Beach.

And then there was to be the Shropshire Minerals Light Railway (SMLR). The intended course is shown on the plan. For the first half mile, as far as Crowsnest, it was to run parallel with the first Snailbeach District Railway, from where it

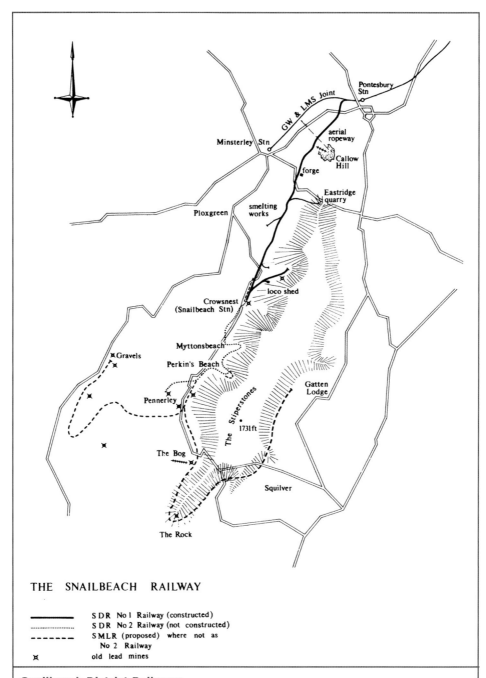

THE SNAILBEACH RAILWAY

————	S D R No 1 Railway (constructed)
··················	S D R No 2 Railway (not constructed)
- - - - - -	S M L R (proposed) where not as No 2 Railway
✕	old lead mines

Snailbeach District Railways

Plan showing the routes of the actual and proposed Snailbeach District Railways. The line from Shrewsbury to Minsterley was a joint Great Western and London and North Western Railway branch line. The latter company became part of the London, Midland and Scottish Railway company. Reproduced courtesy of The Industrial Railway Society from Eric Tonks's history of the SDR.

was to follow, more or less, the route of Railway No 2, with viaducts 100 yards and 93 yards long at Mytton Beach and Perkins Beach, before heading south to The Bog, then all the way down to and round The Rock before coming up the east side of The Stiperstones to Gatten Lodge, presumably with a view to serving the barytes mines on that side of the hill; there was also a branch line planned to the Gravels.

As Eric Tonks, points out:

> 'The SMLR was from the start a much more ambitious scheme than the parent Snailbeach line, totalling more than 11 route miles of track and wending its circuitous way within siding distance of practically every lead mine in the district … a proper switchback throughout … and with but a few hundred yards of level track in the whole of its tortuous length.'

What a train journey it would have made! But it was a pipe dream. Difficulties had been encountered generating adequate capital even for Railway No 1, and neither Railway No 2 nor the SMLR got beyond the drawing board. Royal assent for the SMLR was given in 1891, but by this time lead mining was in severe decline and although the mining of barytes was on the up, the capital required for such ambitious projects was never forthcoming.

Indeed the history of the SDR is one intimately tied to the ups and downs of the mining and quarrying industries. For many years it was run largely as a subsidiary of the Snailbeach Lead Mining Company, its principal customer, and with the slump in lead mining in the last two decades of the nineteenth century, the Railway came close to closure. However, following the opening of the Granham's Moor Quarry at Eastridge, near Habberley, a new spur of the SDR was constructed and came into service in 1905 or 1906; this led to an upturn in traffic. In 1906 the Railway transported a record 20,000 tons, and this rose to over 38,000 tons in 1909, before falling away again.

Dennis the tank engine

Locomotives named 'Sir Theodore', 'Belmont' and 'Fernhill' chugged along the SDR over the years, but 'Sir Theodore', loaned from the Glyn Valley Tramway Company, was prone to de-railment and was soon returned. 'Belmont' was acquired second hand and put in many years of service. 'Fernhill' was acquired new and entered service in 1881; it was built by Barclays & Co of Kilmarnock.[7] The only known photograph of 'Fernhill' may possibly have been taken by Albert Hewitt, older brother of Alfred (see Chapter 2). As a young man Albert worked in the Snailbeach Smelter. He was only 16 when 'Fernhill' arrived, so this photo may have been taken a few years later.[8]

'Dennis' (later also referred to as Number 1) manufactured by Messrs W G Bagnall Ltd of Stafford was also acquired new, in 1906. Its name is taken to be a tribute to the Chairman and Engineer of the SDR, Henry Dennis. He had died in that year, but his son, also Henry Dennis, was the new Board Chairman and may well have initiated this memorial.

Fernhill

The photo is thought to date from the mid 1880s and may have been taken by Albert Hewitt.
National Railway Museum/Science & Society Picture Library.

Colonel Stephens

D H Lawrence saw the SDR in 1924 on his visit to The Stiperstones in the company of Frederick Carter (see Chapter 6), and it earns a brief mention in his novella *St Mawr* (1925):

> 'They [the principal characters, on horseback] rode on slowly, up the steep rise of the wood, then down into a glade where ran a little railway built for hauling some mysterious mineral out of the hill, in war-time, and now already abandoned. Even on this countryside, the dead hand of the war was like a corpse decomposing.'

In fact, as detailed above, the SDR pre-dated the First World War by many years, and by the time that Lawrence saw the railway it was certainly not abandoned, indeed, after some considerable problems its future was looking brighter.

The main problem had been a slump in quarry traffic which led to a temporary closure over the winter of 1912/13, but traffic increased in the war years.[9] In

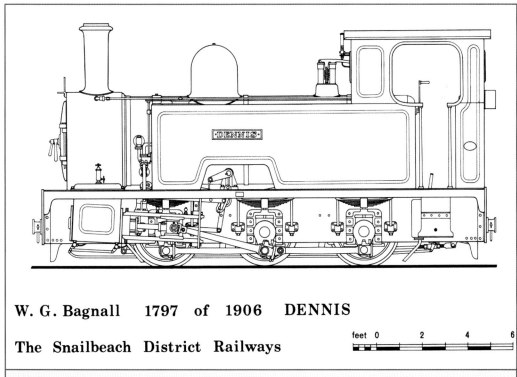

W. G. Bagnall   1797   of   1906   DENNIS

The Snailbeach District Railways

feet 0   2   4   6

Dennis

A drawing by Roger West prepared from the manufacturer's plans. It appeared in Eric Tonks's account of the Snailbeach District Railways and is reproduced here courtesy of The Industrial Railway Society.

1920, 'Dennis', the sole surviving locomotive, had to be taken out of service, and it has been suggested that the Railway succumbed for a while to dependence on horse power and gravity! But, following a further temporary closure in about 1921, a new Board was formed in 1923 under the chairmanship of Colonel Stephens, described by Eric Tonks as 'the first and foremost advocate of the minor railway'. Improvements were made to the line and its rolling stock which led to increased efficiency and a growth in traffic, which reached 26,352 tons in 1938; this was of spar and some barytes, and more importantly of road stone from a new quarry at Callow Hill.

Colonel Stephens (1868-1931) was christened Holman Fred (not Frederick) Stephens; his friends called him 'Holly', to others he became known as 'The Colonel'.[10] He was the son of artists, but his principal enthusiasm was for practical things and he became an engineer. From an early age railways had been a particular interest and they were to become his life's work, although over a long period he served as a volunteer with what was to become the Territorial Army, rising to the rank of Lieutenant-Colonel with the Royal Engineers.

Aged 22, Fred Stephens started his first job in railway construction as resident engineer of the Cranbrook and Paddock Wood Railway in Kent. Over his career he

Colonel Holman Fred Stephens

Courtesy of the Colonel Stephens Museum.

had a direct involvement with 16 light railways, now referred to as 'The Colonel Stephens' Railways', whether as engineer and founder, re-constructor, consultant engineer, operator, chairman or managing director. According to the railway historian John Scott Morgan, he was 'one of Britain's more individualistic and eccentric engineers', responsible for 'some of the more entertaining of Britain's minor railways'.[11] The common threads of his construction projects were 'harsh gradients, lightly engineered with numerous level crossings, stations constructed from cheap materials (wood and corrugated iron) and, above all, a rustic charm that was always going to lead to financial decline once alternative means of transport appeared'. Given these predilections it is little surprise that the SDR appealed to him, even though it only had one level crossing.

'Dennis' was the only engine surviving when Colonel Stephens took over the railway, but it was in sore need of an overhaul, so Stephens acquired 'Skylark' (No 2) second-hand in 1922, and, in 1923, the nameless locomotives Nos 3 and 4, manufactured in the United States and rebuilt after War service in France. 'Dennis', despite its intended overhaul, was never to run again. According to Eric Tonks, though this is questioned by other authorities, the railway's driver, named Gatford, seems to have taken a dislike to the engine and 'in the course of some occasionally caustic correspondence with his chief, put forward a number of reasons why the repairs to 'Dennis' were delayed'. 'Dennis' remained outside the engine shed – partly dismembered – before being officially withdrawn from service in 1936.

From about 1940 the track between Callow Hill and Snailbeach was no longer used for haulage. Traffic continued to operate however between Callow Hill and Pontesbury, and locomotives 2, 3 and 4 remained in service up until 1946, when the boilers of all three were condemned by an inspector, and steam working finally ended. Nevertheless the railway continued in operation, albeit unconventionally. But before covering this aspect of the history of the SDR, more needs to be said about Driver Gatford.

Driver Gatford

In Eric Tonks's account, Driver Gatford (he never gives him a Christian name), having worked on the Bishop's Castle Railway (BCR), became the long-standing kingpin of the SDR. He maintains that by the mid 1930s the railway was being run single-handed by Driver Gatford as driver, stoker, footplate man, fitter and handy-man, 'a unique achievement'. Tonks describes Gatford's cottage as backing onto the railway and recounts that when into his seventies, Driver Gatford permitted himself the perk of leaving the engine outside his garden gate each evening, having first taken on coal and water; it stood there overnight ready for the next day's work.

Eric Tonks maintains that in 1946, when Nos 2, 3 and 4 were all withdrawn from service, the septuagenarian engine driver was required to take the wheel of a Fordson tractor which hauled wagons between Pontesbury and Callow Hill.[12] He adds that 'for a time, Driver Gatford continued in charge of the [surrogate] 'loco', but soon afterwards retired to his cottage at Snailbeach, to watch the weeds creeping over the metals [the rails] beyond the hedge'.

Driver Tom Gatford

He is on the footplate of Terrier No 4 on the Weston, Clevedon and Portishead Railway, September 1937. Note the shine on his boots – Tom Gatford had been a regimental sergeant major. Photo by Peter Strange courtesy of the Colonel Stephens Museum.

Others have come up with a very different employment history. Albyn Austin of the BCR Society has found that Thomas (Tom) Gatford (born 1874) never worked on the BCR and that his time on the SDR was neither lonesome nor particularly long. Apparently the railway generally had four staff, including Driver Gatford, who worked there in the 1920s, being transferred temporarily to the Shropshire and Montgomeryshire Railway (another Colonel Stephens' railway) before becoming senior driver on the Weston, Clevedon and Portishead Railway in Somerset (yet another) from 1936, driving 'Terrier No 4' on the Railway's final run in 1940. He then retired to Kent where he died early in 1946, which was before, back in Shropshire, locomotives 2, 3 and 4 had been condemned and tractor haulage had begun. Eric Tonks's account of Tom Gatford's work on the SDR appears to be largely and mysteriously fictional.[13]

'Awaiting the end'

Returning to the history of the SDR, from 1947 the Pontesbury to Callow Hill section was leased to Shropshire County Council, and thus, after 70 years, the SDR as such ceased to operate any service, although the Council persevered with tractor haulage until 1959. In the interim, the scrapping of rolling stock and lifting of track had begun. Eric Tonks, in the first edition of *The Snailbeach District Railways*, published in 1950, describes, regretfully, the scene:

> 'The track leading from Snailbeach Station is now overgrown and in parts obliterated, and at the top of the slope passes under a frail bridge to the stone engine shed. Loco No 3 stands outside, cold and rusty but covered with a tarpaulin, and Nos 2 and 4 behind the much-patched doors. The shed is an eerie and desolate place in winter, with the wind moaning in the cowl and banging the loose patches of corrugated iron, and how sad it is to look upon the forsaken and silent engines! No more will they snortingly push their trains up the bank to the mines or even clank their way down the curves to Pontesbury; instead, here they are, stranded … awaiting the end.'

The end was imminent: in May 1950 they were cut up on site. The track between Snailbeach and Callow Hill was lifted shortly afterwards, but a short stretch to the loco shed was left intact, as was the loco shed itself, and both survive today. Indeed, when it came to the 1990s and works to consolidate and restore some of the mining remains, the loco shed was the first building to be repaired.

Snailbeach Station

This photograph of September 1941 by R S Carpenter shows the line to Pontesbury lying straight ahead and the one to the locomotive shed and mines uphill to the right. The road from Snailbeach to Crowsnest runs from left of centre in front of the two buildings with chimneys, the nearer of which is the railway weighhouse and office, before disappearing behind the fence on the left. Shropshire Archives (PC/S/17/3). By the time this photo was taken it appears that the rails of the siding opposite the weighhouse (as shown in the accompanying plan) had been lifted, and the weighbridge for rail vehicles, which was linked under the road to the weighhouse, was no longer functional. Eric Tonks states that there was a weighbridge for road vehicles too. The drawing is from Tonks's history of the Snailbeach District Railways and is reproduced here courtesy of The Industrial Railway Society.

Snailbeach District Railway Locomotive Shed

This photo of May 1949 shows the shed and No 3 loco being observed and recorded by a visiting group of enthusiasts. Behind stand the impressive but crumbling mine buildings, the most obvious of which are, in the centre, the roofless Crusher House and, on the far right, the Compressor House and the chimney that served its boiler. Photo by Bernard Roberts, courtesy of The Industrial Railway Society.

For Eric Tonks the SDR and its setting 'inevitably bring to mind some of the Welsh narrow gauge systems, more than any other the Talyllyn, with its climb up the hillside through the woods at Dolgoch'. So it was appropriate that when, in 1961, the track from Callow Hill towards Pontesbury was lifted, some of it went to the Talyllyn Railway which had been kept going thanks to the efforts of railway enthusiasts such as L T C (Tom) Rolt who knew Snailbeach and had indeed written a ghost story set there (see Chapter 4). And, a few years ago, the remnants of two hopper wagons from the SDR were located at Talyllyn. All that remained were the bases and axles but they were brought back home to Snailbeach and the restoration of one of them was completed in 2009.

Amazingly, some fifty years after its demise, a proposal was floated to revive the SDR as a tourist attraction. The notion was greeted with much scepticism, indeed it was dismissed by some as a hoax and little has been heard of it since.

Traction Engines

Whilst the SDR provided transport for minerals won at Snailbeach Mine, the failure to extend the line obliged the other mines to use alternative methods of haulage. George Evans mentions teams of horses and wagons and later:

> 'Foster steam traction engines purchased to convey the minerals [from the Bog Mine to Minsterley Station] in a truck attached to the traction engine with a draw bar. The tractor and truck were on iron wheels and carried 6 tons ... later, Bog Mines hired another traction engine ... it pulled two trucks, each carrying 10 tons. It was named Shamrock and it made ruts in the road all the way from The Bog to Plox Green so deep that a man could lie down in them and not be seen.'

In Mary Webb's *Gone to Earth* the traction engine and trailer from a stone quarry which passed God's Little Mountain two or three times a week 'was never ... so full that it could not accommodate a passenger' (or indeed two). So Mrs Marston and Hazel Woodus book a place for a journey to 'the little country station' (presumably Minsterley) on their way to Silverton (Shrewsbury) to purchase clothes for the wedding of Hazel and Edward Marston:

> 'At last the traction engine appeared, and Mrs Marston was hoisted into the trailer ... They started in a whirl of good-byes, shrieks of delight from Hazel, and advice of Mrs Marston to the driver to put the brake on and keep it on ... They rounded a turn with great dignity, the trailer, with Mrs Marston as its figure-head – wearing

Traction engine of Shropshire Lead Mines Ltd

Ivor Brown gives the date 1917 for this photo and states that the traction engine was used to transport lead ore and barytes in 6-8 ton loads from The Bog to Minsterley. Ken Lock collection.

an expression of pride, fear, and resignation – swinging along majestically ... They went gallantly, if slowly, on through narrow ways ... Carts had to back into gates to let them go by, and when they came into the main road horses reared and had to be led past. Hazel found it all delightful.'

Ropeways

The billeting of German prisoners in the area during the First World War provided a labour force for the construction of the Bog Mine's alternative to the SDR – an aerial ropeway running from the mine to Malehurst (between Pontesbury and Minsterley), a distance of nearly 5½ miles. The ropeway was built under the managership of Lieutenant-Colonel Josslyn Vere Ramsden. George Evans remembers men named Gilderson and Fountain as surveyor and engineer, and Mollie Rowson (born 1908) a Jim Williams who oiled the wheels – literally. Today little knowledge survives of the German labour force, but George Evans reports that they were 'a decent lot of chaps' with one in particular, named Paul Measler, a school teacher, recalled with particular respect. Henry Jones says they were billeted in a big shed called 'the Cabin' (since demolished) on the edge of the hill above Tankerville, 'an outstanding building in its day ... one of the biggest and the best'.

The ropeway was built to carry bucket-loads of barytes down to Malehurst and bring coal back up. The buckets were attached to a steel rope strung between pylons (known locally as 'trussles' or 'trestles') mostly of wood, set in concrete bases; examples of these bases survive today in a number of places. The route ran from near the school at The Bog, crossing over the school yard on its way to Pennerley Hill where, at The Flake, it dropped down through a cutting in the hillside to the back of the Stiperstones School, before crossing over the road and skirting the west side of the hill, on its way to Malehurst. Branches off the ropeway were built serving a quarry at Buxton and the New Venture Mine in Perkins Beach, the latter requiring a pylon as much as 90 feet tall.

Aerial ropeway

This is the leg to Buxton shown looking west from the 'transfer station' on the hill at The Flake, above Tankerville. The road at Burgam Corner is visible to the right of the left hand pylon. Reproduced from *Never on a Sunday.*

According to George Evans there were 127 buckets, and each carried ½ ton of barytes down to Malehurst and ¼ ton of coal back up to The Bog. Michael Shaw states 'around 5 cwt [¼ ton] of barytes down and somewhat less coal back up'. Henry Jones remembers

his grandmother telling him of a time when their family were 'so poor they couldn't afford any coal ... the weather was very bad [and] one of the Germans would get a stick and tip one of the overhead buckets of coal ... Then granny had 4 cwt of coal free'.

The ropeway was taken down some time before 1930, but another, serving the Huglith Mine, ran for a further 20 years. It is probably to this that W Reid Chappell refers in his *The Shropshire of Mary Webb* (1930). He describes the 'peculiar wailing hum' and the 'whirring high-pitched rumble' of the buckets passing along 'a spider thread of cable' strung between the 'gaunt, gallows-like steel masts'. Helen Dickson (born 1937) recalls in *Once Upon a Hill* how, as a young child, she was terrified of the passing buckets: 'There would be this large black sinister shape appearing with a "whoosh" like a great black bird above us, and then it swooped away'.

Perhaps it was knowledge of the Huglith ropeway that inspired the children's writer, Malcolm Saville (see Chapter 6), in his adventure story *Seven White Gates* (1944), to hark back to the former ropeway serving the New Venture Mine, and re-invent it as a 'cable railway' strung across Black Dingle (Perkins Beach). On this cable railway, suspended high above the Dingle, ran 'a cable car – a big round iron container, with two steps or ledges on the outside large enough for a man to stand upon ... suspended by a rather complicated pulley block upon which were two short levers'. The 'cable car' provided a hair-rising ride for Tom Ingles and Petronella (Peter) Sterling in their attempt to rescue Dickie and Mary Morton:

'... suddenly they were out in the evening sunshine ... deep, deep below them the tops of the trees were careering madly backwards and every second the speed of

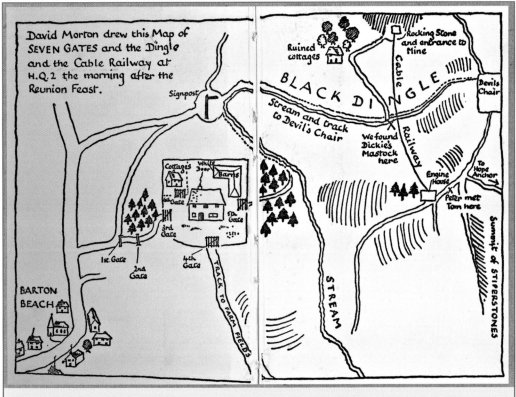

Map from *Seven White Gates*

This map forming the endpapers to Malcolm Saville's story is based extremely loosely on real features and locations, showing (with the parallels given here being open to debate) Barton Beach (Stiperstones Village), Seven Gates Farm, Black Dingle (Perkins Beach), across which runs the 'cable railway' serving the old mine, and the Devil's Chair. Credited to the fictional David Morton, the actual cartographer is not known.

the car increased … [it] swayed violently and the pulley block over Peter's head screeched as the wires tore through it … She screamed … as the great jagged black hole in the rock rushed towards them … and ducked on to the floor of the car as it careered madly into the blackness.'

A boatway

And what of water-borne transport? By 1812 a drainage adit, long referred to as the Boat Level, had been driven from a point north of Tankerville in a southerly direction for 1¾ miles, serving the mines at Burgam, Tankerville, Potter's Pit, Pennerley and The Bog, beyond which it was subsequently extended to attain a total length of about 2 miles. The level was designed as a drainage adit and Fred Brook and Martin Allbutt in their account *The Shropshire Lead Mines* (1973) observe that although 'Its name suggests that boats were used in it as a means of transport … its twisting route and narrow section, together with an absence of any mineral spoil near its portal indicate that it was used for drainage only'.

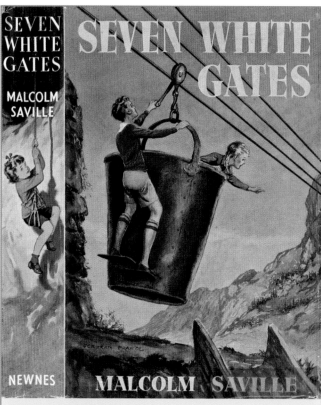

Seven White Gates

The dust cover of Malcolm Saville's story showing Tom Ingles and Petronella Sterling riding the 'cable car' across Black Dingle, and, on the spine, the rescue of Mary Morton from the old mine. Illustration by Bertram Prance, reproduced courtesy of his son, Christopher.

But in *Lone Pine Five* (1949), Malcolm Saville's locally-born character Charles Sterling, when recounting some of the history and legends of The Stiperstones, refers to a story 'of an underground waterway which was built originally to drain one of the mines and later used as a sort of subterranean canal to carry loads of minerals'. Saville was presumably drawing on information that he had gathered locally. His informant may perhaps have been Margaret Corfield, who in 1961, when in her seventies, contributed an article about the Boat Level to the *Shropshire Magazine*. She recalled that when her mother attended the Bog School in the 1850s, her schoolmistress described a trip she had made by boat along the level – the flow of water draining the mines carried boats to the mouth of the level, and a rope fixed to its walls allowed the boatmen to haul them back, hand over hand. In an advert in the *Salopian Journal* of 1830 (reproduced on page 48) details of the auction of the lease of the Bog Lead Mines are given, including the sale of 'Steam Engine, Gins, Boats etc'; the advertisement goes on to list '3 Wood Boats and 1 Iron Boat'.[14]

Motor cars and push-bikes

The little motor car driven by Mrs Edwards, who taught at the Bog School, was the only one that Muriel Jones recalls seeing. To this can be added the first three motor cars that George Evans remembers using the local roads. The first, a Model T Ford was owned by 'the then Manager of the Bog Mines, a Mr Pulean'. Later 'Colonel Ramsden, who was a Director of the Bog Mines, started coming to and from the mines with a little two-seater air-cooled Rover with a dickey seat at the back'; the third was owned by Dr Jameson from Pontesbury. And at some point Nurse Hand from Crowsnest was to be seen riding a motorbike, though Henry Jones remembers her driving an Austin 7 with a canvas roof.

Nurse Hand riding a motorbike

Charlotte Hand (c1885-1953) was District Nurse from 1922 until her death. She lived in the 'Nurse's Bungalow' at Crowsnest. Gertie Oldfield, daughter of Fred Blakemore, the blacksmith at Crowsnest, rides pillion. Reproduced courtesy of Nina Pinches.

As to his own transport, George Evans needed a push-bike to get to and from Shrewsbury, when, as a 17 year old, he went to Withers' Garage to be taught to drive and to do running repairs. But driving in those days was very different. The Model T Ford

> 'had to be started with a starting handle ... there was no gear lever ... there was no accelerator, you had a [manual] throttle under the steering wheel ... there was one lever on each side of the steering column, one for the ignition and one for the fuel ... when you took the hand-brake off, the car was in neutral and right off you were in top gear ... the lights were bright according to the speed you were going ... if you were going slowly round a corner, you had no lights.'

George himself graduated from a push-bike done up by his Uncle Tom, to a brand new 'Rudge Whitworth' bought on HP from Mr Tom Parry at Central Stores, Crowsnest. Next came his first motorbike, which was a second-hand 'Premier', and later a 'Douglas Flat Twin'. In due course George became part owner of an 'old Chev' motor car. Next he drove 'a nice little Rover car with a fabric body', as chauffeur for a Captain and Mrs Dixon of Shrewsbury, before moving up-market as the chauffeur of a Rolls owned by the mysterious Max Wenner of Batchcott Hall on the northern fringe of The Long Mynd.[15]

For the vast majority, a bicycle was the only affordable means of transport, and for some it was a tool of the trade, notably for Bert Evans, the postman. He had lost a leg in the First World War and this made his daily cycle-round heroic. His nephew, Graham France (born 1921), describes Bert's itinerary:

> 'He'd leave Pennerley at half past three in the morning to go to Minsterley [nearly five miles away and some 800 feet lower down] to sort all the letters … He would travel from Minsterley all the way back up to The Bog delivering the mail, he would go home to Pennerley and then he would have to go back down at night collecting all the mail from the boxes to take it back to Minsterley.'

'I can see him now', says Muriel Jones, 'pushing his way through a Christmas morning blizzard struggling with his bike, heavily laden with parcels. And always a warm smile greeted you at the door. What a man! … And with a wooden leg!'

Emily Griffiths used her bicycle to carry an unusual cargo:

> 'Farmers could get a police licence to collect explosives to blow up tree roots [from the Home Office magazine stewarded by her father]. So there always had to be someone at home … to go up to the magazine, about a mile and a half away and collect these explosives … I've gone on my bicycle many a time and carried ten pounds worth of gelignite down the front of my coat.'

Bicycles (of a sort) were used for recreation too. George Evans remembers that

> 'most of us young lads would find an old frame, a wheel and other parts here and there. Usually there would be no spindle in the wheel so a bit of rusty plain fencing wire would have to do. There would be no tyres on the wheels, or brakes, or pedals and it would only go downhill. We would push it up the bank to ride down time and time again.'

Muriel Jones recalls an alternative in wheeled recreation, remembering

> 'the rush of excitement as me, sister Hetty and my best friend Ethel Lewis, towed an aged wooden pushchair up the lane to the hillock by the old mine shaft. Once used by us sisters when babies, this 'chariot' now provided us with an exhilarating 'Ride with Death' down the stony rutted lane to our front gate.'

Lorries, charabancs and buses

The first lorries that George Evans mentions were 'Peerless', reconditioned after the First World War, and in due course he was to drive one. But, as with the Model T Ford, this was a very different driving experience to that enjoyed by the modern lorry driver:

> 'The 'Peerless' lorries were chain driven and had solid rubber tyres … a wooden cab … I'm not sure whether they had a windshield but there were no side windows … if you had the foot brake on long, it used to set the body on fire … you wanted

TEL. 437.

J. STANT & Co., Motor Engineers,
ABBEY GARAGE, Abbey Foregate, SHREWSBURY.

We specialize in Aluminium
Repairs
Modern Machine Shop
Large Stock of Accessories,
Tyres and Oils
We undertake to Overhaul
Motor Cycles, Motor Cars,
Commercial Lorries, and
Farm Tractors

Magnificent 4-Ton Peerless Lorry Reconstructed by Slough Trading
Co., PRICE £500, or may be had on Deferred Payments.
4% CHARGED ON TOTAL (i.e., £520).
25% DEPOSIT, BALANCE IN 12 MONTHLY PAYMENTS OF £32 10s.
Can we give you a Demonstration with a 4-ton load?

Advertisement for a Peerless lorry

Shrewsbury Chronicle 11 March 1921. Shropshire Archives.

a bucket of water to put it out ... we had to use the hand brake and that was very little use ... it was a good job there was not much traffic on the road in those days.'

Sarah Ann Evans (born 1911) remembers that the earliest buses were not tailor-made: 'I remember the first bus, and that was started off by Mr Edwin Hotchkiss from the Cold Hill, him and his son had an old lorry and they put a body on it and two seats across, so the people sat facing one another. That was the first Bog bus,' a charabanc.[16]

Graham France remembers that such vehicles could indeed be multi-functional:

'George Williams had a haulage business up the Ventor. He had a lorry that would lug barytes down to Minsterley during the week but on a Saturday he would fasten a container with windows in it on the flat-bottomed lorry. He would then take people to shop in Shrewsbury.'

Reminiscing in 1990 in the *Snailbeach District News,* T C R (Clifford) Parry (born 1914) recalls charabancs which had

The Bog Busmen

Edwin Hotchkiss, his wife Edith and their family at Cold Hill, near The Bog, in 1906. In later years Edwin and his son, also Edwin, but known as Wilson, were to run the first 'Bog bus'. Wilson is shown in the insert which is dated 1914. His siblings are, from left to right, Stanley, Gilbert, Winnie, Ewart (known as Joseph) and Edna. Reproduced courtesy of Brenda Jones, daughter of Gilbert.

'rows of transverse seats with doors at the ends of each row of seats ... open to the weather, but a covering hood could be pulled over ... and attached to the front windscreen to form some kind of protection ... cans of petrol and water were strapped on to the running boards ... solid tyres made a ride in them very bumpy.'

A school excursion to Aberystwyth was a great adventure: 'Frequently [on the steep ascent over Plynlimon] the charabanc stopped for the engine to cool and to be topped up with water. On these occasions, to lighten the load, we walked to the top of the incline'.

George Evans recalls some of the early buses he drove such as the 26 seater 'Vulcan Duchess'. The carriage of passengers and goods to and from various local markets was a key part of the job. Duties included climbing up the ladder at the back and loading market baskets weighing up to half a hundredweight 'in a double layer almost across the top of the bus', indeed 'one old chap turned up with a calf in a hessian bag with only its head out'.

Longmynd Travel, Minsterley Motors and Mytton Vale

The photo of George Evans which heads this chapter was taken in about 1939 when he was driving for Bernie Bunce at Worthen, three miles northwest of The Stiperstones; by then he and Kitty, his wife, were living at the Black Hole. He recalls the Tilling-Stevens buses he drove then as some of the best he had driven up to that date: 'They were very heavy and crude and all that, but you could really put your foot down and thrape them hard all day and they were still there the next day for more'. A number of driving and mechanic-ing jobs followed, including travelling the country servicing and repairing early Ferguson tractors and driving buses for the County Council.

George retired in July 1973, but in September of that year his son, George Evans junior, set up 'George's Coaches'. He operated out of the Black Hole and recruited George senior as one of his drivers; George continued driving until he was 79. A year or two later the company relocated to Pontesbury and by this time it had been re-named 'Longmynd Travel', not out of any disrespect for 'the hill' under which it had been established, but perhaps because the name of its near neighbour resonated more widely. Today the company operates a fleet ranging from mini-buses to executive coaches out of Lea Cross near Pontesbury.

From trap to coach

This photo of 2010 marks the evolution of passenger transport over the ninety years running from George Evans's early experiences of horse-drawn transport in about 1920, to his son's deployment of luxury coaches, one of which is seen here at Burgam Corner. Reproduced courtesy of Longmynd Travel.

Nor is the name 'Stiperstones' honoured in the names of the other two coach companies established here, 'Mytton Vale' and 'Minsterley Motors'. The former is based in Mytton Beach. It was founded by Don Rowson in the early 1980s and today specialises in running mini-buses on local school runs. The latter was originally established by Bill Swain, a one-time associate of George Evans, as a taxi firm operating from The Bog; it was eventually taken over by Bert Evans, a younger brother of George. Today it is a major concern and from its base in Stiperstones Village it runs more than 20 service buses and coaches on holiday and private hire.

Why should The Stiperstones have spawned this group of coach companies? Clearly the need to carry materials to and from the mines meant that transport, latterly by lorry, was a crucial component of the local economy. But this was a relatively well-populated and relatively remote location, creating a demand for passenger transport as well, at a time when few owned cars. So it seems that some of the lorries morphed into buses and the driving skills and experience gained in haulage were adapted to the transport of passengers.

Today, as the adverse impact of the motor car becomes ever more apparent, new bus services are being promoted. Amongst them is the 'Stiperstones Shuttle' a service first established in 2002, which on spring and summer weekends does a series of circuits round the hill. Passengers can join it from Shrewsbury via either the scheduled bus service to Minsterley, or the train to Church Stretton, boarding there the linked Shuttle Bus service round The Long Mynd. It is an attempt to provide car-free access to and around The Stiperstones. Whilst the Shuttle buses are refined and luxurious compared to the 'Vulcan Duchess' and 'Tilling-Stevens' buses that George Evans knew so well, they are clearly of the same lineage. A mode of transport that seemed at one time to be on the wane is making something of a comeback. But the lady chosen as the figurehead for the next chapter resorted at times to a more basic from of transport – the porter's trolley.

Chapter 4

'Diafol Mountain': lore and legend

Round such aloof and haunting places legends gather
as naturally as cloud on the summits.

Ellis Peters *Ellis Peters' Shropshire* (1999)

Charlotte Burne

Charlotte Sophia Burne

First woman President of the Folklore Society, 1909-10

Charlotte (Lotty) Burne (1850-1923), author of *Shropshire Folk-Lore*, was the eldest of six children, daughter of the reprobate heir to a country estate. She was born in Staffordshire, but her family soon moved into Shropshire, so although, to use her own words, 'Staffordshire is my "native", as the folk say, I am Shropshire's foster-child'. By the age of seven she was collecting details of folklore and customs and continued to do so through most of her life.

In her mid-twenties she met Georgina Jackson (1823/4-1895) author of *Shropshire Word-book, a glossary of archaic and provincial words etc., used in the county* (1879), a major and meticulous compilation. By the time of its publication Georgina Jackson was an invalid and unable to complete her next projected work which was to be about Shropshire folklore. However, she passed the material she had gathered to Charlotte Burne, and the years 1883-6 saw the publication of *Shropshire Folk-Lore: a sheaf of gleanings edited by Charlotte Sophia Burne from the collections of Georgina F Jackson*. It is clear however that Charlotte Burne added considerably to Georgina Jackson's work, and was author, as well as editor, of the final text. It has been described as 'perhaps the best county folklore book we possess as well as the most monumental'.[1]

Charlotte Burne was to become a mainstay of the Folklore Society, editor of its journal *Folk-Lore* and later its President. She certainly looks presidential in the portrait photograph of her in her prime, but there is also a suggestion of the obesity that, in later years, when travelling by train, required her to be wheeled along the station platform on a porter's trolley.

The compilation of works such as *Shropshire Folk-Lore*, drawing as it does on contemporary testimony, suggests that belief in this lore remained widely and deeply held. Perhaps it was; it certainly served Mary Webb's purpose to suggest so, indeed she grounded a series of novels on the assumption that many in the rural communities of Shropshire were in thrall to the supernatural, so that lore and legend, charm and spell, dictate conduct and shape destinies. When, early on in *The Golden Arrow*, Mary Webb describes the Devil's Chair, the core feature of her 'Diafol Mountain' (The Stiperstones), she establishes this over-arching context:

> 'For miles around, in the plains, the valleys, the mountain dwellings it was feared ... So the throne stood – black, massive, untenanted, yet with a well-worn air. It had the look of a chair from which the occupant has just risen, to which he will shortly return. It was understood that only when vacant could the throne be seen. Whenever rain or driving sleet or mist made a grey shechinah there people said, 'There's harm brewing.' 'He's in his chair.' Not that they talked of it much; they simply felt it as sheep feel the coming of snow.'[2]

Shropshire Folk-Lore is a work which Mary Webb credited in her foreword to *Precious Bane* and on which she appears to have drawn freely, embellishing and supplementing its content so as to support her narratives. Gladys Mary Coles (Webb's biographer) states that she wove nearly 200 legends and superstitions into *Precious Bane*; there are many in *Gone to Earth* too, and some 30 in *The Golden Arrow*, her Stiperstones ('Diafol Mountain') novel. The following account of the lore and legend of the 'Mountain' owes most to the work of Charlotte Burne and Georgina Jackson, but draws on the research of other folklorists too, notably Jennifer Westwood, and it explores the way in which Mary Webb incorporates Stiperstones legends into her novels.

Edricus Saluage

Of the many legends linked to The Stiperstones, those attached to Wild Edric are the most interesting, the most individual but also the most universal. Edric is a historical figure round whom legends accumulated: legends with local themes, but legends that fall too into well-known patterns or 'tale types' with oft-recurring themes or 'motifs' found elsewhere in Britain, and indeed abroad.

Charlotte Burne outlines the known facts about Edric, the historical figure. He is named in *Domesday* as Edricus Saluage, 'the savage', 'the wild' Edric. He was a Saxon nobleman, a powerful landowner, with many manors in Shropshire (including in the Shropshire Hills) and neighbouring counties, to his name. In 1067, Edric, in alliance with the Welsh kings Bleddyn and Rhiwallon, fought the Normans, overcoming their garrison at Hereford, and in 1069, with Bleddyn (now the sole King of Wales), he besieged Shrewsbury. Although in 1070 Edric made peace with William the Conqueror, he was later to rebel again, when he may have died in battle, been imprisoned (where he later died), or he may have bowed to the inevitable and ended his days peacefully somewhere in the Marches.

Wild Edric was, according to Walter Map, writing in about 1180, 'a man of great prowess' named 'from his bodily activity, and his rollicking talk and deeds'. In his *De Nugis Curialium* ('Trifles of the Court') Map recounts the best known of these deeds, and in doing so leads us from history into legend:

> '... he when returning late from hunting through wild country ... came upon a large building at the edge of the forest ... he looked in and saw a great dance of numbers of noble ladies ... most comely to look on ... greater and taller than our women. The knight remarked one among all the rest as excelling in form and face, desirable beyond any favourite of a king ... At the sight the knight received a wound to the very heart, and ill could bear the fires driven in by Cupid's bow; the whole of him kindled and blazed up ... He rushes in, catches her by whom he has been caught ... took her with him, and for three days and nights used her as he would, yet could not wring a word from her. She yielded quietly to his will.'

Wild Edric

From a painting by Shrewsbury-based artist Roderick Shaw.

Despite this violent beginning, the first words uttered by this fairy woman are: 'Hail to you my dearest!' She tells Edric that he will enjoy health and prosperity 'until you reproach me either with the sisters from whom you snatched me, or the place ... from which I come'.

Edric vows fidelity and marries her. They (Edric and his new wife, anonymous in Map's account, but named elsewhere as Godda) are summoned to London by William the Conqueror who is eager to see this prodigy of beauty; she duly excites 'the amazement of all' before the two of them are sent home again. After many years the inevitable happens: returning one night from hunting Edric fails to find her; she is summoned but is slow to come, drawing from Edric the fateful reproach: 'Was it your sisters that kept you so long?' She vanishes, and despite much searching, Edric fails to find her and eventually dies 'in unceasing sorrow'.

But it is Wild Edric's resistance to William the Conqueror that fuels most of the legends, a resistance which earned him an enduring and obstinate following. Discussing Wild Edric in her *Folklore of the Welsh Border*, Jacqueline Simpson observes that: 'One remarkable pattern of belief and tale springs from the persistent loyalty with which a dead leader's followers may reject the bitter truth of his death, and cling to a hope that he has only mysteriously vanished'.

The loyalty shown by Edric's followers was indeed persistent; it endured it seems for 800 years! Charlotte Burne, writing in the 1880s, reports that it was

> 'not many years since ... there were people to be found, if there are not some now, who believed Wild Edric to be still alive .... He [Edric] cannot die, they say, till all the wrong [wrought by William the Conqueror] has been made right, and England has returned to the same state in which it was before the troubles of his days. Meanwhile he is condemned to inhabit the lead mines [of The Stiperstones] as a punishment for having allowed himself to be deceived by the Conqueror's fair words. So there he dwells, with his wife and his whole train.'

And whilst incarcerated, Edric and his followers sometimes knocked to indicate to the miners where the best lodes of lead were to be found. Apparently such knockers, or 'fairy miners', were a particular feature of the Cornish tin mines, from where some of those working in the Stiperstones lead mines had come.

The Wild Hunt, The Death Pack

Edric and his followers are best known however as harbingers of war. According to Charlotte Burne, 'now and then they are allowed to show themselves. Whenever war is going to break out, they ride over the hills in the direction of the enemy's country, and if they appear, it is a sign that the war will be serious'.

Charlotte Burne reports on a sighting of Wild Edric and his men at Minsterley by the illiterate daughter of a miner in 1853 or 1854, shortly before the outbreak of the Crimean War.[3] Her description was detailed: they were dressed in medieval clothes, green and white with gold ornaments; the dark-haired Edric rode a white horse, and the hair of his wife (named Lady Godda in this account) was golden and reached to her waist.[4] The miner himself witnessed the apparition too, bidding his daughter to cover her face, except for her eyes, and on no account to speak, or she would go mad. The miner's daughter reported that her father had seen Edric prior to the Napoleonic Wars, and it is said that there were sightings before the Boer War and both World Wars,[5] and, according to Malcolm Saville's *Seven White Gates* (see Chapter 6), before the evacuation from Dunkirk.

The miner's entreaty to his daughter provides a link with another recurrent theme of English folklore, and indeed that of many countries, the so-called 'Wild Hunt': to see the hunt (or, in this case, connect with it through speech) brings death or madness. It is this fearsome element that Mary Webb draws on in *Gone to Earth* (see Chapter 5), in which Hazel Woodus has a recurrent terror of the appearance of what she calls 'the jeath pack'. Mary Webb explains:

> 'It was said that the death pack, phantom hounds of a bad squire ... scoured the country on dark stormy nights. Harm was for the houses past which it streamed, death for those that heard it give tongue. This was the legend, and Hazel believed it implicitly.'

Wild Edric and Lady Godda
From a painting by Roderick Shaw.

Later Hazel expands on her beliefs:

'First comes the Black Huntsman, crouching low on his horse and horse going belly to earth ... And the jeath pack's with him, great hound-dogs, real as real, only no eyes, but sockets with a light behind 'em. Ne'er a one knows what they'm after. If I seed 'em I'd die.'

For the sensible John Arden in *The Golden Arrow*, the 'Dark Riders', as he called them, represented one of 'them wold, unrighteous tales'. Perhaps this is recognition by Mary Webb that she was writing at or beyond the time when a rural society swayed by superstition was giving way to one guided by rationality. She wrote her novels between 1915 and 1924, but, excluding *Armour Wherein He Trusted* (a medieval romance) and *Gone to Earth* (set in her own time) they are set in the nineteenth century. Mary Webb may have felt that her twentieth century readership would more readily accept plots which depended at times on fables and superstitions, if they were set in the previous century. However, the events of *Gone to Earth*, which was published in 1917, occur some time after 1909.[6] Here, in an effort to make credible Hazel Woodus's dated reliance on the supernatural, Webb gives her gypsy blood, an apparent lack of education, unworldliness, and no worldly guidance other than that of her late mother's 'old, dirty, partially illegible manuscript-book of spells and charms and other gypsy lore'. Interestingly, the makers of the film of *Gone to Earth* moved the events back to 1897, reasoning perhaps that rooting them in the nineteenth century might make them more credible.

Seven Whistling Birds

In July 1987, when walking up to Cranberry Rock, I saw six large birds in flight and heard their whistling call. According to the legend of the 'Seven Whistling Birds', if a seventh bird had risen to join them, the world would have ended. Charlotte Burne refers to this as 'the wildest, vaguest, most imaginative of all the superstitions concerning birds'.

There are various conjectures as to the specific identity of these seven mythical birds: geese, Golden Plover and Curlew are amongst the candidates.[7] Another strong one is Wigeon, a duck of inland waters and estuaries, which, perhaps pre-eminently amongst British birds, has a call most obviously like a human whistle. It is to this resemblance that Mary Webb alludes in *Precious Bane* when, at a portentous moment in the novel, Gideon and Prue Sarn, living amongst the meres of north Shropshire, hear 'a sweet scattered whistling ... falling from the dim, moony sky'. Gideon, sure that it is 'the Seven Whistlers', takes it is an evil omen; Prue, 'mortally afeard to think of those ... ghostly birds', seeks to convince herself that it is 'only some magpie-widgeon we'd disturbed at the end of the mere ...'.[8]

But another possibility is Whimbrel, the species seen, heard and recognised by me in July 1987. The Whimbrel, a close relative of the Curlew, visits Shropshire only on migration to and from its northern breeding grounds. Its flight call is a repetitious whistle, described as having seven notes. Edward Armstrong, foremost authority on the folklore of birds, seeks to dismiss the candidature of Whimbrel, describing it as 'almost certainly merely a sophisticated modern attempt to pin a name to the Seven Whistlers', arguing that 'the numeral referred originally to the number of the whistlers, not the character of their utterance'. Yet, how neat if it referred to both! And why not? Whimbrels are most often seen or heard when flying over on migration, their repetitive call could be suggestive of an anxious search or enquiry, their appearances interpreted perhaps as a quest.

Variations of this legend crop up in many parts of the country, and indeed the world. Students of folklore link the 'Seven Whistlers' legend to that of the 'Wild Hunt' or 'death pack' and also to the phantom or 'Gabriel' Hounds – the vision of an aerial night-time hunting pack conjured up, seemingly, as an explanation for the nocturnal gabbling of migratory geese.

The Devil's Chair

The Devil's Chair is not the highest of the quartzite tors that jut up from the ridge of The Stiperstones, but it is undoubtedly the most celebrated, and it might be the most visited were its actual location not wishfully anticipated

The Devil's Chair
Common Cottongrass is prominent in this photo of June 2013 by Gisèle Wall.

by visitors. Tired of the ankle-wrenching walk along the spine of the ridge, buffeted by the wind and rain blowing in from Wales, they are very ready to assume that one or other of the tors that precede the Chair is in fact the object of their search. So they return home satisfied, but without having actually sat in the remote, broad, north-facing, chair-like depression towards the end of the otherwise knife-like crest of the elongated outcrop that is the Devil's Chair.

The name and the legends attached to the Chair make for its celebrity. There are many variations, but there are two principal tales as told to Charlotte Burne:

'Once upon a time the Devil was coming from Ireland with an apronful of stones. Where he was going I cannot say; some say it was the Wrekin he was carrying in his leather apron, some say he was going to fill up Hell [sic] Gutter, on the side of the Stiperstones Hill. But any way he had to cross the Stiperstones, and it was a very hot day, and he was very tired, so he sat down to rest on the highest rock. And as he got up again to go on his way, his apron-strings broke, and down went the stones, and very badly he cursed them too, so I've heard. They lie there to this day, scattered on the ground all round the Devil's Chair, and if you go up there in hot weather you may smell the brimstone still, as strong as possible!'

Charlotte Burne learned the second version from 'old Netherley', 'a lame old man who used to "lug coal" with a cart and two donkeys', who had been told it by lead miners; he recounted that

> 'of all the countries in the world the Devil hates England the most, because we are good Protestants and read the Bible. Now if ever the Stiperstones sink into the earth, England will be ruined. The Devil knows this very well, so he goes whenever he can, and sits in his chair on the top of the hill, in hopes that his weight will flatten it down and thrust it back into the earth, but he hasn't managed it yet, and it is to be hoped he never will!'

His Chair is a fine look-out, commanding extensive views across Shropshire and beyond. It is benign on a fine day, but grim on a bad one, and can often be atmospheric. In October 1986, relatively new to The Stiperstones but well-versed in local legends, I found myself on a lone overnight fire-watch, monitoring the embers of a 'wild fire' which, progressing rapidly uphill from the west on a broad front, had fortuitously been blocked by the wide expanse of the Chair. A look-out location on the Chair itself seemed, at sun-down, to be both a strategic and relatively comfortable choice, but as night wore on, stars sparkled, smoke wafted and sparks flew, atmosphere overwhelmed me, superstition undermined rationality and I beat a retreat.

The demonic reputation of the Chair may sometimes repel, but its scenic splendour is a draw. On one occasion I was asked to guide a group who, on Rogation Day, had chosen to walk to the Chair for an open-air meeting of prayer and contemplation. This was not intended as an exorcism, or the capture for Christianity of a satanic outpost, but as a celebration of God's creation. Bizarrely, on descending I came across a large wooden cross left by some previous visitor of dubious intent, which I shouldered back down to the car park.

I have since discovered that this wasn't the first such open-air meeting at the Devil's Chair. In an article published in 1955 Margaret Corfield relates that 'some 90 to 100 years ago' the Primitive Methodists held a 'camp meeting' at the Chair at which the first preacher's text was from the *Book of Revelation*: 'For the great day of his wrath is come; and who shall be able to stand?'[9]

The Devil and Slashrags the tailor

> 'He was a tailor by profession;
> But that was not his chief obsession.
> By trade he was a swindler born
> And worked hard at it, night and morn,
> He did no sewing, used no thread
> Together gummed his suits instead.'

These are the opening lines of a ballad entitled 'Slashrags the Tailor and the Devil' published in 1937 by the Reverend Richard Ridge of Ridge who lived at Corndon Lodge, Gravels, near Shelve.

Slashrags, the swindling tailor, got his come-uppance when one day a dark stranger ordered a suit. Slashrags couldn't but notice the stranger's cloven

Slashrags and the Devil

Note the latter's Chair on the horizon. A drawing by Fran O'Boyle, a local storyteller, illustrator and artist.

hooves, long tail and sulphurous odour and realised with horror that he had undertaken to dress the Devil himself. Greed overcame trepidation however and he arranged to deliver the new suit to his client in a week's time. But on returning home Slashrags lost his nerve, and according to the Reverend Richard Ridge, decided to enlist the help of the Reverend Brewster, to whom he confessed his many sins. Believing Slashrags to be truly repentant, the Reverend Brewster undertook to accompany the tailor when he went to see his client. In one version they meet near Cranberry Rock, but Ridge's ballad places the encounter between Shelve and Pennerley, at Whitemedale Gate where

'The Devil grinned and paid his bill
Then set the Tailor for the kill,
But saw with horror in his look
That parson reading his Prayer Book.
He dropped the clothes with an awful yell
And in a jiffy took his hook
And hid himself in the lowest hell'.

Here fantasy and fact coincide, because there was indeed a parson named Brewster: from 1872 to 1901 the Reverend Waldegrave Brewster officiated at Middleton-in-Chirbury, four miles west of The Stiperstones. The Reverend was a sculptor too, decorating the fabric of his church with carvings in stone and wood, including the signs of the Zodiac and a depiction of the legend of the witch of Mitchell's Fold, the Bronze Age stone circle which lies nearby. Pillar, pew and bracket, he carved them all; truly 'the church is alive with his work'.[10]

Whitemedale Gate hung at a sharp bend in the road in a deep hollow between Shelve and Pennerley. It is clearly a place of paranormal occurrences. Bill Francis (see Chapter 9) refers to the location as White Way Dale, and wrote that 'Twice, cycling there around midnight [in the 1920s], this gate opened for me of its own accord and closed when I had passed'.

The Needle's Eye

Charlotte Burne refers to a place called the 'Needle's Eye': 'a long narrow channel accidentally formed among the huge fragments of rock which lie heaped round the Devil's Chair. Through this passage visitors must crawl, but I have been unable to learn particulars of person, occasion, or consequences.' No such long narrow channel is known today.

In his novella *St Mawr* (see Chapter 6), D H Lawrence's describes a rather different Needle's Eye: 'a hole in the ancient grey rock, like a window, looking to England.' Presumably he is referring to the point, part-way along the crest of the tor, where a pillar of rock has fallen side-ways and lies jammed across a gap, forming an angular opening, or eye of a needle.

The Needle's Eye at the Devil's Chair or Great Rock

From an old postcard by Wilding of Shrewsbury. Shropshire Archives.

Ghosts, Witches, a Wizard and Nancy Corra

Thomas Wright, the celebrated antiquarian from Ludlow, writing in 1862, identifies The Stiperstones as the annual meeting place of Shropshire's ghosts, and maybe its witches too:

> 'It is, I understand, still believed in that neighbourhood that, every year on the longest night, all the ghosts (including, I suppose, spiritual beings of all kinds, and perhaps witches) of Shropshire "and the counties beyond" assemble round the highest of the Stiperstones to choose their King.'

Wright is referring to the Devil's Chair and assuming wrongly, in common with many others, that this, rather than Manstone Rock, is the highest point of The Stiperstones.

Mary Webb draws on these ghostly connections in *The Golden Arrow*, telling us how in their cottage, just below the Chair, on the longest night of the year, when 'all the ghosses in Shropshire' are meeting, Deborah learns that she has been deserted by Stephen. Deranged by grief she sets fire to all their possessions before stumbling through the night to the sanctuary of her father's cottage on the Wilderhope Range (The Long Mynd). And, in *Precious Bane*, Gideon Sarn reacts angrily to the taunt that his sister Prue will be dancing with him on Diafol Mountain at 'Thomastide', the implication being that Prue, his 'hare-shotten' (harelipped) sister is a witch. 'Thomastide' embraces St Thomas's Day, 21 December, and marks the shortest day and longest night of the year.

Other writers have framed stories around the annual gathering of witches and ghosts at the Devil's Chair. There is John Macklin's *The Dancing Demons of Stiperstones* in which a geologist, George Vardy, investigating the quartzite rocks, becomes conscious of a dramatic change of atmosphere and finds himself witnessing a ritual dance by shadowy figures of both sexes, some naked, all oblivious to his presence.[11]

George Vardy was alarmed, but lived to tell his bizarre tale, not so Harry Wentworth in *The Eve of St Thomas* by W Howard Williams. Wentworth makes light of local advice not to venture onto the hill on this of all nights. Next day a search party finds his unmarked corpse at the foot of the Devil's Chair; his hand still clutched a torch, but the bulb and batteries were burned out, there was a film of smoke on the lens and all was pervaded by the scent of brimstone.

In 'The Mine' a ghost story by L T C (Tom) Rolt[12] the action moves to Snailbeach, where a creature of human shape 'terrible tall and thin' and 'dirty white all over' is seen crouching on top of the cage bringing up a miner, Joe Beecher, from work on a new level where there have been mysterious goings on. The miner hares off, 'for all the world as though Old Nick hisself were after him', pursued by the creature, which is 'as quick and quiet as a cat after a sparrow'. Joe is later found dead at the bottom of an old quarry, his face horribly contorted.

Magdalene Weale, whose *Through the highlands of Shropshire on horseback* was published in 1935 (see Chapter 6), encountered 'the local wizard' who lived near the Boat Level. His remedies appear harmless, and on the back of effecting a cure for jaundice he confides to Magdalene Weale: 'It's like this. They thinkenen as the charms does 'em good, anna does'.

In *The Golden Arrow* we encounter the herbalist Nancy Corra, whose cottage 'stood amongst the white mounds', the grassless mounds of mine spoil, 'huge heaps of lead refuse [which] rose in unwholesome whiteness, like rather dirty sugar, round the deserted mines'. Her 'acknowledged patients' were treated for minor ailments. For the 'unacknowledged' ones, who 'came in the evening, closely shawled', she offered a service which, according to Mary Webb, was viewed by some as being 'unmixed evil', by others as helping 'to right the balance of punishment between the sexes for the sin of "going too far" '. Elsie Rowson (born 1924), an interviewee for *Never on a Sunday*, recalls her mother saying of the fictional Nancy Corra '"That's Granny Jones, that's your Granny Jones", the lady who lived behind the mounds that grew no grass'.

'The Golden Arrow'

In Mary Webb's *The Golden Arrow* John Arden tells Stephen Southernwood of an 'old ancient custom', and of a related song, which lend their names to the novel.[13] But John Arden conveys uncertainty about the origin of the custom of the Golden Arrow, expressing thereby the uncertainty of Mary Webb herself, and of those, such as Charlotte Burne (presumed to be Mary Webb's source), who had sought to connect the disparate strands of a fading legend. John Arden's tentative account runs as follows:

> 'In time gone by the lads and wenches in these parts was used to go about Easter and look for the golden arrow. It met be along of them getting sally-blossom [pussy willow] for Palm Sunday as the story came; but howsoever, they was used to go. And it was said that if two as were walking out found the arrow they'd cling to it fast though it met wound them sore. And it was said that there'd be a charm on 'em, and sorrow, and a vast of joy. And nought could part 'em, neither in the flower of life nor in the brown winrow.'

'Seeking the Golden Arrow on Ponsert [Pontesford] Hill' was apparently a very long-established custom, but it was dying out by the 1880s when Charlotte Burne was writing. The hill, which lies three miles northeast of The Stiperstones, has two humps, Pontesford Hill proper, and Earl's Hill, the taller by some 110 feet. Charlotte Burne relates that

> 'Every year on Palm Sunday crowds of people were wont to ascend Pontesford Hill "to look for the Golden Arrow" and … a regular "wake" or merry-making was carried on there, with games and dancing and drinking … a great annual picnic. Every household was occupied beforehand in baking cakes and packing up kettles and crockery in preparation for "going palming", as it was called.'

The 'palm' was a spray from a solitary, ancient, 'haunted' yew-tree. The lucky gatherer of the first palm, provided he or she kept it safe, would suffer no misfortune over the coming year. And the first to run at full speed down the hill and dip the fourth finger of his or her right hand into the water of a deep pool on its east side would be certain to marry the first person of the opposite sex whom they happened to meet.

But, what is the 'Golden Arrow'? By the time that Charlotte Burne was writing, recollections of the substance of the legend had withered away:

> 'What the Golden Arrow is, the search for which is the professed object of the Wake, or how it came there, none of the folk can tell. Though many very old people have been questioned on the subject for the purposes of the present work, little has been elicited beyond a hazy idea that it was dropped by some great one in days gone by and never found.'

Into this vacuum of recollection Mary Webb inserts her own appropriately imprecise narration, as offered by John Arden in the passage cited above. According to this version, the 'Golden Arrow' is 'true love', a symbol of love found, of love enduring. Deborah Arden and Stephen Southernwood find the 'Golden Arrow', she clings to it and is wounded; he spurns it and flees, before finally turning back and grasping it for good. John Arden, Deborah's father, knows that finally Stephen too has found the Arrow, saying to his wife:

> 'D'you mind the tale of them that found the Golden Arrow, and went with apple-blow scent round 'em, and a mort o' bees, and warmship, and wanted nought of any man? There's no need of fire or can'le for them my dear, for they'm got their light – the kindly light – and the thorn's white over.'

Pontesford Hill on the left leading to Earl's Hill, in the centre

In this photo of August 1956, a thin crest of conifers is just visible near the top of Pontesford Hill; they had made a striking setting for scenes in the film 'Gone to Earth' (see page 117); blanket afforestation was soon to follow. The halo at the summit of Earl's Hill is the bank of its Iron Age hill fort. The hill was acquired from the Chitty family in 1964 by Shropshire Wildlife Trust, becoming its first nature reserve. A keen eye may pick out the roofs of Habberley, where Jack Mytton had an estate, lying below the hill. Photo, taken from Eastridge, by A P Wallace.

Jack Mytton

John (Jack) Mytton (1796-1834) was a country squire with a seat at Halston, three miles from Oswestry, and an estate at Habberley, just to the north of The Stiperstones. He was one of Shropshire's great characters and greatest reprobates, someone around whom legends accumulated, yet someone who was seemingly more eccentric, more outlandish, more outrageous than the most extravagant romancier could have invented. That we have some grasp of the facts and legends of his life is thanks to his biographer and contemporary

Charles James Apperley (1777-1843), known as 'Nimrod', gentleman hunting correspondent of *The Sporting Magazine*.

Jack Mytton was generous to the point of prodigality, warm-hearted but quick-tempered, extravagant in his virtues and his vices, blind to reason, impervious to advice, spendthrift, fearless, and, perhaps above all, reckless. He is said to have drunk four to six bottles of Port daily; he raced, he hunted, was one of the most daring of horsemen, and an excellent shot; he lost a fortune but spent £10,000 to obtain a seat in Parliament, where apparently he sat for no more than half an hour.

A neighbour christened him 'Mango, King of the Pickles' and, as 'Nimrod' says, 'he proved his title to the honour even to the end of his life'. When in Calais, escaping from his creditors, he set fire to his nightshirt in order to frighten away the hiccups; he suffered severe burns and his recovery was slow and painful; deprived of brandy he drank *eau de Cologne* instead. On return to England he was jailed, and a life of wilful self-abuse caught up with him. According to the *Shrewsbury Chronicle* his death, at 37, was attributed to *delirium tremens*

Jack Mytton leaping the pale

'While suffering severely from the effects of a fall, and with his right arm in a sling [the left in this illustration], he rode his favourite hunter, Baronet, over the park paling of the late Lord Berwick, of Atsham [sic], near Shrewsbury, to the astonishment of the whole field.' Frontispiece and quotation from a 1915 edition of Nimrod's *Life of the Late John Mytton* of 1837. Drawn and etched by T J Rawlins and H Alken.

'brought on by excessive use of spirituous liquors'. Despite his extraordinarily wanton life, or perhaps in some measure because of it, his funeral was apparently an occasion for widespread mourning. Although the *Shrewsbury Chronicle* of 11 April 1834 need not be taken literally — 'The road along which the procession slowly moved [to the funeral] was bedewed with the tears of thousands' — it may be that 'Nimrod' does not exaggerate unduly in reporting that the funeral itself was attended by 3,000 mourners.

Local reminders of this extraordinary man include the 'Mytton Arms' (in Habberley) and the steep-sided Stiperstones valley known as Mytton, or Myttons Beach – the lack of an apostrophe reflecting perhaps a want of confidence in its placement rather than a denial of Jack Mytton's right of possession. His right is not clear-cut however, as it has been suggested that the name could be derived, prosaically, from the similarity between the shape of the valley and that of a 'leg of mutton'.[14] I know someone in her 90s whose pronunciation is clearly 'Mutton' not 'Mytton', but Roy Palmer, in his *Folklore of Shropshire*, whilst providing no supporting evidence, confidently links man and place.

Mytton Beach

This photo, taken looking up the dingle, shows its 'leg of mutton' shape. The topography hides 'Jacob's Ladder', which is round to the left, and 'Flooded Wires', just round to the right. Photo, 2013, Gisèle Wall.

The link comes from the claim that Mad Jack drove his second wife down Myttons Beach, at speed, in a two-wheeled carriage drawn by two horses. Those who have stumbled down the valley, or toiled up it, including the final taxing haul, which is the steepest ascent on The Stiperstones and is referred to as 'Jacob's Ladder', will either wonder at the extreme recklessness of Jack Mytton or dismiss the tale as apocryphal. If true, it is surprising that Mad Jack and his wife survived the experience, though it is said to have cost her a broken leg and a permanent loss of nerve.

Scarlet's Bridge

The Scarlet or Scarlett family of Hogstow, on the west flank of The Stiperstones, once owned an extensive tract of the hill. One of their boundaries was marked by 'Scarlett's Wall' which is shown on the 1847 Tithe Map as running down from the ridge to form the southern boundary of the area known as The Paddock. The line of the wall remains evident today as a bank which marks part of the boundary between the parishes of Worthen and Ratlinghope. There were said to be 'Scarlett Stones' as well, marking at various places the extent of the family's ownership.

And what of the stone inscribed 'Scarlet's Bridge', bearing the date 1745, which is said to have been lost for some time before its re-discovery in 1976 at

Scarlet's Bridge

Approximately three and a half feet long by two and a half feet wide, the stone carries both a bold inscription (including the date 1745), and, near its bottom end, a very faint one, where the words 'Scarlets Bridge' are repeated at right angles, along with what looks like 'JJ56' (illegible in the photo). The stone is not thought to lie in its original location and the final 's' of 'Scarlet's' in the bold inscription is incomplete, possibly inadvertently chipped off when the stone was moved. The significance of the lettering and the date at the top of the stone are unknown. Photo, 2013, Gisèle Wall.

Pennerley? This is now thought to be a boundary stone too, though it has been suggested that it served as a stepping stone across a brook for one of the Scarletts:

> 'there was a myry flow in the Footeway to Bishops Castle markett and Peter Scarlett ouer fallinge in it as he came from that markett he gave a planck to Shelve to make Bridge there.'[15]

A more fanciful explanation is that it served to entomb a casket holding the spirit of a nun murdered by a monk at Hogstow in about 1400. The nun was buried at Hogstow Hall, but her spirit had proved troublesome, even when it was exorcised and consigned to a casket buried half a mile from the hall, hence it was taken a further half mile away to Pennerley, buried in the middle of a stream and capped with the flat-topped 'bridge'.[16]

Whose folklore?

The lore and legends of The Stiperstones are a source of fascination to many, including local residents, but back in 1955 in an article entitled 'Some superstitions associated with the Stiperstones district', Margaret Corfield observed of the local community that 'it is a marked feature of the present age that many of these things are scoffed at by the rising generation'. I remember nearly 30 years ago being told by a local lady in her sixties that it was bad luck to cut down 'Witty' (Rowan), but the advice was delivered as a recollection of something learned decades previously, a throw-back rather than a current belief. Incidentally, when clearing trees invading the open heathland, I have ignored the advice on very many subsequent occasions with no self-evident ill effect.

Today the lore and legend of the place is the stuff of tourist brochures and media hype. A guided walk with a 'myths and legends' theme is a sure-fire success, and the 'folklore' is cherished more perhaps by incomers and visitors than by the indigenous community. As such it risks losing its authenticity: it is no longer part of a local oral tradition on which some degree of superstitious belief hangs, but has been written up (including here), as a historical curiosity; it is in danger of becoming codified and fossilised. This trend is countered however by the popularity of storytelling, of which there are a number of local practitioners including Val Littlehales of Prolley Moor and Sally Tonge of Stiperstones. Furthermore, the capacity of writers (hopefully excluding this one) to introduce error and misunderstanding will prevent fossilisation: in one recent account Lady Godda appears as Lady Godiva![17]

And the old legends reappear in new guises. In 1990, the opera *Wild Edric* (music by Charles Dakin, libretto by Peter Cann), had its première at the Ludlow Festival. It was performed by a combination of local musicians, children's choirs and London-based professionals, totalling more than 100 participants in all. It was very much a community project, and walking round Bishop's Castle, Charles Dakin could hardly believe it when he heard children singing his catchy chorus 'Wild Edric, bold Edric, rebel hero proud and free'.[18]

Publicity for 'Wild Edric' the opera, 1990

Reproduced courtesy of the designer, Lin Brown.

Another new guise is the 'Wild Edric Rose', a *rugosa* hybrid introduced by David Austin Roses of Albrighton, Shropshire, in 2005. Clearly this has to be a rose of wild, rambling, indeed rollicking habit, somewhat unkempt, blood red, with a pungent and earthy fragrance. Well, almost: according to the description in the company's catalogue it is 'unusually tough and reliable ... ideal for semi-wild planting'; it has a fragrance which is 'strong and delicious'; the golden-yellow stamens carrying a scent of 'pure clove' and the deep velvety pink petals of 'classic Old Rose with hints of watercress and cucumber'.

And there is more: *Wild Edric*, a narrative poem by Nigel Sustins appeared in 2008 giving new twists to the tale. The Wood Brewery of Wistanstow marked this publication with a celebratory ale 'Wild Edric Legendary Bitter'. And in 2012 Michael J Hands published *The Broken Shield* an 'action-packed historical novel' relating 'facts, legends and myths about Wild Edric'.

Wild Edric Rose

Photo courtesy of David Austin Roses.

The last word goes however to Val Littlehales, who tells the tale of the less well-known 'Mild Cedric': 'As a boy he was quite keen on sewing – he liked making tack for his dolls', and when, as a young man, he is called on to pursue a giant, he sallies forth only after packing his Swiss army knife and a 'nice non-genetically-modified lunch'. On The Stiperstones the short-sighted giant (masquerading as the Devil) trips over the picnicking Mild Cedric and falls, scattering the rocks from his apron: 'I'll tell you it caused quite a stir/One 'ooman in Snailbeach reported/ 'Twas the first time the earth moved for her'.

Chapter 5

'Natural magic':
the novels and nature of Mary Webb

*No one of our day has a greater power of evoking natural magic.
The landscape, the weather, the seasons, are made to crowd in upon us
as we follow the doings of the protagonists.*

John Buchan (1928)[1]

Mary Webb

Mary Webb (1881-1927) is sometimes referred to in a belittling way, as 'the Shropshire novelist'. True, she was born and bred in the county, lived there much of her short life, and was only really happy when within sight of its hills. What's more, all of her six novels are set in identifiable settings in rural Shropshire (two of them in the area of The Stiperstones) and she made extensive use of Shropshire dialect, lore, legend and folklore. Yet she was so much more than 'just' a regional writer.

Mary Webb was born Mary Gladys Meredith at Leighton, under The Wrekin, in 1881. Subsequently her family moved near to Much Wenlock and later to Staunton-on-Hine Heath, north of Shrewsbury, and then to Meole Brace, at that time a village separated from Shrewsbury by fields,

This signed copy is of a photo by Dorothy Hickling thought to have been taken in about 1920. It was given by Mary Webb to the writer, journalist and editor Caradoc Evans, a valued friend and supporter. Mary Webb wears a high collar to hide her enlarged thyroid gland. Reproduced courtesy of Mary and Bruce Crawford and the Mary Webb Digital Archive, Stanford University Libraries.

but now embraced by the town. The story of her short and difficult life, her inspiration and her novels is told by Gladys Mary Coles in *The Flower of Light*.

At the age of 20 she suffered the onset of Graves Disease, in which an overactive thyroid triggers a range of disorders, most obviously protruding eyes and enlargement of the thyroid gland at the base of the neck. At that time there was no effective treatment and she was seriously ill for six months. There were other crises, the unsightly symptoms never entirely left her, and the disease contributed to her early death. Ironically it was doubtless this illness that gave Mary Webb the understanding and the inspiration for her best-known novel *Precious Bane* (1924), the story of Prudence Sarn, disfigured by a 'hare-shotten lip'.

In 1912 Mary married Henry Bertram Law Webb (1885-1939), Cambridge graduate, linguist, philosopher, writer and teacher. They lived successively in Weston-super-Mare, Pontesbury, Chester, London and Lyth Hill near Shrewsbury, where they had a cottage built within sight of the Shropshire Hills. It was a marriage that started so well and brought much mutual happiness, but was to end in separation and heartache.

The novels

Mary Webb published poetry, short stories, essays and reviews, but it is for her novels that she is best known. During her lifetime she published five: *The Golden Arrow* (1916), *Gone to Earth* (1917), *The House in Dormer Forest* (1920), *Seven for a Secret* (1922) and *Precious Bane* (1924); the incomplete *Armour Wherein He Trusted* (1929) was published posthumously. All have rural settings, specifically, in the case of much of *The Golden Arrow* and *Gone to Earth*, the area of The Stiperstones. Both novels are set at a time when mines and mining would have dominated the local economy and scarred the local landscape, but Webb turned her back on industry and concentrated on the rural, making only passing reference to the mines; instead she steeped her readers in the 'natural magic' of the countryside.

Webb's is a unique voice, speaking with a prodigal richness of language and imagery as she develops universal themes of love, lust, fidelity, cruelty, compassion, generosity and greed. As John Buchan observes in his introduction of 1928 to *Gone to Earth*: 'There are moments when it [her prose] seems to be superheated, when her passion for metaphor makes the writing too high-pitched and strained'. Some readers are entranced; just as many find her novels over-blown and melodramatic. And critics, unsure of how to react to her exuberant descriptions of the countryside, are liable to pigeonhole her as 'the Shropshire novelist'. The other frequent put-down is to point out that she was parodied in Stella Gibbons' *Cold Comfort Farm* (1932), a hugely entertaining satire of the rural novel. Indeed she was, but so too were D H Lawrence, Thomas Hardy and others.

Mary Webb's novels are certainly 'rural' – they are steeped in the countryside. Most events of consequence occur outdoors, or in houses where the wind whistles under the door or 'mews in the chimney like a great cat'. Weather, seasons, topography and natural features influence events and outcomes. The novels could equally well have been set in counties other than Shropshire, but Mary Webb always drew on her own county, and not least that part of it which she knew best, the Shropshire Hills. Her narratives are tied tight to the place and its people, providing an identifiable setting against which the universal themes are explored.

She, and her husband Henry, lived for much of the years 1914-1916 in Pontesbury, latterly in a cottage at the Nills, built of and built on the Stiperstones Quartzite, which was quarried close by. At Pontesbury she was within walking distance of the hill, and it was here that her two novels set on and around the hill, *The Golden Arrow* (1916) and *Gone to Earth* (1917) were written.

The Golden Arrow

The Golden Arrow opens with a description of the view from John Arden's stone cottage set on the 'Wilderhope Range' (The Long Mynd). But it reads more like the view from a building on The Stiperstones sometimes called, for unknown reasons, 'Mary Webb's Cottage', but more often 'Tin House', because although now a complete ruin, memories linger of a roof of corrugated iron, otherwise referred to as 'tin'.[2] It lies 250 yards to the northwest of the Devil's Chair above the southern flank of Perkins Beach:

'John Arden's cottage stood in the midst of the hill plateau, higher than the streams began, shelterless to the four winds. While washing dishes Deborah [John Arden's daughter and heroine of the story] could see, through the small age-misted pane, counties and blue ranges lying beneath the transparent or hazy air in the bright, unfading beauty of inviolate nature. She would gaze out between

'Tin House'

This photo is from W Reid Chappell's *The Shropshire of Mary Webb* (1930); see Chapter 6. Note the round chimney stack.

the low window-frame and the lank geraniums, forgetting the half-dried china, when grey rainstorms raced across from far Cader Idris, ignoring in their majestic progress the humble variegated plains of grass and grain, breaking like a tide on the unyielding heather and the staunch cottage.'

Deborah leaves the security of her snug home and loving father to live on 'Diafol Mountain' (The Stiperstones) with her lover Stephen Southernwood, foreman at the 'Lostwithin Spar Mine',[3] in a cottage 'close agen' the Devil's Chair – a menacing presence throughout the novel. The proximity of this building to the unyielding quartzite tor (closer than 'Tin House') suggests that it may have been modelled in part on 'Rock Cottage' which stood at The Rock, towards the southern end of the Stiperstones ridge. Prior to its demolition, this cottage stood tight up against the quartzite. It was the subject of a memoir by Miss Jeanette Merry (see Chapter 9).

In locating Deborah and Stephen close by the Devil's Chair, Mary Webb submerged them and her narrative in the upland heathland environment. A similar one-ness with the natural context is to be found in Thomas Hardy's *Return of the Native* (1878) where the protagonists live surrounded by 'Egdon Heath'. Hardy was considerably older than Mary Webb – he was born 41 years before her – but he survived her by a year. She regarded him as the greatest living novelist and was delighted by his praise and his acceptance of her dedication to him of *Seven for a Secret*.

Both Mary Webb's 'Diafol Mountain' and Thomas Hardy's 'Egdon Heath' become more than just malign presences: they are protagonists in the drama. Yet the two novelists describe their respective contexts very differently. For Hardy the heath is sombre, 'embrowned', 'Titanic'; it repels Eustacia Vye, the vibrant and seductive incomer who pines for gaiety and glamour and 'cannot endure the heath, except in its purple season'. To suit his purpose, Hardy portrays the 'grim old face' of the heathland as uniform, lacking in variety, light and colour, and sparse in wildlife.

The Devil's Chair in profile

A pen and ink drawing by Ethel Hall from Magdalene Weale's *Through the Highlands of Shropshire on Horseback* of 1935; see Chapter 6.

In Mary Webb's novel the satanic presence of the Devil's Chair weighs on the mind and spirit of Stephen Southernwood (also an incomer) with golden hair, 'excited blue eyes and radiant bearing'. It 'towers in gigantic aloofness a mass of quartzite, blackened and hardened by uncountable ages'. Yet, in just one paragraph describing the Chair, Mary Webb mentions Heather, Holly, Cranberry, Curlew, Doves and Black Grouse. She cannot resist drawing on a rich lexicon of plants and birds. And her heath is coloured by the 'startling bright green' of the Whinberry (Bilberry), the 'dull crimson sea of heather' and the 'waxen whiteness' of the Cranberry (Cowberry) buds.

Stephen and Deborah become oppressed by the Chair, the chorus of grouse 'laughter' that goes with it and 'the desolate acres of burnt heather, each bush charred and left like a skeleton above the black-strewn ground'. As the nights draw in, the leaves fall and the frosts bite, Stephen, who is 'lost within', feels imprisoned by his environment and situation, hemmed in by an 'enforced intimacy with every mood of Nature', 'homesick for lighted towns', 'chained to the ridge' by his recent marriage to Deborah. He absconds to America, leaving Deborah near to suicidal despair. But eventually he returns, wiser, more mature, and at last together they clasp the metaphorical 'golden arrow', the symbol of enduring love.

For some, it is the finest of Mary Webb's novels. It is a tale of a girl's love, her sexual longing and fulfilment, her fidelity and maturity; of her father's tenderness, understanding and constancy; of her lover's fickleness, weakness and immaturity; and, after all is nearly lost, it tells of an eventual cautious reunion. It is a narrative of modest, insignificant lives played out in a forgotten corner of England, yet Mary Webb's flood of poetic description and her evocation of The Stiperstones as a place of portent, grandeur and malevolence, creates a backdrop against which these small lives assume dignity and weight, and resonate with a wider significance.

Gone to Earth

The principal setting for *Gone to Earth* is 'God's Little Mountain', modelled closely on Lordshill and Lordshill Chapel, which stand, 1,000 feet above sea level, at the northwestern extremity of The Stiperstones, close to Snailbeach. Whilst the denomination is not made clear in the novel, this is a Baptist chapel, built in 1833 and enlarged in 1873 (see Chapter 2). And in life, the novel and the subsequent film: 'The chapel and the minister's house at God's Little Mountain were all in one'.

Comparisons can again be made with Thomas Hardy, because *Gone to Earth*, like *Tess of the D'Urbervilles* (1891), is about innocence, its loss, and how this impacts on lovers who cherish that innocence; and in both novels there is a degree of redemption, followed by tragedy. In *Gone to Earth* Hazel Woodus is a near wild thing, 'elvish', a child of wood and meadow, yet, at eighteen, she emerges a ''ooman growed', for whom 'to be admired was a wonderful new sensation'. She has become a creature of fascination and beauty who entrances

The chapel at 'God's Little Mountain'

This card, by Wilding of Shrewsbury, pre-dates the filming, in 1949, of 'Gone to Earth'. The changes made for the film are shown in the photo on page 118. Reproduced courtesy of David Evans.

both the gentle, milk-and-water minister, Edward Marston, and the rough, red-blooded squire, Jack Reddin. But she is bemused by her response to both, and resorts for guidance to 'an old, dirty, partially illegible manuscript-book of spells and charms and other gipsy lore' inherited from her gipsy mother. She marries Marston. He wishes to consummate their marriage but fails to do so through his own timidity and out of an exaggerated reverence for Hazel's innocence. By contrast Reddin chases her, stalks her. He is 'so very much alive', exerting both 'a terror and a fascination', triggering her sexual awakening, drawing her to him 'like a jacksnipe fetches his mate out o' the grass', before forcing himself on her. She then has little choice but to go with him, but eventually recoils from his brutishness, his casual cruelties both to people and to the wild creatures which she cherishes – he is a huntsman, she the befriender of a fox cub, her 'Foxy'. She returns twice to Edward. On the second occasion he is at last obliged to acknowledge her loss of innocence, but he nevertheless takes her back and they enjoy a brief, tentative, tender but celibate conciliation before the final tragic dénouement.

At times laboured, often improbable, sometimes melodramatic, nonetheless *Gone to Earth* exerts a fascination on many readers. Hazel, whose 'ways were graceful and covert as a wild creature's', captivates them as she does Marston and Reddin, and, as the pages turn, the reader's dread deepens as the tragedy unfolds. A tragedy of which Mary Webb has forewarned us, identifying Hazel and her 'Foxy' as victims of the casual cruelty that drives the story, describing both as 'fiercely beautiful', 'facing destiny with pathetic courage' with 'a look as of those predestined to grief, almost an air of martyrdom'. Predestined perhaps, but it is a mark of Mary Webb's skill that time and again the engaged reader still wants to cry out to Hazel: 'Don't do it!'.

As always with Mary Webb, her readership is carried along by a forceful tide of nature writing, a nostalgic glimpse of a time when 'the brilliantly varnished buttercups' glowed in all the meadows, when 'silver-crested peewits circled and cried with their melancholy cadences', when there was some point in calling 'Thuckoo!' because there were cuckoos to imitate, and when there was a good chance of finding 'the little spring musherooms as come wi' the warm rain'. Times have changed, but those who seek to promote 'the Mary Webb country' often pedal the notion that a hundred years on it survives, unspoilt, unchanging – if only! It remains a compelling landscape, but much of the texture, the diversity of creatures and plants, the sheer profusion, has been lost.

There is more to this novel however, than a feast of nostalgia and drama. There is a debate about sexuality, female and male; a passionate polemic about man and his cruelty to his fellows and to nature; and a tortured enquiry into the existence, or otherwise, of God. The last was a consequence, perhaps, of the carnage of the First World War which was being fought while Mary Webb, who had brothers on the Western Front, was writing.

'Gone to Earth', 'The Wild Heart', 'La Renarde'

Thirty years later, not long after another war, the summer and autumn of 1949 saw the filming of 'Gone to Earth' at various locations in South Shropshire, including Much Wenlock (as 'the town'), Pontesford Hill (as 'Hunter's Spinney'), Longnor Hall (as 'Undern Hall') and on The Stiperstones, but, most significantly,

Hazel Woodus (Jennifer Jones) at 'Hunter's Spinney' (Pontesford Hill)

From the filming of 'Gone to Earth', 1949. Supplied by the British Film Institute, photographer unknown. These conifers are the ones just visible near the top of Pontesford Hill in the photo on page 105.

A rocky location

Preparations in hand at Diamond Rock for the filming in 1949 of a scene from 'Gone to Earth'. Supplied by the British Film Institute, photographer unknown.

A godly location

Lordshill Chapel with the changes made for the filming of 'Gone to Earth' still in place: a porch incorporating a decorative barge board, which survives to this day, and, also on the gable end, the addition of a non-functional upper-storey bay window; still present in this photo of 1954, it was later removed. This illusory window was necessary in order to establish the fiction that from here Hazel Woodus (now married to Edward Marston) could see Jack Reddin stalking her from amongst the tombstones below. Photo A P Wallace.

at Lordshill Chapel, the inspiration for Mary Webb's 'God's Little Mountain'. Here a fake window was added to the gable end of the chapel house; it was subsequently removed, but the specially built porch with its decorative barge board, and a pool dug for Hazel's baptism, a scene unique to the film, both survive, the silted shape of the latter defined now by 'the yellow cradles of the mimulus', Mary Webb's evocation of the blooms of the Monkey Flower.

The film was 'written, produced and directed by Michael Powell and Emeric Pressburger', a partnership described by Philip French – doyen of British film critics – as 'amongst the greatest in movie history'. Powell, the director, 'an archetypal Englishman', and Pressburger, the screenwriter, a Hungarian-born, Jewish German émigré, collaborated on 19 films in the 1940s and 1950s, encompassing 'some of the finest pictures about a nation at war and the prospects for the post-war world'.[4] 'Gone to Earth' is not regarded as one of their best films, but it captures something of the magical, ominous, troubling quality of Mary Webb's novel and of the dishevelled, only part-tamed texture of the Shropshire countryside that Mary Webb described, much of which survived until the middle of the twentieth century. The film was released in Great Britain in 1950, and it is said to have been a particular success in France, where it was called 'La Renarde' (The Vixen), the title also used for the French translation of the novel and a play of 1951. It was not until 1952, however, that it appeared in the United States, significantly shortened (from 110 minutes down to 82), under the title 'The Wild Heart'.

Casting the elfin

Casting posed two significant challenges: who was to play the beautiful, innocent, elfin, all but wild, eighteen-year-old Hazel Woodus? And what about her 'Foxy'? The first challenge was soon resolved. Powell and Pressburger were working at the time for Alexander Korda and David O Selznick, two of the biggest names in film production, and, according to Michael Powell, Selznick was 'looking for a European subject for Jennifer Jones [the actress he had recently married], whom he was parading about Europe at his chariot wheels'. Jennifer Jones was beautiful, an Oscar winner and a star, but could she capture Hazel's wildness and youth? What about her accent? And what about Hazel's feyness and her complete sexual innocence, followed by her gradual, aching, sexual awakening, factors on which the credibility of the narrative leans so heavily?

It was a tall order for an American woman of 30, with two children, now married for the second time. But Michael Powell recounts how Jennifer Jones threw herself into the role:

> 'She had lost several pounds for the part, and had had corsets specially designed to pinch her in and to push her out ... from the moment that she arrived she threw her shoes away and went barefoot ... she asked interminable questions about everything she saw, felt and smelt ... she wanted to know everything that Hazel, who had been born and bred in the countryside would know ... she never tired of talking to the local people and picking out their accent and their words for everything ... she went through the film as if she were the real Hazel, playing herself.'

The filming of 'Gone to Earth'

The four individuals in the foreground are, from left to right, Christopher Challis (seated, Cinematographer), Jennifer Jones as Hazel Woodus, Michael Powell (co-Director and co-Producer, with sleeves rolled up) and Esmond Knight as Abel Woodus. The device on the left appears to be one of the cumbersome cameras of the time. Photographer unknown.

David Thomson, one of cinema's senior historians, lauds both actress and film:

> 'Jennifer's Hazel is a daring performance, in many ways her freest and least self-conscious … 'Gone to Earth' is often beautiful, eerie, and emotionally powerful, and its vision of a remote rural world where magic and destiny are at work depends upon the barefoot, feral intuitiveness of Jennifer.'

Both Powell and Thomson are perhaps in thrall to the star. Yes, she gives a creditable performance, but not surprisingly, she fails fully to capture Hazel's nymph-like quality, to appear so completely naïve, such a child of nature. And she is directed towards an interpretation in which she appears a more willing victim than the novel suggests, prey to a muscular seduction rather than the rape perpetrated in the novel, and thereafter displaying more tenderness to her assailant than is suggested in the text.

The film has a strong cast, with David Farrar as Jack Reddin and Cyril Cusack as Edward Marston, supported by Esmond Knight as Abel Woodus (Hazel's father),

Hugh Griffith as Andrew Vessons (Reddin's servant), Sybil Thorndike as Mrs Marston (Edward's mother) and George Cole as Hazel's cousin Albert. And these actors revel in the rich supporting roles that Mary Webb had created, characters full of individuality, quirkiness and humour.

Casting the foxy

And what about 'Foxy'? Clearly a tame fox was a requirement, but Michael Powell 'had visions of our 'Foxy' in the film being gobbled up by the hounds before she had started playing her part', so he ordered that three should be found. Apparently it proved easy enough to recruit one tame fox but the second was difficult to find and, though signed up, did not inspire confidence; a third could not be located. The animal-handlers came up with an unlikely fall-back: 'they suggested that they should train and hold in support two or three corgis, a foxy-looking little dog with a low wheel-base, much favoured by our gracious Queen'. Powell was aware of their dissimilar physique and yet he was persuaded that the corgis:

Tally-ho!

Preparations in 1949 for a hunting scene above Lordshill for 'Gone to Earth'. No sign of the hounds, but the field gathers behind the film crew; on the right, Hazel Woodus (Jennifer Jones), with her back to the camera, talks to a huntsman assumed to be Jack Reddin (David Farrar). Note the Resting Hill Chimney and Engine House; Bromlow Callow is on the horizon to the right of centre. Supplied by the British Film Institute, photographer unknown.

'would make a very passable double for a fox, provided that a fox's brush were first attached to the corgi's short and stumpy tail. The proposal was greeted with enthusiasm by me, but not by the corgis … When they found themselves held between the property man's knees while a fox's brush was taped to what other people might call a short, stumpy tail but which was, after all, their tail, down it went like a railroad signal and no amount of persuasion could encourage them to lift the hated fox's brush from the dust in which it trailed.'

A close viewing of the film suggests however that these unpromising stand-ins were never called upon.

Recruiting a pack of hounds is said to have posed problems too, because, fearing a hostile portrayal, the hunting establishment advised against participation in the film by official hunts, and it was Bertie Stevens, a farmer from near Aberystwyth, who brought his own personal pack to take part in the hunting scenes.

Remembering and revisiting 'Gone to Earth'

No such casting problem need trouble directors of the play 'Gone to Earth' because 'Foxy', and much else besides, has been written out of the script. Helen Edmundson's adaption had its first performance in 2004, and she admits to having 'taken great liberties with the narrative, changing the way the story is told'.[5] Reduced to words on a page, the play appears limp and insubstantial, and some of the language sounds laughably anachronistic. But the kernel of the tale is there and it appears to have provided a moving theatrical experience in a production that gained enthusiastic reviews. The part of Hazel Woodus, that other potentially taxing casting problem, went to 19 year-old Natalia Tena. It was her professional stage debut and she is reported to have given a 'phenomenal' performance – 'fierce, graceful, apparently guileless … with the urgency of childhood' yet 'never girlish, coy or watchful'.[6]

But to return to the film, it was re-issued in the mid 1980s, and there were many showings at local venues. These burnished abiding memories of the making of the film amongst the survivors of the 300 or so local people who were 'extras'. Others had assisted in various ways, while many more witnessed the filming on location in Shropshire. A rich seam of reminiscence was mined from this numerous company for a 75-minute video issued in 1998 entitled 'Hollywood Comes to Shropshire'.[7] It is an entertaining collage of scenes from the film, anecdote and factual detail. More recently 'The Lordshill Project' has released two CDs under the title 'Gone to Earth Remembered and Revisited', a fascinating compilation including the recollections of extras and observers.[8] It is full of charm and warmth, of fond recollection of an event that still evokes wonder and excitement in those that it touched. More than 60 years have passed since the film was made, yet, in the words of 'The Lordshill Project' 'the experience is still a vital part of community and family history'.

'Gone to Earth' extras, 1949

Sylvia Jones on the left, then aged 13, outside the Chapel House at Lordshill with her siblings (left to right) Keith (aged 15), Terence (9), Stella (7) and Ken (11), parents Tom (39) and Beatrice (37), and grandparents Jane and William Evans (70 and 72). They all lived at the Chapel House, and were joined on occasion by Sylvia's cousin Basil Hotchkiss (23), top row at right; her grandfather was caretaker for the Chapel. Photo reproduced courtesy of Sylvia Lewis (née Jones).

Mary Webb and the natural world

'Gone to Earth Remembered and Revisited' includes observations on the birdlife that Mary Webb mentions in her novels. Her abundant wildlife references reflect the importance of the natural world to her writing, an importance highlighted by further comparison of her work with that of Thomas Hardy. Although a mechanistic analysis reveals nothing about their merits as writers, it is telling that Mary Webb names 47 flowering plants and 23 birds in the course of *The Golden Arrow*, whilst for Thomas Hardy, in *The Return of the Native*, the count is respectively 22 and 14, despite Hardy's book being almost twice as long.

Clearly Mary Webb was fascinated by nature, but, like many of us, her knowledge, other than of birds and readily recognised plants, appears to have been very sketchy. This is suggested by a close reading of her three 'upland' novels: *The Golden Arrow*, which is set on The Stiperstones and The Long Mynd; *Gone to Earth*, much of which takes place on the northwestern end of the Stiperstones ridge at Lordshill ('God's Little Mountain'); and *Seven for a Secret*, for which the setting is the Clun Forest ('Disgwlfas on the Moors'). Throughout these three novels she never names a single butterfly and only two moths, as against 50 species of birds and 96 of flowering plants.[9]

Red Grouse and Black Grouse

This illustration by Archibald Thorburn is reproduced from T A Coward's *The Birds of the British Isles* (1920).

Curlew (top) and Whimbrel

This illustration by Archibald Thorburn is reproduced from T A Coward's *The Birds of the British Isles* (1920).

Yet, despite the frequency of these wildlife references, they remain relevant to the setting of each novel, they are not simply thrown in for poetic effect but used to give a sense of ecological place. Thus, for example, Heather and Bilberry, both classic upland species, are mentioned 21 and 11 times respectively in *The Golden Arrow*, which is set amongst the upland heathland of The Stiperstones and The Long Mynd. But when it comes to *Gone to Earth*, which is set on the fringe of the hills, in somewhat softer, more low-lying country, one of woods, pastures and river valleys, there is no reference to Heather and only one to Bilberry. By contrast Bluebell and Wood Sorrel rate eight and four mentions respectively in the latter novel, but none in the former. Similarly for birds: Red and Black Grouse, both heathland and moorland specialists, appear in *The Golden Arrow* but not in *Gone to Earth*, whilst it is vice versa for Grey Wagtail and Dipper, both of which are river birds.

Birds: then and now

There is also a historical dimension to Mary Webb's wildlife references. In none of her upland novels does she mention Raven or Buzzard; why is this? Both are common today in the Shropshire Hills, and both are striking birds with, particularly in the case of Raven, rich potential for symbolism and poetic allusion. However, during the greater part of Mary Webb's life, the Raven was extinct as a breeding species in the Shropshire Hills, driven out by relentless persecution through nest destruction, shooting and poisoning. The last breeding record was in 1884, and it was not until 1918, after four years of the Great War, in which many gamekeepers had fought and died, that Ravens bred again in the county. The story was similar for Buzzard; once common, it was all but extinct in Shropshire by 1900 and did not start to recover until after the Great War.

By contrast, Mary Webb mentions other species which, though to be found when she was alive, have since become rare or extinct in Shropshire. One such is Black Grouse: they were present on The Stiperstones in her day, but have not now been found breeding in the county for some 60 years. Another is Woodlark, mentioned five times by Mary Webb in *Gone to Earth*. They are birds of bare ground and short vegetation with scattered trees, and with 'their hurried ripple of notes and their vacillating flights' they accompanied Hazel Woodus as she walked amongst the Whinberries above the chapel. Mary Webb lived at a time when the Woodlark population was expanding to occupy suitable habitats across much of the southern half of Britain, and the heathland fringe above Lordshill Chapel would have been ideal, but a marked contraction southwards was underway by the late 1950s. It is now some 60 years since there was much chance of observing Woodlarks in Shropshire.

Lapwing or Peewit would have been a common sight in the Shropshire Hills in Mary Webb's day. In *Gone to Earth* Reddin curses until 'the peewits arose mewing all about him'. Some twenty-five years later, in Malcolm Saville's *Mystery at Witchend* (1943) – see Chapter 6 – it is Tom Ingles, a London evacuee working on a Shropshire hill farm, who suggests the 'pee-wit' whistle as the Lone Pine Club's secret signal. At that time the Lapwing was still a common breeding species in the Shropshire Hills, it remained so until the 1960s; it is now a rarity.

Whimbrel and Curlew

Amongst the many references to birds in *The Golden Arrow* there are six to Whimbrel. It figures too in another of her novels *Seven for a Secret*, set in the Clun Forest area of southwest Shropshire, and in the following passage evoking high summer she describes the Whimbrels' recently hatched young:

> 'The blackbirds grew silent. The whimbrels rang their elfin peals less often and their pencilled chickens[10] ran amongst the heather near the springs. The wimberries ripened...'

Yet, as H E Forrest states in *The Fauna of Shropshire* (1899), a book which Mary Webb will surely have known,[11] the Whimbrel is 'a rare visitor to Shropshire Moors on its Spring and Autumn migrations. It has never bred here'; nor has it since.[12] By contrast, Forrest states that the very similar Curlew 'is numerous on our Shropshire moorlands and breeds regularly'.

Could Mary Webb have confused the Whimbrel and its close relative the Curlew? No, she would have been familiar with the Curlew and known it well from its onomatopoeic call; clearly she chose to use the name Whimbrel for poetic reasons. The alliteration of 'whimbrels' and 'wimberries' works well in the above quotation, and it comes from a passage which opens with 'Summer drooped warm wings over the moor'. Understandably, in her writing of fiction, poetry weighs more heavily for Mary Webb than science, so with a little 'natural magic' she spirits in the Whimbrel to impersonate the Curlew.[13]

Chapter 6

'The aboriginal hill': literature and tourism

I think it's frantically lovely up here.

D H Lawrence *St Mawr* (1925)

D H Lawrence and Frederick Carter

D H Lawrence

An engraved portrait by Frederick Carter from his *D H Lawrence and the Body Mystical* (1932) in which he describes Lawrence thus: 'A weary red-bearded man with a lean, acrid smile, sardonic from his deep understanding of the old earth and its inner secrets. He had delved deep. Bright eyes, sheer and hard with the luminosity of mountain streams, gleamed from beneath a broad ancient rock of a forehead, scarred with thinking. And over it hung a sweep of mouse-coloured hair'. Reproduced courtesy of Richard Grenville Clark.

D H Lawrence (1885-1930) was a close contemporary of Mary Webb (1881-1927); I wonder whether they read each other's work. But Lawrence's visit in 1924 to Pontesbury and The Stiperstones had nothing to do with his fellow author; he came to visit Frederick Carter (1883-1967) an artist who also had aspirations as a writer.[1] Gordon Dickins describes Lawrence's visit in his *Illustrated Literary Guide to Shropshire* (1987) and Peter Francis adds considerable detail in an article in the *Snailbeach District News* of 2003 to which I am indebted for much of the following account. Other important sources include Richard Grenville Clark's 1998 study of Carter's etchings.[2]

Frederick Carter was born in Yorkshire. He trained as a 'surveyor-architect', but became a book illustrator, took up etching, and exhibited at leading galleries at home and abroad. Carter had a particular interest in apocalyptic symbols, the zodiac and the *Book of Revelation*, and prepared a manuscript and drawings on these subjects. Under the misapprehension that Lawrence had also made a deep study of the *Book of Revelation*, Carter sent him the manuscript. Already an established writer, Lawrence's published works included *Sons and Lovers* and *Women in Love*.

Frederick Carter

This photo from *Frederick Carter, A Study of his Etchings* (1998), is reproduced courtesy of the author, Richard Grenville Clark.

Although not previously aware of Frederick Carter, or his work, Lawrence expressed pleasure and interest in the manuscript. Further correspondence ensued, in which Lawrence, then living in Mexico, suggested that when next he visited England they should meet. They did so in January 1924, when Frederick Carter was living in Pontesbury, three miles northeast of The Stiperstones. Richard Grenville Clark recounts how Lawrence had assumed from Carter's address, 'The Deanery', that he was a layman theologian with a private income.[3] In fact, in order to supplement the uncertain sales of his work, he was travelling each week to Liverpool for a part-time job teaching etching. Carter's decision to rent a house in Pontesbury was influenced by his friendship with the artists Walter and Dorothea Clement, who lived there. Walter made the altar in St George's Church, Pontesbury; it was carved by Dorothea. The altar incorporates three panels, these were painted, a little ineptly in my view, by Frederick Carter.

St Mawr

Carter met Lawrence at Shrewsbury station, from where the two of them travelled to Pontesbury on the Minsterley branch line. During Lawrence's brief stay in Shropshire they discussed the possibility of joint research and publication; they also walked together to The Stiperstones, and Carter states that Lawrence 'was delighted with that wild Shropshire countryside'.[4] It seems that their route took them over Pontesbury Hill, through Poles Coppice and along Eastridge to Lordshill Chapel; from there they went to the top of Crowsnest Dingle and on to the Devil's Chair – clearly a destination for tourists then, as now.

By the spring of 1924 Lawrence and his wife Frieda had returned to America, living on a small, partly derelict ranch close to Taos, near Santa Fe in New Mexico.[5] Once the ranch had been made habitable, Lawrence quickly wrote *St Mawr*, *The Woman Who Rode Away* and *The Princess*. *St Mawr* was published in 1925; it is a novella of some 175 pages. The story starts in London, moves to Shropshire and finally over to New Mexico and the Rocky Mountains, but the pivotal moment occurs close to the Devil's Chair.

The influence of a bay stallion named St Mawr is evident almost throughout the novella. Lawrence's fictional horse, with its 'big, black, brilliant eyes, with a sharp questioning glint, and that air of tense, alert quietness which betrays an animal that can be dangerous' was inspired it seems by a magnificent bay stallion he had seen when in Pontesbury. And St Mawr animates the inter-play between the principal human characters: the American, Mrs Rachel Witt, her daughter, Lou Carrington, and her Australian son-in-law, Rico.

St Mawr is an essay about the wild and the tame – the wild, instinctive, animal spirit of the stallion, and the tame, mannered, self-conscious attitudes of upper class men. The sight of St Mawr makes Lou Carrington want to cry: 'He burns with life. Most men have a deadness in them ... Why can't men get their life straight, like St Mawr'. But the novella is also about the wildness of nature, whether on The Stiperstones or in the Rocky Mountains: 'the marvellous beauty and fascination of natural wild things' contrasted with 'the horror of man's unnatural life, his heaped-up civilisation'.

Pontesbury characters

The bored, idle protagonists, together with their horses, head, as upper-crust tourists, from London (where St Mawr has already proved a handful) to Shropshire. They travel to Shrewsbury and then out to 'a village of thatched cottages – some of them with corrugated iron over the thatch' (Pontesbury) where Mrs Witt has taken 'a tall red-brick Georgian house looking straight on to the churchyard'.

Frederick Carter later commented that *St Mawr* caused great amusement in Pontesbury because the locals, following up their own clues, 'discovered the identity of every other character in the story'. Indeed they will have recognised Carter himself in Lawrence's Cartwright, an artist who was 'just beginning to accept himself as a failure, as far as making money goes', who 'studied esoteric matters like astrology and alchemy' and had a face 'curiously like Pan's' (as indeed has Lawrence in Carter's drawing!). And what about Mr Jones the postmaster, who 'delivered his message in the mayonnaise of his own unction'? And then there was 'the wicked little group of cottagers' ... 'famous for ill-living' ... 'in-bred' ... the 'result of working through the centuries at the Quarry, and living isolated there'. This was, presumably, the Stiperstones Quartzite quarry at the Nills, near where Mary Webb once lived, which Lawrence and Carter will have walked past on their way to The Stiperstones.

'The old savage England'

'An excursion on horseback' is arranged to 'two old groups of rocks, called the Angel's Chair and the Devil's Chair, which crowned the moor-like hills looking into Wales'. Though the name is never used, this is clearly The Stiperstones; perhaps the Angel's Chair is Lawrence's name for Shepherd's Rock. The route followed by the riding party is that taken by Carter and Lawrence in January 1924: 'down into a glade where a little railway [had been] built for hauling some mysterious mineral out of the hill' (clearly the Snailbeach District Railway), and past 'the hollow where the old Aldecar Chapel hid in damp isolation' (Lordshill Chapel). But it is now high summer and there is a 'sea of bracken' ... 'distant bilberry-pickers' ... 'the pinky tops of heather and ling' ... and 'tufts of hare-bells blue as bubbles'. On the skyline there is 'a bunch of rocks: and away to the right another bunch'; they head for the Devil's Chair:

> 'They came at last, trotting in file along a narrow track between heather, along the saddle of a hill, to where the knot of pale granite suddenly cropped out. It

was one of those places where the spirit of aboriginal England still lingers, the old savage England, whose last blood flows still in a few Englishmen, Welshmen, Cornishmen.'[6]

They dismount and scramble over the Devil's Chair and locate 'the famous Needle's Eye' (see page 102); some at least of the party enter into the spirit of tourism and find it 'frantically lovely up here'. Then, back in the saddle, they head on, but soon St Mawr shies, backs and rears at the sight of an Adder. His rider, Rico, who has come to hate the horse, tugs viciously at the reins. He pulls the horse over backwards on top of himself. Ribs are broken, an ankle crushed; another young man is disfigured by a kick in the face.

Should St Mawr be shot? Or gelded? He is saved from both fates by Mrs Witt and her daughter who take the stallion away, pack their bags and eventually, along with St Mawr, but without Rico, head back to their native America. Lou buys a little, semi-derelict ranch, at over 8,000 ft, 'man's last effort towards the wild heart of the Rockies'. The ranch is described in detail – it is modelled on the Lawrences' own Kiowa Ranch where *St Mawr* was written.

Lawrence's principal characters lead privileged, vacuous, decadent lives. They are egotistical and self-absorbed, tedious in their constant self analysis and analysis of others. They serve Lawrence's satirical purpose, and provide the opposite to the natural and vital as represented by St Mawr, but their vacuity rubs off on the novella. It is saved and illuminated however by Lawrence's vibrant descriptions, his wit and intelligence.

Shepherd's Rock framed by part of Scattered Rocks
Photo, 1999, courtesy of Gordon Dickins.

Two Dragons and an Apocalypse

And what of Frederick Carter? By the end of 1925 he was in Liverpool, and the following year he published *The Dragon of the Alchemists*, a series of drawings of figures and symbols preceded by several essays, the preliminary chapters it seems from the manuscript he had originally sent to Lawrence. In 1929 there was a concentrated exchange of letters between the two men, and late in the year Carter visited Lawrence in the south of France. On his return (together with copies of *Lady Chatterley's Lover*, which was banned in the UK) he made the etching of Lawrence reproduced at the head of this chapter. By this time Lawrence, whose health had been fragile throughout his life, was terminally ill; he died of tuberculosis on 2 March 1930. Carter survived him by many years, turning increasingly to literature, as a short story writer, biographer,

'Silence'

From Frederick Carter's *The Dragon of the Alchemists* (1926). Reproduced courtesy of Richard Grenville Clark.

critic, editor, translator and essayist, seeking, in the words of Richard Grenville Clark, 'to explore the philosophical, astrological and religious dilemmas which so overwhelmingly preoccupied him'.

Apocalypse (1931)

Title page from the first edition.

Prior to his death, Lawrence had been working on an introduction to what was to be Carter's second book, *The Dragon of Revelation*. But it seems that Lawrence's pen ran away with him (he drafted some 25,000 words and deleted a further 20,000) and, not surprisingly, he abandoned the notion of this manuscript as an introduction. Instead it became his final book, *Apocalypse*, 'a radical and searching criticism of the political, religious and social structures which have shaped our materialistic and technological age';[7] it was published posthumously in 1931.

Lawrence had, however, written a new and short introduction for Carter, but perhaps because it was not altogether complimentary, it was not made use of when, also in 1931, *The Dragon of Revelation* was published.[8] Instead Carter's publisher includes a note telling the story of Lawrence's involvement with Carter and how it had led to the writing of *Apocalypse*. Carter's *D H Lawrence and the Body Mystical* (1932) describes their relationship and planned literary collaboration. It is a relationship which merits a significant literary footnote: it played an important part in the writing of *St Mawr*, and if, in 1923, Carter had not sent Lawrence his manuscript, and had not remained in contact with him, visiting him in the south of France in the months before his death, *Apocalypse* would surely not have been written.

Artists and book illustrators

Perhaps Frederick Carter painted, drew or etched The Stiperstones, or illustrated books about it, but nothing has come to light during research for this account. Indeed, despite inspiring a number of well-known works of fiction, this spectacular landscape has inspired no similarly well-known works of art. Perhaps it is too extensive, too austere a landscape, not painterly enough. Yet today, as doubtless in earlier generations, local artists have painted works of quality here, capturing the essence of the place. A prime example is Fred Hollands, formerly of Tankerville, now of Pontesbury, who has painted many fine water-colours of the hill, including one reproduced below and another on the cover of this book. Another Tankerville artist is Patricia A Evans whose *Poetic Landscapes* (2002) matches her watercolours with extracts from the

The Devil's Chair in profile

A watercolour of the 1980s reproduced courtesy of the artist, Fred Hollands.

prose and poetry of Mary Webb. The watercolours include half a dozen of The Stiperstones; amongst them is one of the Devil's Chair which is reproduced in the Introduction. More recently, Jackie Astbury, an artist and book illustrator who lives at Welsh Row, has painted a dramatic mural within the Bog Visitor Centre. And there are examples galore of highly artistic landscape photographs, a number of which illustrate this book.

Book illustration has, however, given some more widely-known artists a connection with The Stiperstones.[9] The illustrated edition of the works of Mary Webb which Jonathan Cape published from 1929 onwards, drew in the talents of Norman Hepple and, in the case of *Precious Bane*, Rowland Hilder. Hepple (1908-1994) was a young man at the time, he went on to make a career as an artist. President of the Royal Society of Portrait Painters he was commissioned to portray several of the Royals. His angular vignettes top and tail the chapters of *The Golden Arrow* with distinction but I doubt that he had ever visited The

Whinberrying

A plate by Norman Hepple from the illustrated 1930 edition of Mary Webb's *The Golden Arrow*. Hepple's image has a quotation from the novel as a caption: 'They picked for two hours, absorbed and perspiring'. Absorbed perhaps, but perspiring? And what sort of Whinberry bush is this? Bridgeman Art Library.

Prudence Sarn midst plough and stubble

'It was a fine fresh morning with a damp wind full of the scent of our ricks'. This plate by
Rowland Hilder from the illustrated 1929 edition of Mary Webb's *Precious Bane*, shows a skyline
of the Shropshire Hills, inspired perhaps by The Stiperstones, Pontesford Hill and Earl's Hill,
albeit re-arranged. Reproduced courtesy of Rowland Hilder's son, Anthony.

Stiperstones: his tors are docile slabs rather than fractured hulks; John Arden's
'cottage' runs to three stories, four gables and umpteen chimneys; and whilst
his illustration of Whinberry picking may work as art, it is laughable as rural
record.

Rowland Hilder (1905-1993) was one of England's most popular artists of the
twentieth century, yet many of his drawings for *Precious Bane* are curiously
small, sombre and lifeless. He had however visited Shropshire,[10] and one of
his colour illustrations shows a skyline strongly suggestive of the view looking
south from Lea Cross near Pontesbury. It appears to show the outlines, albeit
transposed, of Pontesford and Earl's Hills and of The Stiperstones; it is a skyline onto which D H Lawrence and Frederick Carter will have looked in 1924 as
they travelled to Pontesbury on the Minsterley branch line.

Stanley Baldwin, Mary Webb and her pilgrims

Stanley Baldwin

A photo from the 1920s.

In 1924, at the time when D H Lawrence was visiting Frederick Carter, Mary Webb was completing *Precious Bane*; it was published later that year.[11] Prime Minister Stanley Baldwin (1867-1947) was to read this, the best known of Mary Webb's novels, over the Christmas of 1926. In the New Year Baldwin wrote to Webb telling her of the 'keen delight' with which he had read 'a first-class piece of work'. Webb responded, delighted in her turn at receiving praise from someone 'notably versed in the classics', and clearly flattered that the man who, she supposed, had the 'least leisure … of anybody in the British Empire', had taken the trouble to write to her. She asked if she might be allowed to dedicate to Baldwin the novel on which she was then working, and promised to post next day a 'little bunch of violets for your writing-table'.[12]

At this time Mary Webb had only a small band of admirers but, as Gladys Mary Coles recounts in her biography of Mary Webb,[13] Stanley Baldwin was to be instrumental in establishing her as a popular novelist, albeit posthumously. Her death, in October 1927, a mere nine months after her correspondence with Baldwin, went largely unrecorded, and it was only the day before a speech to the Royal Literary Fund dinner in April 1928, at which Baldwin intended to talk of Mary Webb's work, that he learned that she had died. He went on to speak of his surprise that he had seen no obituaries, and paid testimony to 'the extreme pleasure' her writing had given him. Next day's papers gave prominence to Baldwin's tribute, under headlines which included 'Neglected Genius'. In an astute move, Jonathan Cape, the publisher, hurriedly bought the rights to all her works, rushing them into print in a new Collected Edition. Mary Webb's novels, which had sold slowly in her life-time, now became best-sellers: *The Golden Arrow*, re-issued in May 1928, had to be reprinted six

The Shropshire of Mary Webb (1930)

The cover of W Reid Chappell's book, in which village, beach and tor are brought together by an unknown designer in a non-existent but evocative combination.

times by March 1930, as had *Gone to Earth*, while within a six-month period in 1928 *Precious Bane* was reprinted five times.

Some of Mary Webb's many new readers were keen to visit the settings of her novels. According to W Reid Chappell in *The Shropshire of Mary Webb* (1930): 'English and American pilgrims commenced to pay homage in the summer of 1928, and it is apparent that what was once a secluded bit of England far from the macadamised track will become the scene of many pilgrimages'. His was the first of the pilgrims' guides. It is an entertaining mix of history, travel guidance, philosophy, homily, nationalism, anecdote and the life and times of Mary Webb, including a description of the locations of each of the novels. And it holds historical interest, not least in the photographs with which it is illustrated and for the light that it throws on the harsh lives of the miners. It includes descriptions of individuals and homesteads, the debilitating work in the mines and the desperate poverty that followed when, inexorably, industrial disease overcame the bread winner.

Shropshire Hills and Haunts: the travel guides

Magdalene Weale

Over the next few decades other writers were to follow Reid Chappell's lead, notably Magdalene Weale, H W Timperley, W Byford-Jones and Vincent Waite, all of whom dedicated a chapter or more to describing The Stiperstones.

Magdalene Weale's *Through the Highlands of Shropshire on Horseback* (1935) is the most characterful. Weale (1890-1961) had previously stayed in various parts of Shropshire and had covered some of the highlands when hunting with The United, but she determined 'to weld my various experiences into a connected whole' and decided that the best way of 'doing justice' to the area was to see it from horseback.[14] But rather than a hunter, she chose a local pony, Sandy, from Hogstow Hall, just west of Crowsnest. Sandy was 'the racing pony of the Mary Webb country, a bright chestnut, trim and elegant and full of idiosyncrasies'. These included the ability to open gates, and part way through the itinerary, while her rider was staying at the Buffalo Inn in Clun, Sandy effected an overnight escape. A 'stalking party in a car, headed by the owner of the Stiperstones Inn' (this will have been William Humphrey) came to the rescue, and thanks to 'examinations, at intervals, of the horse-droppings along the road, their dimensions and date of issue, supplemented by inquiries *en route*', Sandy was tracked all the way back to The Stiperstones, from where Magdalene Weale recommended her travels.

The original departure from Hogstow Hall had been delayed because Sandy had a racing engagement at Minsterley, and whilst on tour she ran also at Kerry (14 miles southwest of The Stiperstones), coming in 'a good second'. But despite her various accomplishments, Sandy has a smaller part to play in the events than did the donkey in Robert Louis Stevenson's celebrated travels, and Magdalene Weale's account is more of a guidebook than a travelogue. Indeed, its final chapter, entitled 'The country of the Mary Webb novels' is a virtual gazetteer

Through the Highlands
Shropshire on Horseback
By MAGDALENE M. WEALE, M.A.

Ethel Hall.

**With twelve pen and ink Drawings and twelve Maps
and Plans**

Through the Highlands of Shropshire on Horseback (1935)

A long life has left the dust jacket of Magdalene Weale's book frayed at the edges and shorn of a word. Designed by Ethel Hall (1894-1940), it is reproduced courtesy of Mark O'Hanlon.

In 'The Land of Dereliction'

A pen and ink drawing by Ethel Hall from Magdalene Weale's *Through the Highlands of Shropshire on Horseback* (1935).

of fictional and actual place-names and locations. The text is decorated by the characterful drawings of Ethel Hall (1894-1940) an artist best known for her flower paintings.

By the time that Magdalene Weale was writing, mining activity was petering out, leaving behind what she describes as 'The Land of Dereliction', 'a great stretch of desolate moorland and bog' where 'from amid the purple gold-flecked heather the gaunt arms of ruined mine-shafts rise like ghostly memorials to the futile cupidity of man'. Her portrait of The Stiperstones and its people gives due weight to the scars and debris of mining, to the stark hardness, as well as to the character and beauty of the landscape, and to the poverty and grind of life here at that time.

W Byford-Jones and H W Timperley

Shropshire Haunts of Mary Webb by W Byford-Jones (1907-1977), a journalist who often wrote under the name 'Quaestor', was published in 1937. It had originally appeared as articles in the *Express and Star*, Wolverhampton, and it is essentially a series of journalistic yarns, ghost stories and legends, coloured by deeply conservative sentiments and nostalgia for a countryside seen as being under attack from urban sprawl. He provides a few biographical details of Mary Webb and descriptions of her homes, interspersed with *faits divers* and traveller's tales. He adds little more than anecdote to the store of knowledge about Mary Webb or The Stiperstones. When visiting the latter he comments, accurately perhaps, that 'One is nearer to Mary Webb on the Devil's Chair ... than anywhere else in Shropshire'. He also visits Rose Cottage, Pontesbury, where Mary Webb wrote *The Golden Arrow*, and it is indicative of the post-Baldwin popularity of her work and her countryside that he reports that under the guise of 'Roseville' it had been made into a boarding house on the strength of its literary connections.

In *Shropshire Hills* (1947), H W Timperley (1890-1964) offers a lyrical portrait of this part of his native county. He regrets the time that he has been obliged to spend away from Shropshire, even though this had given him the opportunity to write *Ridge Way Country* and *A Cotswold Book*. He concedes that 'with me the habit of gradual approach seems ingrained ... I would rather not go straight to a place at first sight but come to it in roundabout stages'. Timperley's writing mirrors his navigation, but despite a tendency to go 'all round the Wrekin', he eventually homes in on the essentials, offering some colourful and evocative portraits of Shropshire hill country, not least The Stiperstones, without, incidentally, a single mention of Mary Webb. For Timperley 'the hill is harsh and often saturnine' and 'against a sky glowing with the rising sun ... its crestline stacks of rocks simplified to a black or purple-toned silhouette ... loom like a barren and jagged wilderness on the edge of the world'. If you wish to share this perspective, approach the hill at dawn from Shelve and observe the long crest, etched, pin-sharp, against the eastern glow.

H W Timperley includes knowledgeable observations of the birds and plants of the hills, some of which assume historical significance today. Note, for example, his comments on the ubiquity of Curlews, which are now in decline, and, by contrast, his surprise at seeing three Buzzards 'which must have drifted across from the Welsh mountains'; today such a sighting is commonplace and invariably involves locally-bred birds rather than strays from Wales.

Vincent Waite and Jim Perrin

Vincent Waite's *Shropshire Hill Country* (1970) tends towards the scholarly, drawing on history, literature and myth, as befits perhaps a barrister-at-law who, for nearly 20 years, had been a teacher. Clearly Waite was a busy man, who wrote a quantity of books including several about other hill country (the Malverns, Quantocks and Mendips), consequently, perhaps, he observes The

Stiperstones only from its periphery, and through the eyes of others including Murchison, 'Nimrod',[15] Walter White and, of course, Mary Webb, about whom he includes extensive biographical notes, together with brief critiques of her novels. He neglects 'the hill', skirting round it without ever pulling on his walking boots, and before long he's off to comment on the celebrated maidens' garlands at Minsterley.[16]

Some claim to have been reluctant pilgrims of Mary Webb; one such is the revered mountain writer and essayist Jim Perrin (born 1947). Whilst acknowledging his debt to 'a balding, slight, fierce, acerbic master, gowned and intense' who, in the 1960s had drawn his attention to Mary Webb, Perrin did not become a devotee. He recognises the 'haunting and memorable' nature of some of her writing, but he is not alone in finding her work 'slightly repellent'.[17] Perrin tells us that for twenty-odd years he shunned her hills, which seemed to him 'doom-laden, bleak and primitive – to be avoided if you wish to keep your peace of mind'. By the time of his first visit, The Stiperstones had become for him one of those places which 'before you ever visit them and whilst they are still *tabula rasa* to the physical eye, are written upon in the most vivid terms by the imagination'.

One passage in particular from *The Golden Arrow* is writ large for Perrin, so that in his mind's eye he sees The Stiperstones, in Mary Webb's words, as a hill of 'flat, white stones that lay about … like tombstones with no name, no date, no word of hope, fit … for the nameless, dateless dead, beasts and men, who had gone into the silence of annihilation'. Little wonder then that when, finally, Perrin drags himself to The Stiperstones he finds a hill 'capped and crested by shattered tors of quartzite, their faces black-crannied, sightless eyes on the road to Basra,[18] blocks and shards lying everywhere about like innumerable white jagged tombstones among the cowberry and the heather'.

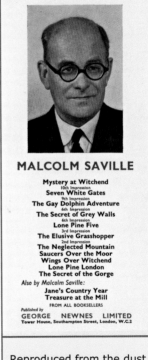

The author of the Lone Pine Books . . .

MALCOLM SAVILLE

Mystery at Witchend
10th Impression
Seven White Gates
9th Impression
The Gay Dolphin Adventure
6th Impression
The Secret of Grey Walls
6th Impression
Lone Pine Five
3rd Impression
The Elusive Grasshopper
2nd Impression
The Neglected Mountain
Saucers Over the Moor
Wings Over Witchend
Lone Pine London
The Secret of the Gorge

Also by Malcolm Saville:
Jane's Country Year
Treasure at the Mill

FROM ALL BOOKSELLERS
Published by
GEORGE NEWNES LIMITED
Tower House, Southampton Street, London, W.C.2

Malcolm Saville and the Lone Pine Club

An enthusiastic Mary Webb pilgrim from an earlier generation was the children's author, Malcolm Saville (1901-82), who declared that 'nothing has influenced me more than the work of Mary Webb'. Saville, who was born in Sussex and was a London commuter, working in publishing, first visited Shropshire in 1936, when he and Dorothy, his wife, stayed at the south end of The Long Mynd, at Cwm Head House, a mile from Priors Holt. It was to here that Dorothy and three of their four children (the eldest was at boarding school) were evacuated for a year in 1941.

Reproduced from the dust jacket of a Lone Pine Book courtesy of the Estate of the late Malcolm Saville.

Saville was a part-time writer, but a highly prolific one, author between 1937 and 1981 of 93 books. He is best known for the twenty books relating the adventures of the Lone Pine Club, so-named because the founders of the Club signed oaths of allegiance in their own blood under a lone Scots Pine, 'H.Q.1', overlooking 'Witchend' (Priors Holt at the mouth of Nut Batch).

Saville's first Lone Pine Book, *Mystery at Witchend*, published in 1943, chronicles, amongst other things, the formation of the Lone Pine Club by the three Morton children, David (club captain) and the twins Dickie and Mary, fictional evacuees to Witchend, together with two children they encounter locally, Petronella (Peter) Sterling and Tom Ingles. The second Lone Pine adventure, *Seven White Gates* (1944), takes the Club to what was to become its 'H.Q.2', a barn at an imaginary farm known as Seven Gates, standing in the shadow of The Stiperstones. Here Jenny Harman, who lives at the shop in 'Barton Beach' (Stiperstones Village), is enrolled.

Seven White Gates was, like *Mystery at Witchend*, serialised for BBC Radio's 'Children's Hour', and editions were published in Australia, and, in translation, in

Dust jacket of *The Neglected Mountain* (1953)

Designed by Bertram Prance it shows David Morton, Petronella Sterling and Macbeth looking up at the Devil's Chair masquerading as the Eiger. Reproduced courtesy of Christopher Prance.

the Netherlands, Spain and Finland.[19] Seven Gates Farm figures in six more of the series: *Lone Pine Five* (1949), *The Neglected Mountain* (1953), *The Secret of the Gorge* (1958), *Not Scarlet But Gold* (1962), *Strangers at Witchend* (1970) and *Home to Witchend* (1978).

Mine workings figure prominently in *Seven White Gates*, *Lone Pine Five*, *The Neglected Mountain* and *Not Scarlet But Gold*, and members of the Club tend to get stuck in them. Underground rivers are a recurrent theme, as is rain and the ominous bulk of The Stiperstones. The older members of the Club are generally too plucky for their own good; the young twins Dickie and Mary are consistently tiresome. There are always villains, to whom the black Scottie dog Macbeth (Mackie) usually takes an instant dislike, but they are generally petty and ineffectual, and, although there are moments of tension and excitement, a satisfactory outcome is never really in doubt.

Our heroes are always doughty and adventurous, friendly and loyal. David and Peter, Tom and Jenny are obviously couples in the making, but it is not until the twentieth and final book of the series, *Home to Witchend*, published in 1978, 35 years after the first, during which time the protagonists age by just four years, that they finally get engaged. Today the Club's adventures seem somewhat tame, slow-moving and repetitive, but the link to landscape and local history make for an enduring interest, and the stories tell us something of the attitudes, language and culture of the educated middle classes in the mid-twentieth century.

Saville's Pilgrims

Saville, in his turn, inspired a new generation of pilgrims; I was amongst them. My sister and I were keen readers of the Lone Pine Books and we were brought to The Stiperstones in 1960 when on a family holiday; sadly I have no recollection of the visit.[20] A more local enthusiast, Peter Francis, remembers reading the books in the 1960s at his home in Minsterley, just a few miles from The Stiperstones. He pored over the maps illustrating the scenes of the children's adventures which appear in duplicate inside front and back covers, seeking similarities with the maps of the Ordnance Survey and his own knowledge of the area.

Whatever their limitations, the Lone Pine Books gained an enthusiastic and loyal readership and are still remembered today with great affection by many who read them decades ago. New editions are now being published and perhaps a new generation of readers will take to them. If so, it will be because the key ingredients of adventure, camaraderie and a hint of romance have an enduring appeal, and because the lure of being party to the exploits of a club whose members are brave, stalwart and attractive, and who get caught up in exciting events in exciting places, is surely as strong as it was when the books were first written.

A particular strength of the adventures was that Saville rooted them firmly in real locations, whether the Shropshire Hills, Rye, Romney Marsh, Dartmoor, Walberswick, North York Moors or London. Peter Francis's experience highlights

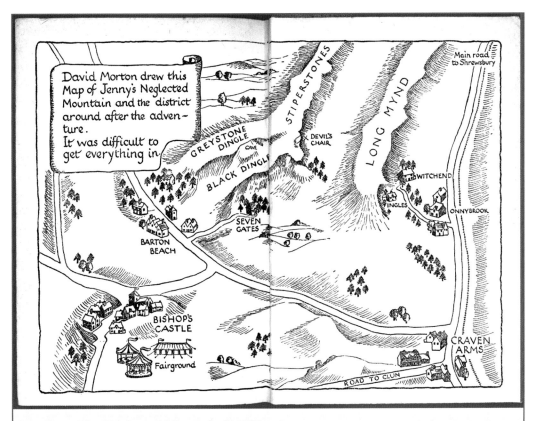

Map from *The Neglected Mountain* (1953)

This map from the endpapers of Malcolm Saville's adventure story, is based extremely loosely on real features and locations. It shows Barton Beach (Stiperstones Village), Seven Gates Farm, Black Dingle (Perkins Beach), Greystone Dingle (Mytton Dingle), the Devil's Chair and Onnybrook (Marshbrook, south of Church Stretton); some of these equivalents are however debatable. Although credited to the fictional David Morton, the cartographer was in fact David Saville, the author's brother. Reproduced courtesy of Hilary Saville, his daughter.

a crucial ingredient: the map of each adventure, printed for ease of reference inside both front and back covers (a feature omitted by witless publishers from some of the later reprints). Armed with the maps, readers could visit the locations, explore the topography and relate fictional to actual place names. Many did so, and told him excitedly in their letters: 'It's just as you said'.

And, to some extent it was 'just as Malcolm Saville said'. The map from *The Neglected Mountain*, reproduced here, illustrates the point. In his foreword Saville states: 'You will find the Stiperstones and the Long Mynd with its Gliding Station … and you can go to Shrewsbury, to Clun and Craven Arms and Bishop's Castle and explore them for yourself'. Then he adds disingenuously: 'But you will not find Black Dingle or Greystone Dingle or Barton Beach, for these places are as imaginary as are all the characters in this story'. In fact, although the geography is much condensed and re-orientated, Barton Beach must be Stiperstones Village, with Black and Greystone Dingles corresponding to Perkins Beach and Mytton Dingle – or vice versa!

Saville's sources: Weale and Webb

Saville normally researched his locations in person, but in the case of *Seven White Gates*, published in 1944, the research was through books and maps, because Saville didn't visit The Stiperstones until 1948. In the absence of first-hand knowledge, Saville turned to other writers, stating later: 'I have special reasons to acknowledge with gratitude two authors whose work has fascinated me for many years and stimulated my interest in the district even before my first visit.'[21] The authors were Magdalene Weale and Mary Webb and the latter's influence is particularly evident in the atmosphere and detail of *Seven White Gates*. The Devil's Chair is a malign black presence throughout Webb's *The Golden Arrow*: 'For miles around, in the plains, the valleys, the mountain dwellings it was feared'. Saville, in his turn, refers to 'the great bulk of the Stiperstones crowned with the black, sinister quartzite rocks of the Devil's Chair', and the superstitious awe of the local people lives on in Jenny Harman. And is there

perhaps a hint of Hazel Woodus of *Gone to Earth* in Jenny? They don't have quite the same hair colour (respectively auburn and red) but they share a terror of 'the Black Riders' – Wild Edric and his huntsmen (see Chapter 4) – whose sorties presage dreadful happenings. Hazel, almost a wild creature herself, would not however have been troubled by bats, whereas Jenny was, and refers to them, like Lily Huntbatch in *The Golden Arrow*, as 'bit-bats'.

In addition to rehearsing the Wild Edric legend, Saville borrows, presumably from Mary Webb, that of the 'Seven Whistlers' (from *Precious Bane*) and the tradition (from *The Golden Arrow*) that The Stiperstones was, on the longest night of the year, the meeting place of 'all the ghosses in Shropshire'.

Miss Edith Pargeter

Later better known by her pseudonym, Ellis Peters, she is photographed in 1936 working in Bemrose, the chemists, in Dawley, Shropshire, surrounded by proprietary medicines. Photo reproduced courtesy of the *Shropshire Star*.

Ellis Peters and Pauline Fisk

In *Shropshire Haunts of Mary Webb* (1937) W Byford-Jones writes of his meeting with an 'ardent admirer of

Mary Webb', another Shropshire-born writer, Edith Pargeter (1913-1995). A mere twenty-three years old at the time, this serious-minded assistant at a Dawley chemist's had already published the portentously titled novel *Hortensius, Friend of Nero* and another named *Iron-Bound*; she went on to write more than 70 other books and publish 16 volumes of translations of Czech poetry and prose. Many of her books were published under the pseudonym of Ellis Peters, and a series written using this pen name was to gain an international readership: it related the unravelling of twelfth century crime mysteries by Brother Cadfael, a former crusader, subsequently Benedictine monk and herbalist at Shrewsbury Abbey. Oddly, although the countryside around Shrewsbury figures in many of the Cadfael Chronicles, The Stiperstones, seemingly an unrivalled back-drop for medieval murder and mystery, never gets a mention.

The Stiperstones does however appear, albeit under the name 'the Hallowmount', in *Flight of a Witch* (1964), a novel in Ellis Peters' less well-known detective series 'George Felse Investigates'. Here we find a boulder-strewn hill, an Iron Age hill fort, a quartzite 'Altar' which is the meeting place of a witch-coven, and, to seal the link, there are lead mines which are home to Wild Edric and his fairy wife Godda. Yet, in her *Shropshire*, Ellis Peters equivocates: 'I had more than one Shropshire hill in mind when I described the Hallowmount, in *Flight of a Witch*. It is a little too gentle for the antediluvian lizard-length of the Stiperstones, but has something of the same menace … I think the Callow [Bromlow Callow, 2½ miles west of The Stiperstones] comes closest to the image.' But her appreciation of The Stiperstones is unequivocal:

> 'The Stiperstones, for me, is the most awesome of all our hills, and the most unmistakably imbued with that sense of generations of human habitation, in a silence and a solitude. Even from the distance, sharp against the sky, its very outline, the long, stark ridge crowned by the jagged outcrops of the Devil's Chair and Cranberry Rock, has a force and significance bordering on the sinister, yet in sunlight, with the sun stroking every fold of ground and sharpening every edge of rock, and the heather and gorse colouring the slopes, it has a variety and beauty impossible to resist.'

Midnight Blue

Cover from a recent edition of this children's book first published in 1990; reproduced courtesy of the author, Pauline Fisk.

And it proved irresistible to Pauline Fisk as a setting for *Midnight Blue* (1990), a book written for children which has captivated many an adult.[22] It is the story of Bonnie, a lonely single child, whose urban existence with her weak, single-parent mother, is dominated by the malevolent and domineering Grandbag (her grandmother). Bonnie escapes into a parallel world in a giant balloon (Midnight Blue) exchanging a home in a block of flats (Highholly House Nos 1-79) for Highholly Farm, an isolated farmhouse from where a sheep track leads through a mass of Bracken and Heather, Brambles and Whinberries onto Edric's Throne on Highholly Hill (The Stiperstones). Here, battling against her own insecurity and jealousy, she finds, at least for a while, the security of a loving adoptive mother, father and sister and the help of the mysterious Shadow Boy, and of Edric and Godda too.

Samuel Horton and Ida Gandy

Pauline Fisk's 'Highholly Farm' surely owes something to the area of elevated holly 'parkland' known as The Hollies, which lies adjacent to Lordshill Chapel at the north end of the hill (see Chapter 7). The Chapel and The Hollies are thought to appear in the 1930s novels of Samuel Horton, *Rainbow Farm* and *The Chapel on the Hill*, as the Rainbow Chapel and Hollis Hill. Horton wrote books of a type popular at the time, in which the world is neatly divided into the godly and the ungodly (the former always triumphing). Geoffrey Stuart is one of the former and when he sees the chapel for the first time it is framed by a rainbow and he learns that it earned its name 'because rainbows often encircled the hill on which it stood'.[23]

In 1930, Ida Gandy (1885-1977), her doctor husband Tom, and three children moved to Clunbury, in south Shropshire, where they stayed for 15 years. It was not until 1970, however, that Ida Gandy, now aged 85, published her memoir of those days, *An Idler on the Shropshire Borders*, but despite the passage of time, the book has the freshness and excitement of a daily diary of discovery.[24] One of the entries is entitled 'On the Stiperstones'. It is a day of walking, of immersion in the 'immensely desolate' landscape, but of encounters too. These include a 'patient-faced farmer … raking together his sodden hay, with a dejected cow and her calf to keep him company', and 'a rosy-cheeked young woman', wife of one of the last miners at The Bog, now on the dole, who provided a tea of home-made bread, butter, whinberry jam and cake. Apparently several people had asked for tea recently, 'all because of that woman Mary Webb'.

The Stiperstones as a tourist destination

Tourism did not however start with Mary Webb. The Stiperstones has long been and remains, a favoured destination for, in particular, field trips by geologists, the 'stwone-tappers' of which Magdalene Weale learned in the 1930s (see Chapter 1). Such parties had been following in the footsteps of Roderick Murchison for many decades. Amongst them was the Dudley and Midland Geological and Scientific Society and Field Club who visited in the summer of 1877;[25] one of their number appears to have been Alice Scott, who was to become the mother of Mary Webb (see page 12).

This party took the opportunity to visit the mines, as did the Geological Association Meeting of 1894. On the latter occasion the Stiperstones Quartzite

Here come the tourists

A murky but historic photograph of tourists at the Devil's Chair in about 1890, with the Needle's Eye behind them. Reproduced and digitally enhanced from Trumper (2001).

quarries at the Nills, above Pontesbury, were visited too, as was Mytton Dingle, where fossils were collected. The Shrewsbury-based Caradoc and Severn Valley Field Club came in 1896 when the Snailbeach Mine was the object of their visit. In addition to such educational or recreational parties, and they may well have been numerous, there were those whose principal purpose was to see the mines into which they had, or were thinking of, sinking their money. As many as three such parties in one day are mentioned in a piece in the *Mining Journal* of 1870.

But others, such as Thomas Poole, who records in his 'Log Book' visits to the mines in 1834 and 1836, appear to have been motivated simply by curiosity.[26] Walter White's curiosity may have been triggered by Murchison, and in his book *All round the Wrekin* (1860), White describes his visit to the hill, including taking a 40 minute nap at the Devil's Chair; he was perhaps the first of the Stiperstones travel writers.

Some of these visitors will have required accommodation, and a series of recommendations of where to stay are given by Jasper More MP, of Linley Hall (1836-1903) in a piece published in *The Advertiser* in the year of his death. Eager presumably to attract potential

Jasper More (1836-1903)

Reproduced courtesy of Justin Coldwell.

147

investors, he added details of train times from Euston, tips as to the best sources of on-site guidance and a reading list.[27] Over the years income from visitors has been vital to sustaining local public houses. Walton Humphrey (born 1921, son of William) remembers in *Never on a Sunday* how his mother, Esther, who ran the Stiperstones Inn, 'used to rely on the visitors ... We would be sleeping in the garden shed so she could make money in the summer months. They [his parents] used to advertise in the *Liverpool Echo*, bed and breakfast, lunch and evening meal'. And visitors continue to make an important contribution to the local economy. A study commissioned by English Nature in 1999 concluded that the total number of jobs supported through expenditure by those visiting the Stiperstones area as a whole, might be in the order of 20.

Nowadays a significant local attraction is the Bog Visitor Centre which occupies the former school at The Bog. Here, through the services of a band of enthusiastic volunteers, information, refreshments, cakes, books, cards, craft and art work are all on offer. Some 17-18,000 visits are recorded per year.

Charabancs to the Mary Webb Country

Whilst tourism pre-dated Mary Webb, the popularity of her novels undoubtedly brought the area to the attention of a new audience, and the resulting visits did not meet with the universal approval of local people. One who did not approve was T J Mytton More (1872-1947) of Linley Hall, near Bishop's Castle, as we learn from the highly readable memoir *A Tale of Two Houses* (1978) written by his son, Sir Jasper More MP (1907-1987).[28] Sir Jasper quotes from a letter written by his father in 1934 to the Rt Hon Stanley Baldwin MP, no longer PM by this time but Lord President of the Council, number two to Ramsay MacDonald in the National Government of the day. Clearly Sir Jasper's father held Baldwin responsible for popularising 'the Mary Webb country':

'My family made many miles of roads: one over Shelve Hill and thence to Stiperstones. This is the Mary Webb road. It was dedicated to the public on condition that the five gates should be kept shut. So they were until the Mary Webb public began to arrive. Their mind was directed on to Mary Webb and could not reasonably be directed to closing of gates. Limited to time, the chara patrons had no minute to spare in which to close a gate, still less to open it. So the chara crashed through the gate, to the intense hilarity of the passengers.'

Baldwin replied from 11 Downing Street in his own hand:

'The unforeseen results of my remarks on Mary Webb have been a lesson to me ... I can only hope that in time you may forgive though you may never forget. But seriously I should have thought that you could have got damages from the charabanc company. Their behaviour is quite intolerable. But it is tragic to think there are millions in our towns who believe a gate is put up of malice to stop passage; they never think of beasts straying or if they did they wouldn't think it mattered. They probably think a walk is good for them and that they always come back to tea ... I remember your father well ...'.

Magdalene Weale reports Baldwin's 'regrets' on hearing of charabancs marked 'To the Mary Webb country', but she did not share them. She declared that if her own book 'adds to the number of those seeking healthy and beautiful surroundings as well as literary and historical interest in the hill country of Shropshire, I shall feel but little compunction, for this part of England is wild and spacious enough to suffer no real injury therefrom'. Malcolm Saville was to go further: he was 'happy to know that my Shropshire stories have sent thousands of families to explore country which means so much to me'.

Charabanc to the Malcolm Saville Country

Amongst Saville's explorers was a group of Lone Pine enthusiasts who, in February 1994, met outside The Lion Hotel, in Shrewsbury. Led by the late Richard Walker, storyteller and freelance radio programme producer, they boarded a 1950s coach and headed for the hills; their exploration is described by Mark O'Hanlon in his *Beyond the Lone Pine* (2001). Reaching The Long Mynd was no problem, but the nearer they got to The Stiperstones the slower their progress, indeed they had to get out and walk while, relieved of its burden, the ailing vintage bus was coaxed up the steep hills. Unsurprisingly, the Devil's Chair was shrouded in mist, and in any case time was running short, so the intended ascent was postponed and the party headed on, before a definitive breakdown at Pontesbury, where they transferred to a 1990s coach for tea and crumpets back at The Lion. Amongst those present was Chris Eldon-Lee, another radio producer, and, in collaboration with Richard Walker, he put together a BBC Radio 4 'Kaleidoscope' feature entitled *Witchend Once More*, which included an

Charabanc to the Malcolm Saville Country

The excursion which led to the formation of the Malcolm Saville Society pauses in the Cardingmill Valley, Church Stretton, on a damp and misty day in February 1994; this was prior to a tour which included The Stiperstones. Photo courtesy of Mark O'Hanlon.

account of the day. From this was born the Malcolm Saville Society which now has a world-wide membership of hundreds, and continues to thrive, organising trips to many Lone Pine locations, not least The Stiperstones.

Foiling the Devil and liberating Wild Edric

In *Quietest under the Sun* (1944) John Wood offers a take on countryside access far more radical than that of Magdalene Weale or, indeed, Malcolm Saville. He invokes the spirit of Wild Edric in suggesting that the descendants of the Saxons should

> 'throw off that remaining relic of the Norman Conquest: class privilege … The day that the English – or Scots or Welsh – tramper [ie 'walker'] can cross the moors of his native Britain without fear of impediment from game-preserving landholders or their hirelings, that day will the Devil be finally foiled and the spirit of Wild Edric be liberated for ever from its dungeon beneath the Stiperstones.'

Perhaps then, with the passage of the Countryside and Rights of Way Act (2000), which confers the so-called 'right to roam' over The Stiperstones, and other areas of mountain, moor and common up and down the country, we have seen the last of Wild Edric!

'Give us back our land'

Invoking the spirit of Wild Edric

A vignette by Donald Foster from *Quietest Under the Sun* (1944). Note the profile of The Stiperstones.

Going to the Devil: visitors and their impact

Was Magdalene Weale right in thinking that Shropshire was wild and spacious enough to suffer no real injury from tourism? Some think not. But are they simply keen to keep a good thing to themselves? Potential 'injuries' might include caravan sites and large car parks – but neither is a significant issue in the Shropshire Hills. There can, however, be issues about gates being left open, dogs running wild and vehicles obstructing gateways, leading to significant problems on occasions for farmers. But it can be argued that these are occasional, not invariable problems, and that by a wide sharing of special places such as The Stiperstones, a consensus is established both for their conservation and for the funding needed to sustain them, including for stewardship payments to farmers.

For many Salopians, indeed for many from further afield, The Stiperstones is a very special place. It has been estimated that in the order of 30,000 visits are made to it each year.[29] Most come to enjoy a quiet walk, but there are few places for a gentle stroll and the walking tends toward the demanding.[30] To reach the ridge requires a bit of an effort, but some seek to do it at speed. Every October The Stiperstones is a major leg in the Longmynd Hike, a 50 mile competition hike taking in eight local summits and involving 8,000 feet of climbing. It is organised by the 2nd Longmynd Scout Group and has been held every year since 1967, with the exception of 2001 when it had to be cancelled due to Foot and Mouth Disease restrictions. The event currently attracts more than 450 participants, with the quickest completing the course in less than 8½ hours and some 350 doing so within 24 hours.[31]

The Longmynd Hikers toil past the Devil's Chair and, as Magdalene Weale observes: 'Going to the Devil in Shropshire is by no means the easy thing it is represented [as being] elsewhere. Contrary to Biblical directions, narrow is the way and steep the path that leads thereto'. Nevertheless, since 1979, the Boxing Day 'Dawdle or Dash' from the Stiperstones Inn to the Devil's Chair has drawn both keen competitors and relaxed participants from near and far, raising worthwhile sums for local charities. The event, which is organised by Geoff and John Sproson of the family who run the Stiperstones Inn and shop, nowadays attracts in excess of 300 official entrants (runners, joggers or walkers) with another 100 or more

'Dawdle or Dash'

Father Christmases and their anxious-looking rivals lead the way up Perkins Beach on the 2001 event. Photo courtesy of the *Shropshire Star*.

tagging along. Tim Davies, the quickest of the 'dashers', returned a time of just 20 minutes and 46 seconds in 2006 for the 5km-long course. Some of the 'dawdlers' do just that, but 250 or so complete the course within an hour.[32]

Paths, birds and dogs

These annual events are soon over, but what about the day-in day-out impact of 30,000 visitors? The path from the car park at The Knolls to Cranberry Rock and on to Manstone Rock is broad, over 30 feet wide in places, and worn, and getting wider and more worn with the passage of time, feet and water. It is the first experience that most visitors have of the pathways over the hill and it concerns some of them, who may conclude that the plant life and soils of The Stiperstones are under threat from relentless trampling. But this path is not typical, some paths are less than three feet wide and despite there being more than 11 miles of rights of way running through or alongside the heathland, paths occupy less than one per cent of the total heathland area. Eroded paths may be regarded as unsightly and can be awkward to walk on, but they have a limited impact overall on the plant life of the hill.

What then of the impact on birdlife? This issue raises more difficult questions. There is little doubt that if all visitors were to be excluded from The Stiperstones then crag-nesting birds, most notably Peregrine Falcon and Raven, would, within a year or two, start to nest on one or other of the tors. Other birdlife might benefit too, particularly from the exclusion of dogs, as would the sheep which on occasion they chase. An English Nature review of disturbance to breeding birds at sites up and down the country by visitors and their dogs, concluded that it exposes eggs and young to a greater risk of loss to opportunistic predators, especially the crow family, and that this is the greatest risk arising from disturbance at sites like The Stiperstones where visitor and dog numbers are high.[33] But clearly it is not feasible, nor desirable, to exclude visitors. Furthermore, a walker has a legal right to be accompanied by a dog provided it remains on the right of way.

Some bird species are notably resilient to disturbance, others are notably susceptible. An example of the former is Red Grouse which, despite its obvious vulnerability to straying dogs, may sometimes be found nesting close to paths. At the latter extreme is the Curlew, which, it is said, may be disturbed when a walker with a dog is still as much as 1,000 metres away.[34] Curlews have decreased markedly in the area over recent years; a number of factors are involved, but dog walking is likely to have played a part. It would certainly help to safeguard bird life and livestock if dogs were kept on a lead, but clearly in the case of Curlew this would not be a complete answer.

Here, as on other nature reserves, it proves difficult to convince dog-walkers that, in the interest both of livestock and of wildlife, they should keep their pets on leads. Peremptory notices have been tried, persuasive ones too, and humorous cartoons as well, but the problem persists. Lateral thinking may be required along the lines of the novel approach to visitor management adopted

Dogs on leads please!

Cartoons commissioned by English Nature from Bill Pinder for leaflets and signs about The Stiperstones National Nature Reserve.

by the late Sir Jasper More, whose father had expressed to Stanley Baldwin his exasperation with unruly visitors. In More's obituary in *The Independent*, his nephew, Justin Coldwell, the current owner of Linley Hall, records that Sir Jasper, was 'ever ingenious with ways of discouraging unwanted intruders without wishing to give obvious offence; he was ... reputed to have posted signs in his woodlands admonishing visitors to refrain from feeding the snakes'.[35]

Chapter 7

'The natural web': habitats and wildlife

Once more the bracken pushed out soft fingers,
and cuckoos cried from orchards at the foot of the cwms.
The snipe summoned his love from his airy circles,
and curlews ran along the hilltops with their forlorn, elfin music.

Mary Webb *The Golden Arrow* (1916)

Charles Sinker

This photo of Charles Sinker was taken at Preston Montford Field Centre in 1961. He has his son Mark on his shoulders and a botanist's lens around his neck. Reproduced courtesy of his daughter, Rebecca.

Charles Sinker (1931-2010), a botanist and teacher of distinction, had a particular liking for The Stiperstones and contributed much to our knowledge of the place and to its conservation. Born in Cambridge, he was a pupil at Shrewsbury School from 1944 until 1949 when he returned to Cambridge as a student. After graduation he worked for the Field Studies Council (FSC) at Malham Tarn, where he developed his talents as an inspiring teacher. He came back to Shropshire in 1956 as the first Warden of the FSC's Preston Montford Field Centre, a post he held for 16 years before becoming the FSC's first director.[1] Parkinson's Disease forced his early retirement, in 1983. He was a founder of the Shropshire Conservation Trust (1962), its first Secretary, then its President and for many years its Patron.[2] In 1979 he was appointed OBE for his services to nature conservation.

Right from the start Preston Montford Field Centre made extensive use of The Stiperstones as a site for fieldwork, and over the years thousands of students and children have come to experience and learn about the hill. In his introductory talks Charles Sinker drew on the cultural as well as the natural aspects of The Stiperstones, and over the years it has offered teaching opportunities, at levels running from primary through to adult and professional, in a wide range of topics – geology and landscape, history and customs, literature and poetry, conservation and restoration, habitats and wildlife.

Charles Sinker first visited The Stiperstones when at Shrewsbury School, and he was to draw on knowledge gained at that time when, years later, he became lead author of the *Ecological Flora of the Shropshire Region* (1985), which was acclaimed as setting a new standard for county floras. It had ecological content at a scale not previously attempted,[3] and Charles Sinker's novel idea of 'coincidence mapping' (facilitated, as were other novel aspects of the *Flora*, by the growing availability and ease of computer analysis) is now a widely used technique.[4]

Another of Charles Sinker's important publications was his paper on Shropshire's meres and mosses,[5] but The Stiperstones is thought to have been his favourite place in Shropshire, one that inspired him and which became a regular choice for family walks and picnics. On his 75th birthday his family took him on 'his last proper expedition', a wheel-chair ride along the 'All-ability Trail' at The Stiperstones.[6]

Charles Sinker's name is associated in particular with The Hollies, at the north end of the hill, which became a Site of Special Scientific Interest in 1964 following a report he had written. The Hollies was well known to another founder member of the Shropshire Conservation Trust, the Shrewsbury rose grower, Hilda Murrell (1906-1984), whose delightful nature diaries Charles Sinker edited for publication in 1987.

This chapter describes the habitats and wildlife of Charles Sinker's favourite place. It is, in general, a broad-brush description, but it touches on some more specialist aspects as well. Hopefully there is something here to interest both the general reader and those, including perhaps students at Preston Montford, who may be seeking pointers towards a more in-depth exploration.

The heathland

Charles Sinker's coincidence map for a group of 11 species which normally grow on dry heathland or in acid, heathy woods, underlines the importance of The Stiperstones for this group of plants. During fieldwork for the *Ecological Flora* seven of these species were found in two tetrads (areas 2km x 2km square) on The Stiperstones, eight in one tetrad and nine in another. The maximum number of these species recorded in any other tetrad in Shropshire was seven and this from only one tetrad (on Catherton Common in the southeast of the county). The *Ecological Flora* provides a number of such insights into the botanical interest of The Stiperstones, and knowledge has subsequently been enhanced by the publication in 2009 of a site-specific *Flora of The Stiperstones* by Sarah Whild and Alex Lockton.

Common Heather in flower

Photo taken near the Devil's Chair, August 2001; courtesy of Ben Osborne.

The commonest heathland plant on The Stiperstones is Common Heather. Confusingly, 'heather' is both a generic name, referring to a group of similar plants, and a specific one, being the name given to the commonest of its type, a plant otherwise known as 'Common Heather' or 'Ling' and, botanically, as *Calluna vulgaris*. Common Heather dominates the vegetation of the hill, as it does many other upland heathlands and moorlands, and lowland heaths too. Common Heather is most at home on poor, acid and peaty soils, but its widespread distribution across the country is due to its tolerance of a wide range of conditions: dry to damp; cold to warm; coastline to mountain; pH3.5 to pH6.5; moderate woodland shade to full hill-top exposure.[7] What it will not tolerate is excessive grazing, cultivation, persistent trampling, soil fertility improvements and blanket afforestation.

The habitat range of Common Heather is wider than that of the other two heathers which occur on The Stiperstones – Bell Heather and Cross-leaved Heath. The former is a plant of dry areas, the latter of wet. Common Heather's requirements are intermediate between, and overlap, those of the other two. Bell Heather comes to prominence on the thin soils of the south-facing slopes, notably of Mytton Dingle and Perkins Beach. The name is derived from its bell-like flowers; they are red-pink and appear earlier than those of Common Heather, giving these slopes a vibrant mantle in July which contrasts with the rich but more sober pink-purple blanket of the August-flowering Common Heather. There is little wet ground on The Stiperstones and few places, therefore, where Cross-leaved Heath flourishes, but the shy pink of its downy flowers may be

Bell Heather in flower, Mytton Dingle

Photo courtesy of Paul Glendell/Natural England

seen from June onwards in boggy spots on both the west- and east-facing flanks of the hill.

These rare wet places are worth searching for some local treasures. One of the most abundant and arresting is Bog Asphodel; its bright yellow and orange, star-like flowers, turn a deep saffron after flowering. Only a diligent search will locate the leaves of the few Round-leaved Sundews with their sticky, red, insect-trapping tentacles. And a real challenge is to hunt for another insectivore, Common Butterwort. In 1965 Charles Sinker spotted its basal rosette of leaves, once likened to a greasy green starfish, in a flush below Cranberry Rock, but it has not been recorded since.

The 'National Vegetation Classification'[8] describes plant communities according to the relative abundance of the more frequently occurring species. Almost all of the heathland vegetation of The Stiperstones falls within the community referred to as 'H12 *Calluna vulgaris-Vaccinium myrtillus*', reflecting the general dominance of Common Heather and of Bilberry *V myrtillus*. Bilberry, known locally as Whinberry,[9] is virtually as ubiquitous as Common Heather, forming dense stands in places and elsewhere growing alongside or beneath its co-dominant.

When fresh, Whinberry leaves are, as Mary Webb says, 'startlingly bright green', sprouting from the plant's tough stems which are aptly referred to locally as 'wires'. For her, their flowers are like 'small, rose-coloured tulips upside down, very magical and clear of colour' and, in *Gone to Earth*, Hazel Woodus picked them and 'sucked out the drop of honey from each flower like a bee'. The small, rounded, deep-purple fruits ripen from July onwards. In *Never on a Sunday* Doris Hewitt (born 1916) recalls finding a patch of white Whinberries, but in other respects they will have been like the usual purple ones, carrying a belly-button-like scar at their base where parts of the flower have fallen away

Heathland plants

Plate by Anne Gilbert from the *Ecological Flora of Shropshire*, illustrating, with Cranberry Rock in the background, the characteristic species of heathland on The Stiperstones. From left to right: Crowberry (the straggling stems), Common Heather, Whinberry, Wavy Hair-grass, Bell Heather, Match-stick Lichen *Cladonia floerkeana*, Common Cow-wheat, Mat-grass and Cowberry. Reproduced courtesy of Shropshire Wildlife Trust.

as the fruit has formed. And, as explained in Chapter 8, the berries and The Stiperstones community were once umbilically linked.

Cowberry, Crowberry and more

Amongst other heathland plants of note are Cowberry and Crowberry. Both are classified, like the heathers and Whinberry, as 'dwarf-shrubs', and both are common on The Stiperstones but virtually unknown throughout the rest of the county. Mary Webb refers to Cowberry buds as 'of most waxen whiteness' (though once open the flowers are often flushed pink) and describes them as 'venturesome', reflecting their tolerance of the highest, stoniest parts of the hill. The fruits are scarlet-red and similar in size to those of the Whinberry; they ripen a month or so later. Cowberry (referred to locally as Cranberry) is evergreen, Whinberry deciduous, but they are closely related. In 1970 Charles Sinker identified three plants of the hybrid between them, *V x intermedium*, and more have been found since.[10] But he was pre-empted: Doris Hewitt recalls that Emily Griffiths (then Corfield), a contemporary of hers, 'found a Whinberry crossed with a Cranberry [= Cowberry] once, and brought it to Girl Guides' (this will have been in about 1930).

The last of this trio of berry-bearing shrubs is the Crowberry. It has straggling stems and heather-like leaves; the flowers are tiny and pink, with male and female flowers occurring on separate plants; the fruits are smaller than those

Cowberry in flower

Photo taken on The Stiperstones, May 2007. Courtesy of Dan Wrench.

Crowberry in fruit

The berries glisten with the dew of an August morning on The Stiperstones, 2013. Photo Gisèle Wall.

Lichens on Stiperstones Quartzite

A photo taken by Charles Sinker in 1967, reproduced courtesy of Rebecca Sinker.

the Whinberry, deep black, diminutive and pumpkin-shaped. Though edible, the berries are rather insipid and pippy; in quantity they are said to cause fearful flatulence.

Other common plants include Wavy Hair-grass, present throughout, and often a prolific early colonist after the burning or cutting of Common Heather. Pale patches of *Cladonia* lichens cover areas of otherwise bare ground, looking, according to the species, like beds of diminutive corals, forests of miniature leafless trees and tiny red-headed matchsticks. The lichen list runs to some 180 species including several county rarities, and the lichen community growing on the tors and boulders has been described as remarkable and of national importance. Some notable species have been lost, however, over recent decades, seemingly as a result of the aerial deposition of nitrogen; it has been suggested that the likely source is ammonia from animal dung, a consequence of high livestock levels in surrounding areas.[11]

In June, wetter areas are whitened by tufts of cottongrass plumes; there are two species and both are in fact sedges rather than grasses – the multi-tufted Common Cottongrass and the less frequent and single-tufted Hare's-tail Cottongrass. As their seed-bearing plumes come loose they are swept away by the wind, catching here and there on the stems of Common Heather. In the closing pages of *The Golden Arrow* Stephen Southernwood, returning from afar, notices for the first time his tiny child, born, unbeknownst to him, during his long absence — 'the white bundle, frail as the cotton-grass down that wandered from hill to hill, a poor white waif blown along the steep, dark mountains'.

Clubmosses and Mosses

Charles Sinker delighted in vernacular names and he would have known instantly that when, in the late 1980s, Emily Griffiths (born 1917) told me that she used to find 'Knives and Forks' at the top of Perkins Beach, she was referring not to lost cutlery but to Stag's-horn Clubmoss; both names are descriptive of the plant's branched stems.[12] Charles Sinker himself recorded this clubmoss in Perkins Beach between 1968 and 1970, after which it was only seen on the opposite side of the hill until spotted by David Hatfield at Nipstone Rock in 2002.[13] There are currently just three other sites in Shropshire.

The first 'Knives and Forks' record for The Stiperstones had been in 1727, when it was spotted by the Rev Littleton Brown of Bishop's Castle. Littleton Brown was said to have 'an excellent eye', and a year earlier he had used it to identify Alpine Clubmoss 'on ye top of ye Stiperstones', but it took another 286 years before it was next recorded, near Nipstone Rock, by another keen-eyed Shropshire botanist, Dan Wrench; this is currently the only Alpine Clubmoss site in the county. Remarkably, nearby, and on the same day, Dan spotted Fir Clubmoss, last recorded on The Stiperstones a mere 212 years previously, in about 1800, by the Rev Edward Williams of Shrewsbury; this clubmoss occurs at only one other site in Shropshire. Dan had gone to Nipstone to view one clubmoss, the Stag's-horn, by the end of his visit he had notched up three.[14]

To the layman a clubmoss, by appearance as much as name, is a moss, but botanists note that it has vascular tissues which distribute resources through

The three clubmosses at Nipstone Rock

Clockwise from top: Stag's-horn Clubmoss *Lycopodium clavatum*, Fir Clubmoss *Huperzia selago* and Alpine Clubmoss *Diphasiastrum alpinum*. Photos, January 2012, courtesy of Alex Lockton.

the plant, a characteristic which is not shared by what they call bryophytes – the mosses and liverworts. Systematic surveys and casual records have yielded a list of bryophytes for The Stiperstones which now exceeds 170 species.[15] In the past these mosses and liverworts lurked anonymously behind impenetrable Latin names and a seemingly uniform, amorphous, greenness and mossiness, but they have had their profiles raised through the recent publication of a brilliant field guide, with photos which reveal just how variable and colourful they actually are.[16] The attribution of sometimes endearing 'common' names, such as Norwegian Earwort, Dusky Rock-moss, Slender Fringe-moss and Greater Pincushion, has helped too.[17] All of these species are found on The Stiperstones, favouring acidic, generally rocky, substrates; they are species which are most frequent in the uplands and the west of Britain. As so often, across a range of wildlife species, The Stiperstones is an eastern outpost of their distribution.

Bryophyte interest is not however confined to rocky habitats, and despite this being generally a dry site, the 'flushed' area above the National Nature Reserve car park is home to 11 species of *Sphagnum*, the so-called 'bog-mosses'. Their highly descriptive 'common' names, including Red Bog-moss, Cow-horn Bog-moss and Flexuous Bog-moss, indicate that these plants are far from being uniform and amorphous.[18]

Fungi

Like mosses, the generality of fungi have only quite recently been granted 'common' names. But their variety of shape and colour, edibility and toxicity, have always saved them from anonymity. Amongst species impossible to ignore are the waxcaps, showy fungi of old, unfertilised grasslands such as those of the National Nature Reserve. These waxy, often conical fungi are notably colourful, as the names of those occurring on The Stiperstones suggest: these include the Scarlet, Butter, Blackening and Honey Waxcaps, though the last is so-named from its smell not its colour, which is bright orange. The heathland fungi are less glamorous and, to date, have been little recorded. The Moor Club is one of the commonest. The name might suggest a surrogate upland weapon, big and bold, but it relates to shape only – this club is tiny, pale and fragile. Moor Clubs are said to be edible – should you find otherwise, I disclaim any responsibility – but they are so small that you would have to gather dozens just to flavour an omelette. The Earthy Powdercap, another heathland species, of ochre hue and mealy texture, is not much larger, and although described as 'edible', this goes with the rider 'but not worthwhile'. Liberty Caps (pale pixie-caps on spindly stems) which occur where sheep congregate on the boundary of the heathland, should however be left untouched, not because of the dung-enriched habitat in which they occur, nor because they are said to be peculiarly revolting to eat, but because, under the name Magic Mushrooms, they became notorious in the 1970s, and since 2005 they have been classified as a Class A drug.

Non-specific 'mushrooms' and a 'toadstool' are the only fungi mentioned in Mary Webb's *The Golden Arrow* and *Gone to Earth*, but her repeated references in the former novel to red leaves on the Bilberry plants in late summer may refer to the effects of a parasitic fungus. Bilberry Rust occurs commonly, but would not account for the leaves being a 'ladybird red'. The leaves of the closely related Cowberry, often found growing alongside the Bilberry, can however be coloured bright red by another parasitic fungus, Cowberry Redleaf which has been recorded on the hill. Mary Webb, who knew both plants well, may in this case have chosen to conflate the two.[19]

Perpetual Gorse and a Bracken bed

Colourful carpets of flowering heather bring the hill to life in summer, but, come winter, heather looks dark and drab, its sombre uniformity enriched only by the rusty brown of frosted Bracken fronds and, dotted about here and there on the lower slopes, the occasional intense yellow glint of gorse.[20] The adage 'When gorse is in blossom, kissing's in season' is rooted in the knowledge that European Gorse *Ulex europaeus* produces pioneer flowers as early as mid-winter, then builds towards a glowing climax in May/June, after which the plant can't quite give up and continues to brighten the heath with the occasional flower right through to year end.

Western Gorse in flower on The Stiperstones

Photo courtesy of Ben Osborne.

However, on The Stiperstones, the perpetuity of the kissing season is assured by the abundance of another species, Western Gorse *Ulex gallii*. This has a flowering season which peaks in July/August, but it continues to flower sporadically through autumn into winter. Like the Bell Heather, it basks in the warmth of the south-facing slopes, and in July its flowers, glinting golden amongst the crimson of the heather bells, draw the eye. Here the plant community tends towards what is referred to as 'H8 *Calluna vulgaris-Ulex gallii*'.

Richard Mabey, in his cultural compendium *Flora Britannica*, suggests that there is a 'where' implied in the 'when' of the gorse adage, because 'gorse is one of the great signature plants of common land and rough open space, places where lovers can meet, walk freely and lose themselves, if need be, in its dense thickets'. But there are better places in which to get lost than amongst the censorious spininess of gorse thickets. Bracken, known here as 'Fern', grows in patches where the soil is deeper. Having, in Mary Webb's words 'pushed out soft fingers' in spring, it may climb to reach six sturdy feet in height in prime sites; this is the place where lovers may wish for the licence to wander and get lost, and why a condom is referred to locally as a 'fern ticket'.[21]

Pastures

As explained in Chapter 5, Mary Webb was not averse to tinkering with the names of Curlew and Whimbrel to suit her poetic purpose, and it was the same with flowers. In *The Golden Arrow*, John Arden and his daughter Deborah come to 'the slopes of short grass from which the round yellow heartsease was disappearing like a currency withdrawn – as the old mintage of painless and raptureless peace was disappearing from Deborah's being'. The 'round yellow' flower would actually have been Mountain Pansy *Viola lutea* for which old grasslands round The Stiperstones are well-known.[22] Heartsease *V tricolor* has not been recorded on The Stiperstones and, as its Latin name suggests, is normally three-coloured, but the poetic similes on which Mary Webb is playing, require what is, presumably, a deliberate misnomer.

Mountain Pansy is a signature plant for the herb-rich grasslands growing on the moderately acidic soils which fringe the heathland. These grasslands will have been won in the past from heathy, gorsy and bracken ground, in areas where soils were perhaps deeper and marginally better and, most importantly, water was available, permitting human habitation. Here miners and their families succeeded in carving out tiny smallholdings. Hay was cut, livestock grazed and,

Plants of unimproved hill pastures

Plate by Anne Gilbert from the *Ecological Flora of Shropshire*, illustrating, with the Devil's Chair in the background, the characteristic species of The Stiperstones. From left to right, in colour: Heath Speedwell, Mountain Pansy, Heath Milkwort, Bitter Vetch, Common Bird's-foot-trefoil, Moonwort; as line-drawing: Sweet Vernal-grass, Common Bent and Sheep's Fescue. Reproduced courtesy of Shropshire Wildlife Trust.

with applications of manure, and perhaps of mine waste with a calcium content higher than the heathland soil, the agricultural fertility was improved, if only marginally.[23]

In some places this grassland type covered more extensive areas and was rich in low-growing flowers. These areas are grassland still today, but are bereft of blooms. We are indebted to Charles Sinker for knowledge of their former extent and splendour:

> 'As recently as the late 1940s it was still possible to walk from The Long Mynd through Ratlinghope to Shelve and Bromlow Callow over a succession of large, well-grazed fields whose ancient turf was rich in flowers: Heath Bedstraw, Bitter Vetch, Bird's-foot-trefoil, Good-Friday-grass, Tormentil, Heath Milkwort, Germander Speedwell, Moonwort and the hauntingly beautiful Mountain Pansy were all common. Turf of this kind still occurs in a very few small crofts associated with miners' cottages and smallholdings.'[24]

The former smallholdings to which Charles Sinker refers are to be found at Blakemoorgate, Blakemoorflat and Pennerley. The best of the grasslands here are still a spring-time joy – not a riot of colour, but a restrained palette principally of yellows, whites and blues in a plant community described prosaically by present-day botanists as 'U4 *Festuca ovina-Agrostis capillaris-Galium saxatile*'. In these

Flower-rich turf

Mountain Pansies jostle with Bird's-foot-trefoil (orange and yellow), Germander Speedwell (blue), Clover (pink and white) and Heath Bedstraw (white) at Rigmoreoak, June 2007. Photo courtesy of Dan Wrench.

grasslands of fescue *Festuca* and bent *Agrostis*, Mountain Pansy flourishes amongst the tiny white flowers of Heath Bedstraw *Galium saxatile* (Mary Webb's 'minute starry carpet'), along with the blue specks of Heath Milkwort (sometimes purple, alternatively pink or white) and the yellow and orange which give Common Bird's-foot-trefoil its popular name of 'Eggs and Bacon'. Germander Speedwell beams blue, outdoing the pale lilac of its demure cousin Heath Speedwell; Pignut opens white umbels in spring and Harebell pale blue pendants in high summer. Tormentil glows gold and Mouse-ear Hawkweed lemon yellow, its flowers sprouting from a ring of small, hairy, felted leaves that give this hawkweed its specific name, while the miniature fronds of Moonwort rise furtively from the turf.

Moonwort on The Stiperstones

Photo by Charles Sinker, summer 1972, reproduced courtesy of Rebecca Sinker.

Hay Meadows

Each smallholding would have had its hay meadow; doubtless they too were flower-rich, and a few survive. The best meadows, which are to be found at various locations in Pennerley, have been notified as a composite Site of Special Scientific Interest, but other, still-colourful meadows, flourish outside the designated area. The technical description of these meadows is 'MG5 *Cynosurus cristatus-Centaurea nigra*' grasslands. The hay yields, dominated by grasses such as Crested Dog's-tail *Cynosurus cristatus*, Common Bent, Red Fescue and Sweet Vernal-grass, are niggardly,[25] but in terms of flower power the returns are prodigious. Indeed, flower-rich hay from these meadows has often been sold, at a premium, for the creation of new flowery meadows in the Wolverhampton area. The experimental techniques developed there since the early 1980s by Ian Trueman of the University of Wolverhampton, using green 'hay' from Pennerley Meadows and elsewhere, have now become mainstream.[26]

In these meadows at Pennerley, Cowslips are the April harbingers, followed by a succession of other flowers through to late July, Harebell time, when the hay is cut. Between-times whites and yellows predominate: Oxeye Daisy overtops the crop, but look down through the galaxy of blooms and the white of the low-growing Eyebright stares back piercingly; layered in between are the yellows of Cat's-ear and Yellow Rattle, and later in the season the red-purple of Common Knapweed (the *Centaurea nigra* of the plant community's name). Yellow Rattle (the ripe seeds of which rattle in their pods) and Oxeye Daisy, are the 'rattle boxes' and 'dog daisies' that Tom Pinches (born 1924) remembers as such a feature of hay meadows prior to war-time ploughing. Amongst these commoner plants are notables such as Moonwort and Greater Butterfly Orchid; the latter's flowers, though modestly coloured green and cream, sprout a showy jumble of extravagantly long lips and spurs.

Hayfield at Pennerley Meadows

Photo, June 2007, courtesy of Dan Wrench.

Laburnums

The former smallholdings are places to look for a tree that is a particular feature of The Stiperstones, the Laburnum. This is not a native plant, it comes originally from the mountains of central Europe, and, though naturalised, its presence here is due largely to deliberate planting. There are in fact two species, the 'Common' and the 'Scottish', *Laburnum anagyroides* and *L alpinum*. The latter is much less frequent, flowers a little later and when mature is more imposing, with a stout trunk. It was not formally recorded here by botanists until 2002, but had been noted some years previously by an acute local observer and Pennerley resident, Cliff Lewis (born 1923).[27] Perhaps it was to this species that Mary Webb referred in her description of Abel Woodus's cottage at 'The Callow' in *Gone to Earth*: 'Two laburnums, forked and huge of trunk, fingered the roof with their lower branches and dripped gold on it'.

There are many single Laburnums, and few of the numerous abandoned holdings on and around the hill are without one, but at Pennerley, there are entire hedgerows too. Yet, despite much conjecture, no one has come up with a convincing explanation as to why Laburnums should have been planted here, particularly as their seeds are said to be highly poisonous.[28] The assumption is that the purpose was utilitarian, but could it in fact have been ornamental?[29] What a joy it must have been to emerge from the blackness of the mines in the June flowering time to see what Deborah Arden in *The Golden Arrow* refers to as 'the seynty tree … we call it golden showers about our way, from the shine of it'.[30]

Woodlands

Woodland fringes the hill. Here Silver Birch and Rowan are early colonists forming wooded belts in the side valleys, notably Tankerville Hollow, Perkins Beach and Mytton Dingle, where the damper, deeper soils of the north-facing slopes favour germination. These areas of woodland appear to be of recent origin, favoured

'When the hedgerows drip with Laburnum,/Through the sunny days of June'

Lines from Brenda Shaw's poem 'To Barbara' in her posthumous collection *Shropshire Poems*. Photo taken at Pennerley in June 1976 looking south along the road from Tankerville to The Bog with a sliver of the telephone box (since removed) at the former Pennerley Post Office just visible on the left of the bend, and Welsh Row showing white directly in front. These hedges are still dominated by Laburnum but were, and continue to be, cut back hard and hence no longer flower profusely. Photo courtesy of Paul Wagner; he regrets that it is not sharper, but fortunately he took the photo before it was too late!

perhaps by a decline in grazing pressure. They may have sprung up in the mid-1950s when the Rabbit population collapsed as a consequence of myxomatosis, coinciding with a time when smallholders were turning fewer livestock out to graze and looking less to the hill as a source of fuel. Whatever their origin, these new woods are now well-established and ever-eager to expand.

Woodland in Mytton Dingle

Stiperstones Village lies beyond the wood; Western Gorse is flowering in the foreground. Photo, October 2013, Gisèle Wall.

At Resting Hill the woodland is older and more extensive. Here there is a virtual mono-culture of oak and it may well be that other tree species were once weeded, or grazed, out of existence. The community type is described as 'W16 *Quercus-Betula-Deschampsia flexuosa*', reflecting the abundance of what in this case is Sessile Oak *Quercus petraea* along with its normal companion, birch (here Silver Birch *Betula pendula*), over a sparse ground flora in which Wavy Hair-grass *Deschampsia flexuosa* is frequent. The trees have been coppiced in the past and have come again, multi-stemmed – straight and leggy on the lower ground, contorted and squat near the top of the slope. Shade and livestock-grazing have virtually eliminated any understorey, but, where light is let in and livestock excluded, Holly soon flourishes. The herb layer is heathy, with Bell Heather, Common Heather and Bilberry in evidence as well as Common Cow-wheat and Wavy Hair-grass. Elsewhere there are panoramas of Bluebell and vignettes of Wood Sorrel.

A Hollin

Close by the gate to the chapel of Mary Webb's 'God's Little Mountain' (Lordshill Chapel) lies a relict landscape, what she called a 'ragged holly spinney', an area of veteran Holly trees, one of the oldest stands of Holly in Britain. The Hollies, as it is called, is a survival from the period before the last century when it was common in the north and west to use lopped Holly as winter fodder for livestock and, occasionally, for deer. In some areas such Holly wood-pastures (often marked as 'Hollins' on maps) were extensive, but most have now been cleared.

The significance of The Hollies was recognised in the 1960s by Charles Sinker and by George Peterken, who was researching Hollies and has since become a leading national authority on woodlands. As George Peterken observes, 'the antiquity of The Hollies is not the only remarkable feature of the site, for Rowans have become established in the Holly crotches, giving a chimerical effect, part evergreen, part deciduous, to the crown of the composite "individual"'. They are seen to best effect in spring when the creamy blossoms of the Rowans stand out, or in August and September when the 'witan-trees', as Mary Webb calls them, are 'burning with scarlet berries'.

A Holly at The Hollies overtopped by a Rowan in full fruit

The Rowan germinated in the top of the Holly's trunk, but has worked its way downwards; now rooted in the ground, it is becoming the dominant partner. Photo, September 1997, Tom Wall.

The Hollies lay within the so-called 'prison farm' (for years Upper Vessons Farm had been worked by trusty prisoners from Shrewsbury jail), but in 1968 the Home Office decided to sell up. An attempt by the Shropshire Conservation Trust to purchase some of the site came to nought, but, when ownership changed, Charles Sinker helped persuade the County Council to impose a temporary Tree Preservation Order whilst an understanding was reached with the new owners. They retained the trees, entering into an agreement with the Nature Conservancy Council for their safeguard, and, in 2008, forty years after its first attempt, the Trust, now known as the Shropshire Wildlife Trust, was able to purchase much of The Hollies, which it now manages as a nature reserve: 'If at first you don't succeed ...'.

Birds

Many of us listen eagerly each April for 'the Cuckoo', individualising the songster as if there is just one that calls throughout the district; sadly, with numbers in decline, this may soon be so! On The Stiperstones, Cuckoos parasitise Meadow Pipits. This is the commonest of the heathland birds, Skylarks are next in frequency, and twenty or so pairs of Red Grouse hold out at what is the southern extremity of their natural range in England – they were introduced to Exmoor and Dartmoor. Their 'go-back, go-back' calls, interpreted by the protagonists of Mary Webb's *The Golden Arrow* as laughing and mocking, ironic and derisive, punctuate the novel.

Curlews were once common breeding birds on and around these hills. Local poet Brenda Shaw spoke for many in the community when she described their 'plaintive yet familiar cry' as 'that sure and steadfast symbol' of Spring.[31] Today numbers are much reduced, but they still thrill resident and visitor alike each spring, with what Mary Webb called their 'forlorn, elfin music', as do the Snipe which in some years 'bleat' in 'airy circles' over wetter spots.

Amongst other heathland birds, Stonechats, whose numbers plummet when winter weather is hard, have benefited until recently from a run of generally mild winters; in good years there are at least 25 pairs and wherever one walks in summer they pop up, 'chatting' frantically from Gorse bush or Bracken frond; 25 years ago there were probably a mere five pairs on the National Nature Reserve and only 25 pairs in the entire county. The related, and almost equally neurotic Whinchat escapes the winters but runs a migratory gauntlet instead. This may be a factor in the recent steep decline nationally, which has reduced numbers on the hill from about eight pairs towards impending or actual extinction. Whinchats favour areas where there is both Bracken and damper ground, terrain which they share with a few pairs of Reed Buntings. Wheatears are migrants too, homing in on close-cropped grassland where relict stone walls or rabbity banks offer nesting holes near which they squeak and tut with anxiety. Whitethroats, Tree Pipits and Redstarts are other migrant animators of the heathland fringe, needing areas where there are scrub and trees. Redstarts are related to Stonechat, Whinchat and Wheatear and are perhaps the most

The neurotic chats

Clockwise from top left: Stonechat, Whinchat, Wheatear and Redstart. Photos courtesy of John Robinson.

manic of this anxious quartet, keeping up an almost hysterical succession of alarm calls – 'huit, huit, huit' – however negligible the danger.

A genuine source of danger would be a Kestrel, Mary Webb's 'windhover', hanging hopefully over the heathland. It is most likely however to be hunting for small mammals, particularly Field Voles, although Common Shrew and Bank Vole may be taken too, as well as caterpillars, beetles and earthworms. Buzzard and Raven are both now seen frequently and a few pairs nest round the periphery of the hill. In the woods there is a smattering of Pied Flycatchers, Great Spotted Woodpeckers and Nuthatches. Lesser Spotted Woodpeckers have disappeared, reflecting a significant national decline, but Green Woodpeckers hang on.

Invertebrates

In Crowsnest Dingle the Green Woodpeckers raid the voluminous nests of the Upland (Hairy or Northern) Wood Ant *Formica lugubris*, something of a speciality here at the southern edge of its range. Speckled Wood butterflies flit through woodland glades and Holly Blue butterflies flutter round that tree's blossoms in April and May. In wet patches on the eastern side of the hill the rufous-winged Small Pearl-bordered Fritillary butterfly dances between the flowers of Marsh Thistle and Ragged-robin, and lays its eggs on the leaves of Marsh Violet; The Stiperstones is a hot-spot for this uncommon butterfly. On the heathland itself, May is the month to look out for Green Hairstreak butterflies; even the vivid green of the young Bilberry leaves pales beside the emerald of the butterfly's underwings as it alights on the foliage, closing its wings as it does so.

Star butterflies

Photos, courtesy of John Mason and Nigel Jones, show clockwise from top left: Grayling (JM), Small Pearl-bordered Fritillary (on Marsh Thistle at Brook Vessons, NJ), Holly Blue (JM) and Green Hairstreak (NJ).

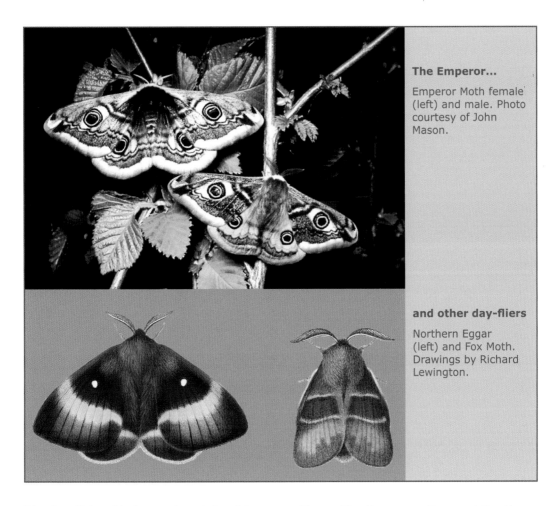

The Emperor...

Emperor Moth female (left) and male. Photo courtesy of John Mason.

and other day-fliers

Northern Eggar (left) and Fox Moth. Drawings by Richard Lewington.

The heathland is home to a trio of large moths — the Emperor, Fox and Northern Eggar. The males of all three may be glimpsed as they career over the heather in daylight searching for females; but you are more likely to see their caterpillars. The full-grown Emperor Moth caterpillar is long (well over two inches), plump, and bright green, with black bands spotted pink or yellow. Is this the 'huge green caterpillar crowned with gold' that Stephen Southernwood threatens to squash unless Deborah Arden allows him to kiss her — on the arm? The Fox and Eggar caterpillars are big, brown and hairy.

A notable Stiperstones first was registered in 1994 when David Poynton, a local entomologist, recorded the Cowberry Marble *Stictea mygindiana*, one of the numerous so-called micro moths. It had not previously been identified in Shropshire and will remain a rarity because Cowberry, the plant on which it lays its eggs, occurs virtually nowhere else in the county. The following year David reared *Glypta gracilis*, a host-specific parasite of the larvae of this moth, from larval spinnings on Cowberry. This is thought to be the first British record of this species.

In addition to recording on and around the hill since 1970, David has run a Rothampsted moth trap at Pennerley for about 20 years,[32] and his very many records, along with those of other recorders of moths and other invertebrates, have been collated by Pete Boardman of the Field Studies Council in *The Invertebrate Fauna of The Stiperstones area.* The *Fauna* lists the 1,294 species that have been recorded, of which the most numerous are the Lepidoptera, which number 449, mostly moths, but including 26 species of butterfly.

Amongst species highlighted in *The Invertebrate Fauna* are a series of so-called 'axiozoans', those that have a strong association with habitats considered to be of high value for nature conservation. It is a concept that the entomologists have borrowed from the botanists who, over recent years, have drawn up lists of 'axiophytes', a term from the Greek meaning 'worthy plants'. The plants and invertebrates in question are not extreme rarities; they are useful indicators of good quality habitat in which they may be found relatively frequently, whilst being scarce elsewhere. Amongst the many 'worthy creatures' of The Stiperstones, four photogenic examples illustrate the concept: the Bilberry Bumblebee is found in the uplands above 300 metres, where there is Bilberry; the Chimney Sweeper Moth lays its eggs on Pignut , an indicator of old grassland; the Golden-ringed Dragonfly patrols streams and runnels on heathland and moorland; and the Giant Tachinid Fly, whose larvae parasitise large hairy caterpillars, notably those of heathland, like the caterpillars of the Northern Eggar Moth. None of these species is a rarity, but all are quite exacting in their habitat requirements, and the habitats in question are no longer widespread.

Many other species are worthy of mention, but the following trio, the first two of which have also been nominated as axiozoans, will have to suffice: the Green Tiger Beetle (iridescent green with yellowish spots), a predatory beetle found on bare ground in heathland; *Mecynargus morulus*, a spider of high ground in the north and west; and the cranefly *Gonomyia dentata*, another upland species, recorded here by two celebrated entomologists, F W Edwards of the Natural History Museum, who found it in 1921 and 1928, and Alan Stubbs, founder of Buglife (The Invertebrate Conservation Trust), who did so in 1987.[33]

Wildlife of mine and spoil-heap

Destructive though mining is, and barren though some of its spoil-heaps may remain, even a hundred years after they were deposited, elements of the mining landscape provide habitat for a number of wildlife species.

If you look into the darker recesses just inside the old mine-workings (or into Rabbit burrows) you may spot a luminous glow; it is Goblin Gold *Schistostega pennata*, a moss which, uniquely amongst British and Irish species, possesses this luminous quality. Further into the mines, beyond the point to which the eye penetrates, there may be winter roosts of bats. In some sites dozens of the uncommon Lesser Horseshoe Bat hang, plum-like, from the ceilings; elsewhere there are smaller numbers of Long-eared, Daubenton's, Natterer's and Whiskered Bats. The bats are recorded and safeguarded by members of the Shropshire Bat

Worthy creatures

Golden-ringed Dragonfly and Chimney Sweeper Moth (courtesy of John Robinson), Bilberry Bumblebee (David Whitaker) and Giant Tachinid Fly (courtesy of Gary Thoburn). The Bilberry Bumblebee is working the Bilberry flowers, Mary Webb's 'small, rose-coloured tulips upside down, very magical and clear of colour'.

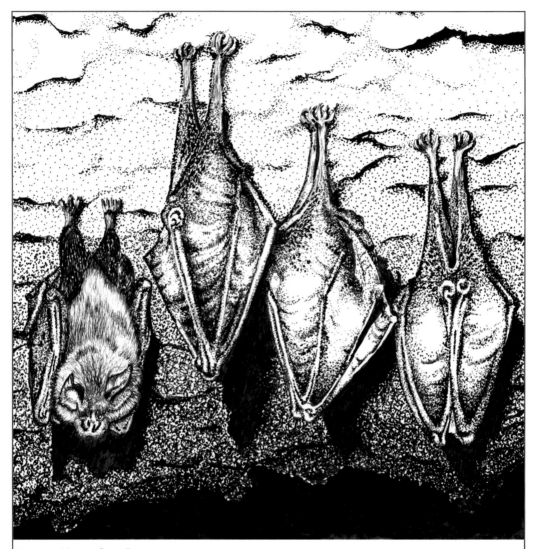

Lesser Horseshoe Bats

A drawing by Pam Curley of Snailbeach.

Group, the Shropshire Caving and Mining Club and the Shropshire Mines Trust, and where, for safety reasons, access to mineshafts and adits is blocked, grilles have been installed so as to allow their continued use by bats.

A survey of other mine wildlife, was organised by the Shropshire Mines Trust in 2005. In addition to finding overwintering Herald and Tissue Moths and resident Cave Spiders, the survey revealed the presence of a springtail (a minute wingless invertebrate) named *Folsomia fimetaria*, an organism which, unlike the moths and spiders, spends all of its life in the dark.

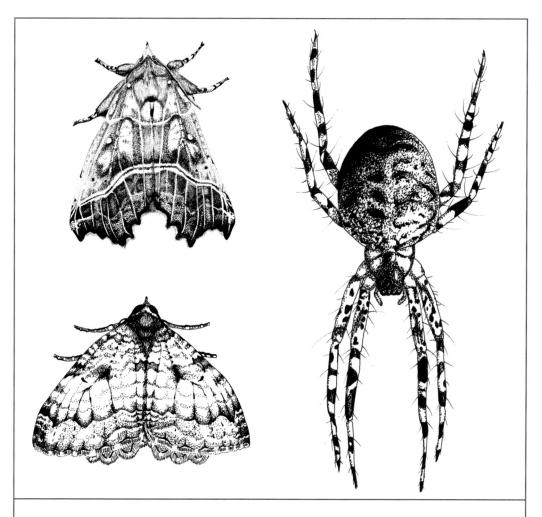

Three part-time troglodytes

Herald Moth (top), Tissue Moth and Cave Spider *Meta merianae.* Drawings by Pam Curley.

Out in the sunshine of high summer the Grayling, a butterfly of restricted distribution in Shropshire, may be found on and around spoil-heaps at a number of places, as well as on the fringes of the heathland. It seeks bare, sun-baked ground, such as the mine spoil, on which to bask, wings closed, cryptically-coloured underside exposed. The old spoil-heaps are in general a hostile environment for plants, being friable, deficient in nutrients and toxic, but eventually, even on the most toxic sites, Sheep's Fescue, which shows some lead tolerance, may gain a toe-hold. Over time it may be followed by Common Heather, and trees may colonise too. Tolerance of heavy metals is highly variable, both between and within tree species, but some examples of pioneer species such as Birch and Goat Willow appear to possess the necessary characteristics.[34] But the heaps are not uniformly barren: *Cladonia* lichens

Mine reservoir at The Bog

This photo was taken in 1985 when the reservoir had a dense cover of Water Horsetail (the green area beyond the walkway). Today this reservoir, which lies south of the former school, is largely overgrown; it cries out for re-instatement. Photo courtesy of Gordon Dickins.

cope well on spoil at The Bog, Harebell and Eyebright enliven the stonier parts of the old spoil-heaps at Snailbeach and Common Spotted-orchids flourish at Pennerley.

The need for water at the mines, whether for the steam engines or for the washing of minerals, led to the construction of mine reservoirs. Some still hold water today, others are now just muddy, rushy hollows or are being overgrown by willows; all are important wildlife features in what tends otherwise to be a relatively dry and quick-draining landscape. The best of the pools are at The Bog, where aquatic life includes Frogs and Palmate Newts, Emperor Dragonflies, Black Darters and Azure Damselflies.

The fragile heath

Heathland is a transitional habitat. It is fragile. Leave it alone and what ecologists refer to as 'succession' will take place: shrubs and trees will colonise and woodland will take over. Manage it too intensively, through grazing and burning, and it will become grassland. This dynamic is illustrated by the notion of heathland as a ball of habitat rolling down an incline, at the bottom of which lies woodland. In order to sustain heathland conditions, 'management' needs to hold the ball on the incline, but not to push it too hard or it will move up the slope to the grassland habitat which lies above.

In recent years at least, conversion of heath to grass has not been an issue on The Stiperstones, but trees and woodland lurk round the heathland periphery, creeping, and indeed jumping back in, at every opportunity. Given half a chance broadleaved woodland would, without any human assistance, engulf the hill within a few decades. Here, as on many heathlands, Birch takes advantage of any relaxation in grazing and burning, its tiny seeds planing on papery wings far from the parent tree to germinate in gaps in the Common Heather. By

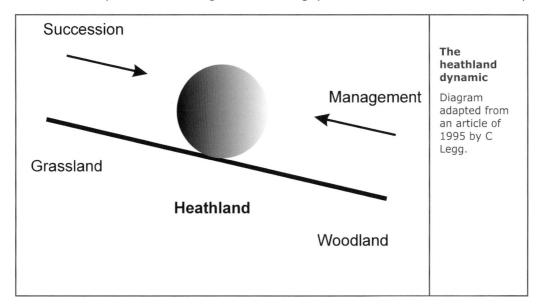

The heathland dynamic

Diagram adapted from an article of 1995 by C Legg.

contrast, Rowan berries drop straight from branch to ground; what chance have their seeds got of distant colonisation? Plenty. The seductive orange-red berry tempts us once only, but the extreme acidity which causes us to wince and spit clearly appeals to Foxes; they hoover up fallen fruits, the pips of which reappear in undigested clusters in their scats, dropped far and wide over the hill. Doubtless Red Grouse shop and drop too, and, if any berries are left on the arrival from Scandinavia of the over-wintering Fieldfares, they are swallowed and air-freighted to distant roosting sites in deep Common Heather, where the seeds are discharged overnight. With all this assistance, it is not surprising that seedling Rowans crop up all over the hill, including in the highest and stoniest of locations. Comparable itineraries could be mapped for the seeds of other common local colonists such as Holly, Crab and Oak, so, without the habitat management to be described in Chapter 10, the fragile heath would soon become wooded. But in the past this management was carried out not as a deliberate act to further the conservation of nature, but as an integral part of the local subsistence economy, elements of which are outlined in the next chapter.

Chapter 8

'Picking our clothes off the hill': heathland harvests

We'd go whinberrying and cranberrying up by the Devil's Chair.
We'd have a little fire and cook bacon and have a picnic. It was right nice.

Wilfred Andrews in *Never on a Sunday* (2000)

Wilfred Andrews

This photograph of Wilfred is reproduced courtesy of his niece, Joyce Pryce.

In the past, for one purpose or another, the mining community harvested virtually all of the common heathland plants, but the Whinberry harvest was of particular importance. Anyone born locally before 1950 has Whinberry picking locked in the memory. One such was Wilfred Andrews: 'They'd say we'd have to pick our clothes off the hill – pick whinberries to sell to buy clothes to go back to school'.

Wilfred Andrews (1925-2010) lived at Snape Cottages on the east side of the hill, where his family ran a small-holding. He continued to work the land until late in life, doing much of the work by hand, just like his forbears, brushing his hedges, scything the rushes and much else besides. He was a quiet, gentle and charming man, remembered with affection by family, friends and neighbours. In the following account, Wilfred's recollections of the various heathland harvests are linked with those of his contemporaries in order to outline the importance that the heathland had to the livelihoods of those who lived on and around the hill.

Whinberries

Wilfred's testimony to the importance of the annual Whinberry (=Bilberry *Vaccinium myrtillus*) harvest is repeated time and again amongst people of his generation. Enjoyable though Wilfred found it, 'whinberrying and cranberrying' was no idle past-time; he was making a vital contribution to the family budget: 'picking his clothes off the hill'. As Doug Boulter (born 1939) points out, this was a community activity: 'The hill would be covered with people, they'd come in droves', or, in the words of Mary Webb's Mrs Arden in *The Golden Arrow*: 'There's a power of folks coming, greedy as rooks in the fowl yard'.

Unlike Wilfred Andrews, many a youngster found the annual harvest a penance. One such was Les Hotchkiss (born 1927): 'I hated Whinberry picking. You never got a wet day them summers', and even if you did, Sue Hartshorn (born 1926) remembers that a truce wasn't necessarily called:

> 'Granny would go Whinberry picking with a big old umbrella and all of the children. If it rained they thought they'd be going back home but "Oh no! Come and get here ...". She'd put this great big umbrella up and all these kids would scuttle underneath it. "Get under me apron", she'd say, if it was only a shower, and it would dry up and they'd go on picking'.

Whinberry pickers

This photo is of a group from Pennerley including Flossie Hughes (married name Dean) on the far left, and her mother Mercy, on the far right; it was taken in about 1920. They are standing next to a Whin (ie a Gorse) bush rather than the lower growing Whinberry. Photo courtesy of Shropshire Mines Trust.

Emily Griffiths (born 1917) recalls the use to which the fruit was put: 'The Whinberries were mostly used for dyes … Buyers, known locally as "higglers", collected with a horse and cart. The ripe fruit was packed into small round wicker hampers, known as "wiskets", which were lined with newspaper and taken for despatch to Minsterley Station'.

And, according to Mary Webb's *The Golden Arrow*, quantities also found their way to Silverton (Shrewsbury) to 'the great wimberry market … in hampers that needed two men to lift them, and the purple juice dripped from them as in a wine-vat'. But they were of course consumed at the point of harvest too, and still are today. Indeed, courtesy of several large deepfreezes, they are available as pie or crumble throughout the year at the Stiperstones Inn.

As well as being delicious, many medicinal properties have, justifiably or not, been ascribed to the Whinberry. These include the treatment of bladder stones, lung and liver disorders, diarrhoea, gout and rheumatism. They have been used as a diuretic, as well as to induce menstruation, sooth mouth ulcers and relieve symptoms of typhoid fever. And they are said to improve vision – a quality remarked on, apparently, by Second World War pilots and since demonstrated, it is said, by a number of experiments. Further experiments have demonstrated that consuming Whinberries improves brainpower – in rats.

But it is the presence of organic chemicals in the skin of the fruit, acting as antioxidants, helping to cleanse the body of toxins, which have led many to recommend the eating of Whinberries. In her book about the *Vacciniums* Jennifer Trehane advocates eating at least half a cup a day, claiming that this should provide benefits in terms of general health and a delay in the onset of degenerative diseases associated with ageing. As a grower she has a vested interest, but few would find her recommendation a hardship.

Whinberry in fruit on The Stiperstones

Photo courtesy of Ben Osborne.

Cranberries, Blackberries and Cowslips

Wilfred Andrews refers to 'cranberrying' alongside 'whinberrying', and at one time the tart little fruits of what, locally, is called Cranberry, but is to be found in flower books under the name Cowberry *Vaccinium vitis-idaea*, were picked in quantity. The scarlet, Whinberry-sized fruits are most prolific on the higher, stonier ground, and have given their name to one of the tors, Cranberry Rock. The confusion over the plant's name is compounded by botanists giving the name Cranberry to a related plant which has the Latin name *Vaccinium oxycoccos*. This occurs on bogs and very wet heaths, including in the Shropshire hills; the last Stiperstones sighting was in a flush below Shepherd's Rock in 1986.

Cowberries have a number of culinary uses and it is surprising that so few are picked today. What's more, they are quicker to pick than Whinberries, coming, as they do, in little bunches of twos and threes rather than singly. In Sweden the plant is known as 'Lingon' and the berries are referred to as 'the red gold of the forest'. Up to 200,000 tons are harvested in a good year and their popularity has led to farmed production in a number of countries.

On The Stiperstones, as in Sweden, Cowberries were kept fresh simply by immersing them in spring water. This was possible because ascorbic and benzoic acid in the fruit gives it good keeping qualities. When it was time to use the berries, the water was poured off and drunk, providing, like the fruits

Cowberry in fruit on The Stiperstones
Photo courtesy of Ben Osborne.

themselves, a valuable supplement of vitamins A and C. In Sweden Lingonberry jam is the classic accompaniment to meatballs, a traditional Swedish dish. This use of the jam is reminiscent of our own use of the American Cranberry *Vaccinium macrocarpon* as a sauce to accompany Christmas turkey. But the Lingonberry/Cowberry jam is excellent too as a spread or filling, and, provided not too much sugar is added, the natural sourness of the fruit comes through, teasing the palate with bitter/sweet contrasts. This delectable quality is lost from some commercial versions, such as that sold by Ikea, because excessive sweetening overwhelms the piquancy of the fruit.

Blackberries growing round the heathland fringe provided a prolific harvest too. Doris Hewitt (born 1916) remembers picking blackberries for 1d a pound: 'We'd pick bucketfuls, seventy years ago they were very plentiful,' and George Evans (born 1908) recalls that 'the buyers would put them on the train by the hundredweight'. Roger Chidley (born 1942) says 'You had to pick Whinberries, but I liked picking Blackberries best – you didn't get as much for them as Whinberries but you didn't have to walk so far', and, as Derek Rowson (born 1934) points out, 'they were easier to pick, even with a few thorns in your fingers'.

Nora Pinches (born 1916) is one of many to recall winemaking: 'We would go picking Cowslips. My mother used to make wine with them. Beautiful it was. She used to make wine with everything – Dandelion wine, Cowslip wine, Elderberry wine and there is a nice wine you can make with Elderflowers as well'. Cowslips still flourish in the old, unimproved hay meadows at Pennerley, but nowadays they are sacrosanct.

Turves, Fern and Rushes

However, as George Evans relates, the hill harvests went beyond the picking of wild fruits. He remembers how his father would cut turves to protect tumps of potatoes from the frost, going amongst the 'whinberry wires' to cut a sod about two foot wide by three foot long which he then rolled up like a carpet. And he describes the use to which Bracken was put: 'When I was a boy, straw was a thing unheard of in this part of the country. We used to go on to the hills and cut with the scythe loads and loads of fern or what is now better known as Bracken, for winter bedding for the animals'. Henry Jones (born 1930) sets the harvest scene: 'The people from The Paddock would be cutting fern, old Mr Cook [from Blakemoorgate] … everybody would be out, all sizes, lugging it away on the little carts'. One of them was Tom Garner (born 1931): 'Every year we'd be cutting fern for days and lugging it home'.

Wilfred Andrews remembers the fern harvest with some amusement:

> 'We would cut fern for bedding. Cut it down in the autumn just as it went brown at the end of October. It would be … left to wilt … then we would roll it up and tie it with string. We would roll the rolls of fern down the hillside – they would be rolling so fast they would jump the hedges! We liked the fun but I don't know that Dad would have called it fun.'

George Evans and others recall using rushes to thatch Bracken stacks, and Wilfred their use for thatching stacks of hay. Doris Hewitt remembers similar uses and develops the theme: 'We used rushes for thatching the hay stacks and fern for bedding and tumping the potatoes, heather stalks for the fire and moss for the florist'.

Moss and Holly

Betty Hordley (born 1933) recalls that her parents 'would gather moss up on Rhadley [Black Rhadley Hill], fill sacks of moss, they used to supply Murrell's, Weaver's and Nichols' with moss. They would go twice a week to Shrewsbury with moss because in those days funeral wreaths were made with wreath frames and moss'. In Mary Webb's *Gone to Earth* Hazel Woodus returns from Silverton (Shrewsbury) with 'a tuthree wreath frames'. Her father, Abel, cuts Holly and she makes a 'prickly wreath' for the coffin of 'old Samson at the Yeath … sewing on the variegated holly-leaves one by one, with clusters of berries at intervals'.

Muriel Jones (born 1920) recalls the use of Holly at Christmas: 'Our "tree" – like everyone else's in the area – was the upper-most branch of a Holly tree, cut from the hedgerow and suspended upside down from the ceiling'. Doug Boulter remembers as a 12-year-old the cutting of Holly at the north end of the hill, in

Christmas Holly wreaths at Whixall, Shropshire

The upturned examples show something of how they are made. The display example on top is adorned with 'stabs' of variegated Holly and berries. Photo courtesy of Joan Daniels.

the area known as the The Hollies, for sending to Manchester for the Christmas market. Sometimes visitors would come on harvesting trips to the area: Bill Allmark (born 1942) recalls how, in the 1960s, he used to travel down from his home at Fenn's and Whixall Mosses near Whitchurch to cut berried Holly at The Hollies for the making of Christmas wreaths. Wreath making using bog-moss (*Sphagnum*) which is wrapped round wire frames onto which bunches of Holly are attached (much as outlined above by Betty Hordley), has, for a century, been an important source of income for 'peat families' at Fenn's and Whixall Mosses, and a thousand or more are still made each year; in common with The Stiperstones, the Mosses are now a National Nature Reserve.

Bees and Rabbits

Mary Webb's Abel Woodus was a bee keeper: 'In summer the garden was loud with bees, and the cottage was full of them at swarming-time. Later it was littered with honey-sections; honey dripped from the table, and pieces of broken comb lay on the floor and were contentedly eaten by Foxy [his daughter Hazel's pet]'. Harold Roberts (born 1925) who was brought up in a cottage, now ruinous, high up Perkins Beach, was another practitioner. He started as a child, and was self-taught, learning from books, but also from Jack Poole, the teacher at Stiperstones School. Joe Roberts (born 1894) of Crowsnest Dingle (see Chapter 2) was a beekeeper too and doubtless there were others, but it is not known how widely the craft was practised. Harold Roberts took to it in a big way, with as many as a hundred hives at various places, including on the hill. His bees produced honey from the heathland flowers, notably from Whinberry, which he says yields honey with 'a sweet flavour', and Common Heather, which gives 'a darker, thicker honey'. Hazel Woodus intercepted the whinberrry 'honey' at source:

Crowsnest Dingle

Here Joe Roberts kept bees and his daughter Doris helped with the hay harvest (see Chapter 3). 'A gem of a place … from the top a steep narrow path led deep down below to a fairy tale cottage right in the hollow and there you could buy honey' (Jeanette Merry, *The Rock*, see Chapter 9). The roof of Joe Roberts's cottage is in the middle of the picture. Photo, May 2009, courtesy of Gordon Dickins.

she picked the flowers, then 'she sucked out the drop of honey from each flower like a bee ... when she found an unusually large globe of honey in a flower, she sang'.

Prior to the spread of myxomatosis in the 1950s, Rabbits were exceedingly common in the fields around the hill. George Evans recalls that 'there were that many Rabbits that we were almost walking over the top of them'. Henry Owen (born 1918) remembers that 'a lot of people lived on Rabbit, especially the big families. The skins would be dried and hung up, then sold to people that came round, and Mole skins, I've sold hundreds'. Wilfred Andrews says that: 'I was making more money at home on Rabbits than I was by going to work. The fields was walking with them. We had rabbitting dogs – two hounds and a little lurcher. I'd rear ferrets and sell them at a pound a piece'.

Fair game?

Wilfred Andrews was less successful with other quarry, recalling that 'in the bad winter of 1947 there was grouse all under the rocks, hundreds of them there were and there was nothing for them to eat. We thought we'd creep up on them with a .410 but they heard us'. Others had more luck, and the Gatten Estate's game book shows a total bag of 115 brace of Red Grouse for The Stiperstones in 1911. The strong population at this period is reflected in the frequent allusions made to Red Grouse by Mary Webb in *The Golden Arrow*. Their cackling call, 'a loud, raucous, mocking laugh', becomes a malevolent motif in the novel.

Birds other than Red Grouse did figure however in the poor man's diet: George Balmer (born 1916) recalls enjoying Rook pie; Gordon Cook (born 1920) roasting Fieldfares (or 'Feldefars' as he called them)[1] and Johnny Butler (born 1920) that the Pheasant had 'only got to squawk and he was signing his death warrant'.

Timber, firewood and other firings

Wilfred Andrews remembers that during the War he worked 'on the forestry', notably in the 'Big Wood'. Many woods have been given this name but this was presumably the Big Wood on the eastern flank of Nipstone. Henry Jones remembers that his mother, Mary, worked there processing felled timber: 'Mr Gilbert Hotchkiss from Welsh Row had some heavy horses and he tushed it up the steep bank on to the flat piece where four women would saw it up into pit props which went to the Lancashire pits'.[2] Timber was harvested from Resting Hill too, here older members of the community remember major fellings in 1925 and 1946/7.

Elsewhere the returns were more modest, but Birch, Rowan and Hawthorn were all cut for firewood. Heber Rowson (born 1921) remembers how 'we fetched birch trees and I sawed them with a cross-cut saw with my sister to save the coal', while Tom Garner recalls that his cousin Harold Tomlins's first job every night was 'to saw an old birch tree down off the hill and lug it home for firewood'. The tough stems and twigs of gorse bushes were a valued and popular burning wood too: 'We always lit the fire with gorse sticks' says Tom. He also recalls the

Aerial view looking northeast from beside Oak Hill, June 1950

The 'white hillocks' of Snailbeach are visible left of centre. Beyond them lies Snailbeach
Coppice and beyond it, Maddox's Coppice (both were then broad-leaved woodland but were
subsequently coniferised). Resting Hill is on this side of the hillocks and, closer still, the
cottages of Gorsty Bank face the camera. The west-facing slope of Resting Hill still looks bare
following the coppicing of oaks here in 1946/7. Presumably the re-growth evident on the
south-facing slope dates from the coppicing of 1925; here the small pale patch is evidence of
a mining adit. Over the winter of 1989/90 rotational re-coppicing of small coupes began on the
west-facing slope, followed in 2004/05 by the first of a series of coupes on the south-facing
slope.

Photo from Cambridge University Collection of Aerial Photography (ref FA56).

use of turves of peat as fuel: 'Siah [Josiah] Wood [who lived above the chapel at Pennerley] used to have peat … stacked in the house, and that was all he burnt; he got that off the hill'.

It is only the hottest of heathland fires that burns the heather stalks right down, and quantities left over from cooler fires ('each bush charred and left', in Mary Webb's words, 'as a skeleton above black-strewn ground') were gathered and stored for domestic use. Wilfred Andrews remembers the fuels burned at his mother's old home at The Knolls: 'They would cut turves to put on the fire – well, they was more heather roots than turves. And they would heat up the bread oven with burthins of heather and bake 24 loaves and cakes and pies'.[3] The use of heather stalks for firing the bread oven is recalled too by John Francis (born 1923), while Henry Jones adds that 'If you wanted to sharpen the fire up under the kettle you would use a few heather stalks'. George Evans recalls that even the dead stalks of Nettle were gathered and tied in little bundles for use as fire-lighters: everything had a use.

Working the heath: sheep and shooting

The historic relationship between the community and The Stiperstones is neatly summarised by George Evans: 'We seemed to be part of them [the hills], and we used them for whatever purpose we required'. This included a significant

Smallholder sheep management

Joe Roberts with his sheep in Crowsnest Dingle, in a photo thought to have been taken in the 1950s. Reproduced courtesy of his granddaughter Margaret Price.

economic activity yet to be mentioned: the grazing of livestock. In 1972, 19 registrations were made of a right of common-grazing, running to a total of three ponies and 807 sheep (or 146 cattle), even though by this time fewer small-holdings were being actively worked. There were also four registrations of a right to cut and take Bracken, and two to 'cut and take heath', along with 84 registrations of a right to pick Whinberries, a number of which included 'other wild fruits'. Although the Commons Commissioner found in favour of only three claimants, all of grazing rights, the extent of the claims made at this time reflects the historical importance of the hill as a grazing resource.

The grazing of livestock was important economically and was instrumental in the establishment and retention of the heathland, helping to keep it free from invasion by pioneer trees. Old photos of the hill used to illustrate this book show how very open and un-wooded the landscape was up until the 1960s. And it was a landscape ideal for the nurturing of Red Grouse for shooting. As stated above, 230 grouse were shot in 1911, the first year for which there are records. These are good numbers and adequate to justify significant input to game keeping and heather burning. Johnny Butler, whose father was a keeper, recalls that 'Jones the Gatten would come with a horse and cart to fetch the game that had been shot, there'd be a market for it'.

It is likely that, at this time, much of the flatter land of the hill would have been burned on a short rotation of perhaps 8-10 years' duration, stimulating the

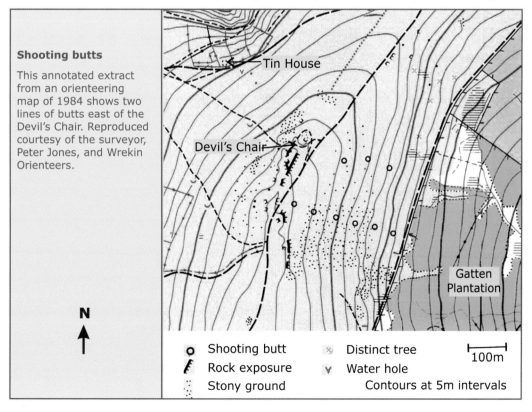

Shooting butts

This annotated extract from an orienteering map of 1984 shows two lines of butts east of the Devil's Chair. Reproduced courtesy of the surveyor, Peter Jones, and Wrekin Orienteers.

Tin House

Devil's Chair

Gatten Plantation

N

o	Shooting butt	×	Distinct tree	100m
ʄ	Rock exposure	v	Water hole	
⋮	Stony ground		Contours at 5m intervals	

Common Heather to produce plenty of nutritious young shoots for the grouse (and sheep) to eat. It was a 'driven' grouse moor, one on which the birds were sufficiently numerous to justify the deployment of beaters. They walked in line in order to flush and drive the grouse to guns waiting in rows of shooting butts strategically placed across the hill. As many as 25 such butts were identified in a recent survey; the most obvious lie east of the Devil's Chair.[4] Recalling the 1930s, when he was involved in game-keeping, Henry Owen says: 'There was a lot of grouse on The Stiperstones then … You could drive grouse easily … We could make up four or five good drives'. At that time, shooting would have included the area running down to The Rock, where a certain Bill Francis had been born. His story is told in the next chapter.

Chapter 9

'A boundless heath':
paradise, devastation and preservation

And here a boundless heath before me lies,
Warmed by the sun and watered from the skies.

Bill Francis *Hasty Pudding and Kettle Broth* (1992)

Bill Francis

Bill Francis (1896-1989) was born at Rock Farm, at the southern end of The Stiperstones, where four generations of the Francis family had lived and farmed since the 1780s. He served with the King's Shropshire Light Infantry throughout the First World War, and in the 1920s he worked in the Bog Mine; thereafter he was a bricklayer and jobbing builder, living at the Grit, Asterley, and later Minsterley.

Bill Francis kept a diary over the last seven years of his life. In 1992 extracts were edited and published by his grandson, Peter Francis, under the title *Hasty Pudding and Kettle Broth*; the title honours two basic but nutritious staples of Bill's youth.[1] The diary is wonderfully forthright, highly entertaining, full of love for humanity, scorn for hypocrisy and humbug and rich in reminiscence, which is nostalgic but not romanticised.

In a diary entry for 9 July 1986 Bill Francis recalls his youth at Rock Farm:

'During this summer weather and the loneliness of old age, one's thoughts revert to the days of one's childhood, remembering the good things and forgetting the bad ...
I had a thousand acres of mountain and moorland and field to wander in ... one hundred springs of pure water to satisfy a thirst and above all the pure air of heaven.'

Reproduced courtesy of Bill's grandson, Peter Francis.

Off to war, 1914

Bill Francis aged 18.
Reproduced courtesy of
Peter Francis.

Rock Farm in about 1905

Bill Francis is the middle one of the three children in the centre of the photo; his parents William and Clara are the adults to his left. The identity of the other individuals is not known with certainty, but the boy to Bill's left may be his brother Jim, who died aged 15 when Bill was away at the war. Photo reproduced courtesy of Peter Francis.

Bill Francis recalls the dairy at Rock Farm, where there would be a barrel or two of home-brewed beer, shallow pans of milk and a large dish of cold potatoes to be taken at will when hungry. He also recalls the lack of money, the patched clothes, the darned socks and shoes with worn out soles, the midden in the yard and the smelly earth closet. Yet beyond the midden and the earth closet lay his thousand acre playground, to which he refers again in his poem 'Lyric to the Stiperstones by one of its sons': 'And here a boundless heath before me lies,/ Warmed by the sun and watered from the skies'.

This chapter recounts something of the origins and history of Bill Francis's 'boundless heath'. It carries the story through to the changes in land use and management proposed, and in large part realised, on the heath and its surroundings, in the 1960s and '70s, changes which had a significantly damaging impact on the landscape and its wildlife. It concludes with an account of how a degree of safeguard came into play.

The 'boundless heath': origins and extent

In this area 'heath' – land where heathers dominate – is not a natural habitat, but one derived from man's activities over recent millennia. The abundant plants of heathland – notably heathers, other dwarf-shrubs and gorse – are plants that were here long before man arrived, but they would have grown in an essentially wooded setting and less abundantly than today. Early Bronze Age people striding the rocky ridge between Cranberry Rock and the Devil's Chair four thousand years ago, would have looked out through a thin cover of hardy, stunted trees, below which there lay more densely wooded slopes. This was broad-leaved woodland in which Birch in particular flourished, Oak was frequent and Hazel widespread, along, doubtless, with Rowan and Holly; Lime and Elm may have occurred in places on the lower slopes but Pine, though it may have been present in earlier times, had probably died out by now.

Bit by bit, starting presumably in the Bronze and Iron Ages (there is no direct evidence of human activity on the hill before the early Bronze Age period, c2400-1400 BC), this woodland was cleared, for, and by, grazing animals. The evidence of Bronze Age presence along the ridge is to be found in what Shropshire archaeologist Michael Watson has described as 'the remains of a cairn cemetery': 22 prehistoric, or possibly prehistoric, cairns have been identified, mostly around Cranberry and Manstone Rocks.[2] Some are small, as little as 0.4m tall and 5.2m in diameter, and are easily overlooked as natural humps and bumps, but the largest is imposing, 'an island of bare stones gleaming in a wine-dark sea of heather; this great cairn stands 1.7m high and 24m in diameter'.[3] Five of the cairns are Scheduled Monuments. None has been excavated but, by analogy with cairns excavated elsewhere, experts confidently identify them as funerary monuments covering single or multiple burials, dating from the second millennium BC.

The great cairn

Looking along part of the ridge from just north of Manstone Rock, with, in the foreground, the largest of the Bronze Age cairns. Ahead, and to the left of the path, is the Devil's Chair. On the right, in the far distance, lies Shepherd's Rock and close by, to its left, on a line back to the Devil's Chair, Scattered Rocks can just be made out. Across to the left are the 'beaches'. Photo May 1993, courtesy of Clwyd-Powys Archaeological Trust (ref 93-C-586).

One of the many cairns was first recorded in an account of 1968 by Shropshire's most celebrated archaeologist, Miss Lily F Chitty (1893-1979) of Pontesbury. Miss Chitty's renown extended far beyond the county, it was built on her archival work, her particular interest in prehistoric artefacts, and her skill in drawing them. This skill is evident in her sketches of a find made in 1964 at Ritton Castle (¾ mile west of The Bog) by eight year old Richard Machin. He picked up what Miss Chitty described as a 'small (3¼ inch long) hourglass-holed stone implement', used perhaps as a hoe, presumably with the tapered hole accommodating a wooden shaft.[4] It is likely to date from the early Bronze Age; Richard Machin had stumbled across an implement untouched perhaps for four thousand years.

Castle Ring, standing on the summit of Oak Hill, at the north end of The Stiperstones, is of later date; it too is a Scheduled Monument. A large, univallate (one-banked) Iron Age hill fort, it was constructed some time between the eighth century BC and the first century AD. Described succinctly in the *Victoria County History of Shropshire* as 'a stronghold, simply contrived in an impregnable position',[5] it takes advantage of a narrow rocky isthmus across which was thrown a defensive ditch and bank of impressive size; elsewhere, the already steep slopes were cut back and defences mounded up, re-enforcing the natural protection afforded by the precipitous promontory. The only entrance was via the isthmus, and it was aligned so that, in the words of the *Victoria County History*, 'to pass into the camp an invader must face the defenders with the perils of the steep hillside at his back'. The earthworks are imposing, suggesting construction by a numerous and cohesive social group able to mobilise and

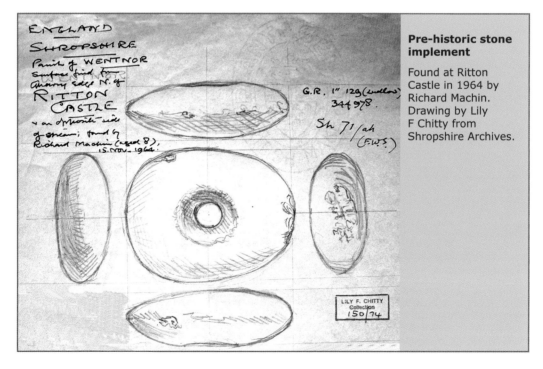

Pre-historic stone implement

Found at Ritton Castle in 1964 by Richard Machin. Drawing by Lily F Chitty from Shropshire Archives.

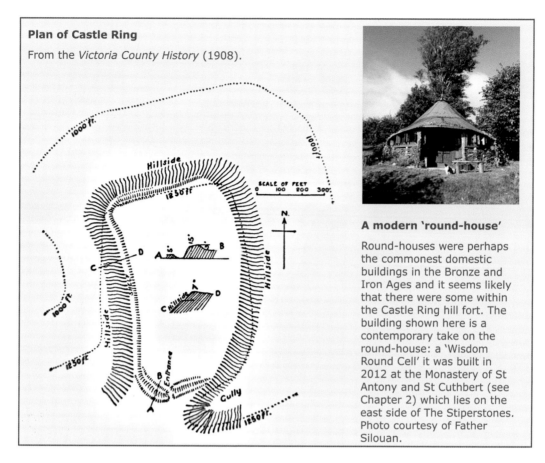

Plan of Castle Ring

From the *Victoria County History* (1908).

A modern 'round-house'

Round-houses were perhaps the commonest domestic buildings in the Bronze and Iron Ages and it seems likely that there were some within the Castle Ring hill fort. The building shown here is a contemporary take on the round-house: a 'Wisdom Round Cell' it was built in 2012 at the Monastery of St Antony and St Cuthbert (see Chapter 2) which lies on the east side of The Stiperstones. Photo courtesy of Father Silouan.

sustain a significant work force. Although the fort has not been excavated, archaeological investigations of similar forts elsewhere suggest that Castle Ring will have been inhabited, and a number of probable building platforms or terraces were identified in a recent non-intrusive survey.[6] This then was probably the first upland settlement on The Stiperstones.

These people of the Bronze and Iron Age initiated an ongoing cycle of felling, burning and grazing. Progressively, over the centuries, the woodland cover was removed, making way for the dominance of dwarf-shrub heathland on the poor, stony soils of the hill. Areas they cleared will have been extended in Roman and later times, creating an open landscape. Nevertheless, what may be floral reminders of the former woodland survive here and there: Wood Sorrel, Wood Anemone and Great Wood-rush lurk still, particularly in shadier, cooler spots; Bluebell persists in un-ploughed enclaves round the heathland fringe, and the fragile fronds of Oak Fern are confined by the munching mouths of livestock to a rocky retreat.

Over subsequent centuries there will have been an ebb and flow of heathland and woodland. In medieval times The Stiperstones became a hunting forest, and this might be taken as evidence that the hill was more wooded at that time,

Woodland survivors?

Clockwise from top left, Wood Sorrel (courtesy of John Robinson), Wood Anemone (beside the All-ability Trail, May 2013, Gisèle Wall) Great Wood-rush (Laurie Campbell) and Oak Fern (beneath a cairn on the ridge, May 2007, courtesy of Dan Wrench).

when deer, probably both Red and Fallow, were chased over the hazardous terrain. However, the term 'forest' indicated then a place of deer rather than a wooded landscape, and it may be that the higher ground of the thirteenth century Stiperstones Forest was no more wooded than the Stiperstones hillscape that Bill Francis's ancestors knew when they set up home at Rock Farm in the 1780s.

The bounded heath

In the 1780s, much of the higher ground for miles around would have been very open. Drawing on the earliest Ordnance Survey mapping of 1816, David Pannett, well-known locally as a historical geographer and geologist, has identified extensive areas of unenclosed land, presumed to have been common (ie land with some communal as well as private use):

> 'On the ridge of the Stiperstones itself, about 1,400 acres, stretched [a continuous band of unenclosed land] the 4½ miles from Habberley Office [by Snailbeach], to Black Rhadley Hill, beyond which detached blocks also existed on isolated hills in More, Linley and Norbury … To the west a parallel band of over 2,000 acres stretched … from Bromlow Callow across the hills of Stapeley, Shelve and Mucklewick and the intervening marshes as far as the Montgomeryshire (Powys) border. Here, further open land spread over Corndon Hill and Hyssington Marsh and down to Todleth Hill in Churchstoke.'[7]

On the poor upland soils these extensive unenclosed areas are likely to have been heathland, but subsequent enclosures and encroachments progressively took in much of this open land. The process accelerated with the expansion of mining in the nineteenth century, when this became a populous area. Settlers spilled out from the mines of The Bog, Pennerley, Tankerville, Perkins Beach and Snailbeach, occupying land at the heathland fringe, nibbling away at it and establishing smallholder settlements. To the young Bill Francis the heath appeared 'boundless' but it was a smaller area than that known to his forbears when they first occupied Rock Farm.

Miss Merry

The enthusiasm that Bill Francis expressed for the 'boundless heath' was shared by a contemporary, but an incomer, Jeanette Merry (1897-1982), generally referred to locally as 'Miss Merry'. In 1948 she took a let on Rock Cottage, which stood just a few hundred yards north of Rock Farm.

On her first visit to The Stiperstones, in the 1930s, Miss Merry had chanced upon the area further to the north known as Rigmoreoak.[8] She remembers this, and later visits, in *The Rock: reminiscences to share with those who enjoy the Stiperstones* (1979):

Miss Eleanor Jeanette Merry

Photographed in the uniform of the Queen's Institute of District Nursing and reproduced courtesy of Eleanor Welham (née Merry), her great-niece. From Dorothy T Merry (1974) *A Merry Family Omnibus*.

'There was not a house in sight nor sign of habitation, only God's earth created as at the beginning, timeless, peaceful, soul satisfying. I fell in love with the Stiperstones … we slept on camp beds in the heather and the brilliant stars seemed to drop out of a dark purple velvet sky onto us. Each night we saw shooting stars. Sheep were our only companions and the call of the grouse.'

They played Beethoven's 'Fifth' and Handel's *Messiah* on a wind-up record player, only to find next morning that the sheep had trampled the records, breaking two of them, one of which included the passage *All we like sheep have gone astray.*[9]

A gramophone on the hill

This gramophone was taken there not by Miss Merry, but by Mary Rowson (bottom left), her aunt Nellie Broadhead (behind her), brother Jesse, mother Alice (right), and, directly behind the gramophone, Miss Ingram, housekeeper for the Robertses at Lordshill. Photo taken on top of Resting Hill in about 1930, reproduced courtesy of Mary Challinor (née Rowson).

The cottage at Rigmoreoak, tight up against the open hill, had been occupied by the Hotchkiss family, but by the late 1920s they had moved downhill to Bog Hill Farm. Miss Merry recalls seeing Mrs Hotchkiss

'on a clear and windy day in the farmyard outside the kitchen with her four lovely children holding between them at all four corners, a sheet.[10] Their mother held above it … buckets of whinberries and poured them into the sheet … allowing the wind to blow away the loose whinberry leaves and chaff, to leave the berries as clean as possible for market.'

Miss Merry was Assistant Superintendent of District Nursing for Shropshire from 1933 to 1935, and in this capacity visited District Nurse Charlotte Hand who served the Stiperstones community from 1922 until her death in 1953.[11] But by the time she leased Rock Cottage, Miss Merry was working in London. She held a number of senior posts in the Queen's Institute of District Nursing, of which she was appointed General Superintendent in 1951. With Miss Iris Irven she co-authored *District Nursing: a handbook for district nurses and for all concerned in the administration of a district nursing service* (1955), said to have been the standard work on the subject. She was appointed OBE on her retirement in 1958. During her career, and after retirement, she travelled widely in an advisory capacity, notably to Malta, Malaysia, Singapore, Jamaica and British Honduras, including, in her own words 'among many primitive peoples living in jungle villages with dwellings made of bamboo and banana leaves'.[12]

Rock Cottage

Recollections of holidays at Rock Cottage occupy the bulk of Miss Merry's short memoir. We learn that the Cottage nestled up against a quartzite tor, and in that respect could well have been the model, in part at least, for the cottage that Stephen Southernwood and Deborah Arden occupied in *The Golden Arrow* (see Chapter 5). The rental was £3 per year, plus a further £2 for an adjacent one and three-quarter acres of ground.[13]

Rock Cottage in 1954

The cottage nestles beneath The Rock. Photo A P Wallace.

When Miss Merry leased the cottage, it was surrounded by heathland, marsh and rough grazing:

> 'At times Buzzards flew over ... mewing and wheeling. Rarely one could hear the deep ominous croak of a coal-black Raven ... The Grouse surprised us often by crying "Go back, go back, go back" as they rose in fright ... From the marsh below came the [sound of] Curlews, Snipe and many Peewits. Occasionally we could hear ... the soft purring of the Nightjar.'[14]

The cottage, although not 'partially ruined', like the fictional one near the Devil's Chair taken on by Stephen and Deborah, still needed work to make it habitable, and the 'bare necessities' had to be added, including an Elsan toilet in the hut up the abandoned garden. Water was drawn from 180 paces away at what Miss Merry knew as 'Bessie's Well' (Bill Francis called it 'The Well of Salvation'); for tea-making it was boiled in the kettle hanging from a chain over the fire. Despite

Water from 'Bessie's Well'

Jillian (left) and Jennifer Wallace in 1956 walking the 180 paces to the well to collect water for Rock Cottage. Photo A P Wallace.

Jeanette Merry (left) and her sister Dorothy (Dolly) at Rock Cottage

This photo was taken in about 1960 and is reproduced courtesy of Eleanor Welham.

(or perhaps because of) such relatively primitive living conditions (experienced of course throughout the year by the resident population), Miss Merry, escaping from the strains of work and of London, felt she was in 'Paradise', and she had no greater delight than to spend a day picking Whinberries and Cowberries, pausing from time to time to look around and enjoy the beauty of the hills.

Paradise Lost

Sadly 'Paradise' did not endure. Miss Merry chronicles the changes that took place: 'The Miners' Arms' at The Bog ceased trading, the school closed and, following the sale of the local Ritton Estate, the 'bog land' attached to Brookshill Farm, to the west of the cottage, was drained, limed and seeded with grass. The cottages at The Bog were demolished. Ironically the demolition was the work of a Shrewsbury builder, Roy Fletcher, and although this destructive tendency is difficult to comprehend, his widespread drainage and 'improvement' of agricultural land is understandable, being underwritten by generous Ministry of Agriculture grants, but deeply regrettable. These doubtless offset the cost of clearing Laburnum, Hawthorn, Birch and other trees as bemoaned in verse by Brenda Shaw (born 1917) who lived at Ritton Place:

> 'The Fletcher men they laugh and joke
> As Ritton trees go up in smoke,
> Ah me! I feel emotion choke
> What memories those trees evoke.'[15]

But it was Roy Fletcher's <u>planting</u> of trees that brought about what Miss Merry calls 'the final devastation'. He now owned her cottage and the surrounding heathland, and in 1969, courtesy presumably of forestry grants, the land around the cottage was planted with conifers: 'Small fir trees sprang up wherever the ground made planting possible … in rows, orderly, artificially regimented'; ten years on they were 'as tall as human beings and the ground beneath them like waste land'. Miss Merry had by then retired, and along with her sister, had settled in Minsterley. 'The conifers grew bigger and bigger and the area was transformed and no longer had the same natural unspoilt beauty'. Miss Merry surrendered the tenancy.

'Where have all the flowers gone?'

I will return to the damaging transformation wrought by afforestation and agricultural 'improvement', but wish first to mention other new impacts of landscape management, less obvious perhaps, but equally damaging, starting with a grassland plant. Mountain Pansy, the perky and endearing yellow grassland pansy of the uplands, has already been referred to in Chapter 7. In the *Ecological Flora of the Shropshire Region*, Charles Sinker, drawing on personal knowledge, recalled that 'In the 1940s it was still possible to walk from Ratlinghope via Squilver and Shelve to Bromlow Callow [a distance of some six miles] through field after field washed pale with Mountain Pansies'. They were still around in 1964 when the well-known Shrewsbury rose-grower and botanist, Hilda Murrell, came across them when driving up the road to The Stiperstones

Here come the conifers, June 1960

A composite of two photos taken from above Rock Farm by A P Wallace. It shows Black Rhadley on the right, Heath Mynd right of centre, and in the centre, The Knolls, now part of Linley Big Wood, but then much more open (note that this should not to be confused with another The Knolls which lies between Nipstone and Cranberry Rocks). Below the road, and at right angles to it, lie the furrows ploughed prior to the planting of conifers; nearer to the camera further furrows run across the photo above the bank. This afforestation pre-dates the planting of 1969 around Rock Cottage as reported by Miss Merry. Most of the conifers planted following this 1960 forestry ploughing persist, and a belt of broad-leaved trees has become established on the flank of Black Rhadley.

Rock Cottage in about 1982

Note the burgeoning conifers to right and left. Photo courtesy of Gordon Dickins.

from Ratlinghope.[16] Her diary entry for 16 May records how she sought out a grassy bank and had a good snooze – a nap in the sun and brewing tea outdoors were amongst her greatest pleasures – and there she found 'beautiful little clumps of Yellow Pansies in the grass'. But today one would have to look hard to find a single Mountain Pansy along the entire route from Ratlinghope to Bromlow Callow, and the rich mix of associated plants detailed in Chapter 7 has gone too, victim of the agricultural intensification that has swept through the countryside.

Since the Second World War the drainage, ploughing, liming and re-seeding of agricultural land have proceeded apace, not least in the uplands, stimulated by government grants and by the very understandable pursuit by farmers of livelihood and profit. Loss of flower-rich grasslands has been one of the consequences. In a survey of the area surrounding The Stiperstones it was found that just in the years 1979-1982 some 22% of the area of 'rough', but flowery, grassland was destroyed.[17] This was neither the start nor the end of the process, and over the period 1979-1989, 35% of Shropshire's 466 grassland 'Prime Sites for Nature Conservation' were damaged or destroyed, amounting to more than 20% by area, a total of 2,280 acres, the equivalent of 84 miles of football pitches laid end to end.[18] The most damaging local loss came in 1983 with the draining of a flush at Marehay Marsh (below the National Nature Reserve car park). It harboured such treasures as Butterwort, Bogbean, Tawny Sedge and Round-leaved Sundew, and was habitat for Snipe, Lapwing and Curlew.

'One of Shropshire's Curlew places'

Curlew is another example of wildlife in jeopardy. In the period 1939-42, a young birdwatcher, Ken Stott (born about 1924), was a regular visitor to a Scout camp at Wentnor. He tramped the hill-slope running from Ratlinghope up to The Stiperstones, a slope which included Marehay Marsh. 'Besotted with Curlew and Snipe', he remembers finding five Curlew nests in the area in one season, hearing Snipe 'drumming' (their mating display) all night and watching the Lapwing that abounded. And he says that across the ridge, the area from The Bog to Shelve Pool was equally alive with these wading birds.[19]

Plants of Marehay Marsh

Butterwort and Round-leaved Sundew, top and bottom left, courtesy of John Robinson.

Bogbean, top right, courtesy of John Mason.

Tawny Sedge, David Fenwick, www.aphotoflora.com.

In *Shropshire Hills* (1947) H W Timperley (see Chapter 6) describes the valley between The Long Mynd and The Stiperstones (Ken Stott's tramping ground) as one of Shropshire's 'Curlew places':

> 'All through the spring and early summer there are few moments when no Curlew can be heard there. If one is not close by, beating round in circles over the rushy roughs, or hovering just clear of the ground where his mate is down, then there will be one above a far hillside or away behind a hill-shoulder. When the mating frenzy is at its height the valleys often resound with the wild calling which, though still finding an echoing wildness in the land, suggests other times, far off, when these valleys that man can now scarcely hold for his cultivation were wilderness untouched.'

Farm machinery has improved enormously since then, and man no longer has a problem 'holding this land for his cultivation'. Almost all of it has now been drained, ploughed, limed and re-seeded, reducing habitat for many of the birds of the upland edge, including Curlews. Now they often nest in mowing fields where their nests risk being destroyed when the grass is cut. Small numbers persist, but sadly today there are many moments in the spring and early summer when none can be heard. Unless new nature conservation initiatives come to fruition, the Curlew may well be lost to the Shropshire Hills over the next ten years.

The case of Lapwing is even more pressing. It would have benefited from the mixed farming regimes of the past, when occasional root crops and cereals were grown, but it likes damp ground too; today there is a monoculture of grass and fewer wet patches. It is now close to extinction in the Shropshire Hills, but Bill Tuer recounts that in the 1930s, when his father Ted was gamekeeper on The Long Mynd, there were so many to be found in the Ratlinghope area that their eggs, an acknowledged delicacy, were collected and sent to Fortnum and Mason's, London, in boxes of 36 at a time; yet the birds returned each year in good numbers.[20]

Snipe are similarly beleaguered. One or two birds 'drum' in some years, on or near the eastern flank of the National Nature Reserve, but they have been lost from swathes of ground to east and west of the ridge which were havens for them until the 1950s.

Ken Stott was born at a time when Mary Webb was writing lyrically about the Shropshire Hills. Were she to return, she would notice enormous changes. The topography remains the same of course, but the loss of the detail, the grain of the countryside, the richness of its wildlife, has been dramatic. In terms of agricultural livelihoods there have been considerable improvements – production has greatly increased and subsidies have underwritten profitability – but in terms of habitats and wildlife, texture and colour, the enriching fabric of the countryside has been torn away. Writing of Mary Webb's Shropshire, Paul Evans, nature writer and broadcaster, observes that 'so much of the ecological weave of the countryside has unravelled that the once commonplace is now extraordinary'.

Further forestry frustrated

To return to the issue of afforestation, Miss Merry's 'final devastation' of 1969, the coniferisation of The Rock, was the work of a private landowner, but elsewhere on The Stiperstones the Forestry Commission was carrying out similar works and planning further conifer planting. Indeed, as early as 1962, the Commission had planted land surrounding the tor known as Nipstone Rock, just to the north of The Rock. Miss Merry tells us that 'wonderful were the whinberries there until afforestation choked them out', calling to mind the words of Mary Webb: 'the fir trees reared their tarnished blue-green – sullen, archaic, sentinels of death'.[21]

In 1966, the Forestry Commission went on to lease some 350 acres lying between The Knolls and Crowsnest. Most of the Commission's leasehold was on the west side of the ridge, and the intention was to plant conifers on the lower slopes from below Cranberry Rock through to Blakemoorgate, including the flanks of Perkins Beach, Mytton Dingle and Crowsnest Dingle. This was in addition to the re-planting of the Gatten Plantation on the east side, which had

Here come more conifers, 1961

A P Wallace's photograph shows Nipstone Rock on the left and Corndon in the distance. In the foreground are furrows ploughed by the Forestry Commission prior to planting; the ploughing gives the conifers a head start by suppressing potential competitors.

been afforested with pine and larch in the nineteenth century but had been left as open ground since the felling of that timber crop in the 1930s. Only the rock-strewn heights of The Stiperstones were to be left unplanted.

In 1967 another threat loomed: a proposal by the BBC to site an Ultra High Frequency Television Station consisting of a building and a mast, a staggering 550 feet tall, either on the ridge to the north of Shepherd's Rock, or on The Wrekin.[22] The Rural District Council raised no objection to the Stiperstones site, but others did. In the end, and despite protests, The Wrekin was blighted and The Stiperstones spared.

Meanwhile, local opposition to the Forestry Commission's planting plans was growing. The Stiperstones Preservation Society was formed in 1966, seeking to safeguard both the amenity of the hill and what were considered to be the community's common rights; its secretary was Mrs Emily Williams (she has often been referred to in earlier chapters as Mrs Emily Griffiths, which she became when she re-married following the death of her first husband).

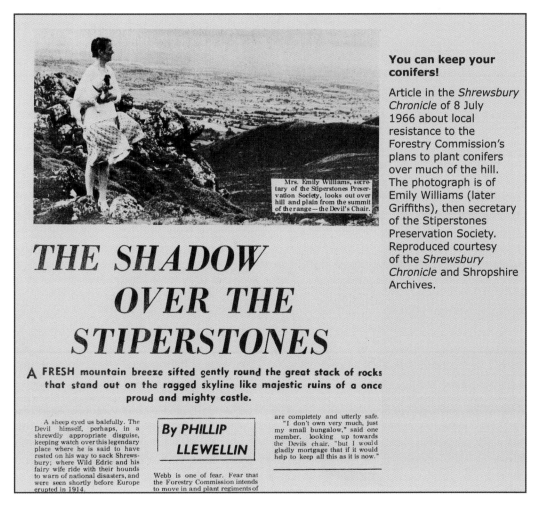

Mrs. Emily Williams, secretary of the Stiperstones Preservation Society, looks out over hill and plain from the summit of the range — the Devil's Chair.

You can keep your conifers!

Article in the *Shrewsbury Chronicle* of 8 July 1966 about local resistance to the Forestry Commission's plans to plant conifers over much of the hill. The photograph is of Emily Williams (later Griffiths), then secretary of the Stiperstones Preservation Society. Reproduced courtesy of the *Shrewsbury Chronicle* and Shropshire Archives.

THE SHADOW OVER THE STIPERSTONES

A FRESH mountain breeze sifted gently round the great stack of rocks that stand out on the ragged skyline like majestic ruins of a once proud and mighty castle.

A sheep eyed us balefully. The Devil himself, perhaps, in a shrewdly appropriate disguise, keeping watch over this legendary place where he is said to have rested on his way to sack Shrewsbury; where Wild Edric and his fairy wife ride with their hounds to warn of national disasters, and were seen shortly before Europe erupted in 1914.

By PHILLIP LLEWELLIN

Webb is one of fear. Fear that the Forestry Commission intends to move in and plant regiments of

are completely and utterly safe.

"I don't own very much, just my small bungalow," said one member, looking up towards the Devils chair, "but I would gladly mortgage that if it would help to keep all this as it is now."

Achieving recognition of common land status and of common grazing rights, through the Commons Registration Act of 1965, was worthwhile in itself, but it was also the best way to prevent afforestation. Registration was a complex and lengthy process and, on the invitation of Worthen Parish Council, it was facilitated by David Pannett, then working at the Field Studies Council Centre at Preston Montford. Registration required knowledge of current ownerships and how these had evolved over the centuries, and David's expertise as a historical geographer meant that he had a particular aptitude for the task. With the encouragement of Charles Sinker, Warden of the Centre (see Chapter 7), who regarded 'getting to know your area' as a professional requirement, he researched the history of land ownership and tenure going back to the seventeenth century, sharing his findings with the applicants, and the Parish and County Councils.

Finally, in 1979, after rights had been claimed and representations made at a public hearing, the Commons Commissioner concluded that thanks to prescription (uninterrupted usage over many years) common rights had been acquired over 608 acres of the main area of the hill, including the major part of the Forestry Commission's leasehold. This effectively frustrated their planting plans. The re-planting of the Gatten Plantation (which lay outside the common) had gone ahead in 1968-1970, predominantly with Sitka Spruce, but the representations of local people and the registration of the common had been instrumental in saving the core of The Stiperstones from afforestation.

Jolly Green Giant opens National Nature Reserve

Following the decision by the Commons Commissioner, there was little point in the Forestry Commission maintaining its leasehold interest; furthermore, the freehold owners, the Hulton-Harrop family of Gatten Lodge, were increasingly conscious of the responsibilities and liabilities of the land. The Stiperstones had long been recognised as of particular importance for its heathland and geology, indeed, as early as 1953 the Nature Conservancy had notified a considerable acreage as a Site of Special Scientific Interest. So, in the light of the new situation, the Nature Conservancy Council (successor to the Nature Conservancy and predecessor of English Nature and Natural England) negotiated for the surrender of most of the Forestry Commission's leasehold, and for the purchase of the freehold of this and additional land amounting in all to 1,015 acres. Purchase was completed in 1981; it was subject to the rights of common and, at the vendors' insistence, retention by them of the shooting rights. A further 63 acres of oak woodland at Resting Hill and Crowsnest were purchased from Shropshire County Council.

The combined area was declared a National Nature Reserve in 1982 and opened by David Bellamy.[23] Professor Bellamy, the erstwhile academic, was by then the 'jolly green giant', a leading presenter of natural history programmes, but at the opening he shared the starring role with children from Stiperstones School.[24] He was a particularly appropriate person to open this botanical refuge, the first National Nature Reserve in Shropshire, because he records that it was 'on

David Bellamy and friends

A cartoon drawn by Jim Gammie on the occasion of the opening of the National Nature Reserve; he was an employee of the Nature Conservancy Council but drew his cartoons out of hours! Reproduced courtesy of the artist.

the flower-decked habitat [of Shropshire] that I first cut my botanical wisdom teeth'.[25]

Whilst some of The Stiperstones was now a National Nature Reserve, its conservation depended not on this designation but on its future management. The next chapter touches on the management of the reserve and on progress towards extending the conservation of landscape, heritage and wildlife to the rest of The Stiperstones and its surrounds.

David Bellamy and further friends

He is seen at the opening of The Stiperstones National Nature Reserve, November 1982, accompanied by children from Stiperstones School. Marie Jones gets the starring role, the supporting cast are: 1. Lara Sproson, 2. Stuart Bennett, 3. Jeremy Zihni, 4. David Morris, 5. Tim Bradley, 6. Robert Evason, 7. Peter Evans, 8. Gareth Ingram, 9. Gail Groves, 10. Julie Potter, 11. Lisa Williams, 12. Vicky Heath, 13. Zena Haynes, 14. Daniel Sproson, 15. Verity Harrison, 16. Carla Holz, 17. Jacob Tjellesen, 18. Nicky Holz, 19. James Richardson. Just out of shot are Nicky Hampson, Diane Powell, Caroline Bradley and Julie Perkins.

Chapter 10

'Back to (and beyond) purple': conservation and restoration

To each of us a sacred trust
'Protecting earth' should be,
This heritage preserve we must
For all posterity.

Emily Griffiths 'A Hymn for Conservation' (1990)[1]

Flagships

Each section of this book has started with a single figurehead with which I have kicked off that part of my narrative. All but one, the Man Stone, have been animate, the others have been writers or narrators around whom I have sought to write my own tale.

For this final chapter I am nominating not one, but three figureheads, all illiterate: Emperor Moth, Curlew and Mountain Pansy. Each is a 'flagship' or 'signature' species, nominated to represent and carry the flag for a particular wildlife habitat which is of importance on and around The Stiperstones — conserve this species and a whole innumerable cohort of other species will be conserved as well. The Emperor Moth carries the flag for Bill Francis's 'boundless heath', the Curlew for H W Timperley's 'rushy

Flagship species

Emperor Moth caterpillar (at The Bog, courtesy of Nigel Jones), Curlew (courtesy of John Robinson) and Mountain Pansy (at Blakemoorgate, courtesy of Paul Glendell/Natural England).

215

roughs' and the Mountain Pansy for what the authors of the *Ecological Flora of the Shropshire Region* refer to as 'living grassland museums'. But first, an exploration of some of the issues surrounding the management of the National Nature Reserve which the Jolly Green Giant had opened in 1982.

Conservation

Managing the heath for nature conservation: wildlife and sheep

The importance of The Stiperstones for nature conservation lies in the outstanding quality of its open heathland landscape and its singular geological interest. This open landscape came about through sustained levels of grazing, through the scavenging of the many woody products that a small-holder economy needed, and by the burning of Common Heather (hereafter referred to simply as 'heather') designed to maintain a high population of Red Grouse for shooting, and to stimulate the growth of fresh browse for livestock. Grouse and grazing were the main drivers in the management of the hill.

By the time that The Stiperstones became a National Nature Reserve these traditional activities were losing their economic purpose. The Nature Conservancy Council (NCC) took on a landscape shaped by activities which were no longer viable. Small-scale grazing enterprises were uneconomic, small-holding and

Sheep at Blakemoorgate

Bob Cook and his son Gordon with their sheep, probably in the late 1930s. Reproduced courtesy of Gordon's daughter, Margaret Tate.

part-time livestock farming had ceased to be a necessity for local people, and grouse shooting was not profitable. The NCC needed to encourage the Commoners to continue grazing the hill, indeed to graze it more intensively, because grazing levels had declined over the years. The relationship between the NCC and the Commoners was not always an easy one. Issues of territoriality and control compromised cooperation in the early years, but recognition of mutual dependence has grown over time.

The NCC also needed to institute nature conservation management as a replacement for what previously had been self-sustaining activities carried out in pursuit of livelihood and profit, such as the felling of invasive trees and the management of Bracken. It is a surprise to some that nature reserves need management – are they not natural places where nature can and should be left to get on with it? In fact, in this country, where man's hand is omnipresent, many nature reserves are places fashioned by man through the exploitation of naturally occurring plant species (think, for example, of coppiced woodland, hay meadows and chalk downland) and this is the case with the heathland of The Stiperstones. A cessation of human activity, above all an end to the 'turning out' of livestock to graze, would soon allow woodland to re-colonise, taking this landscape back to a semblance of its pre-Bronze Age wooded state. The result would be fascinating and exciting, but it would see the loss of the special qualities that marked out The Stiperstones as a place worthy of becoming a National Nature Reserve. The sweeps of purple heather and banks of golden gorse would be lost, Red Grouse exiled and Skylarks silenced. There would be no open ground on which Grayling butterflies could bask, and Cowberry and Crowberry would be confined to the rocky ridge from where the visitor would peer out through tree branches, striving to discern landmarks and landform. It would be a very different place.

Numbers of livestock need to be held at a level which will ensure that the heathland is well grazed, slowing heather growth and keeping trees at bay. Currently the aim is to graze 440 ewes and their lambs on the hill from May to October. This is now being achieved by Higher Level Stewardship agreements with two of the three Commoners, through which they are paid to run the required numbers.[2] But the livestock graze some areas preferentially and neglect others; here trees soon get away and then have to be uprooted or cut down and their stumps treated with herbicide to prevent re-growth. Large areas, mostly on hillsides, have been tackled, with the assistance in some cases of the Commoners through their Stewardship agreements.

When management for nature conservation started in a concerted way in 1986, it was some years since there had been much controlled burning of patches of heather, though there had been extensive uncontrolled fires. There was a lot of old and leggy heather in which fires can soon get out of hand, and few areas of short heather where fire control is much easier and which can therefore be used as firebreaks. It was decided therefore to cut some of the heather in order to speed up the management and to create a network of firebreaks. Cutting, with a tractor and swipe (a mower with blades that rotate horizontally), can, unlike burning, be done in most weathers but, for obvious reasons, it can't be done on steep slopes or stony ground, conditions typical of much of The Stiperstones. Nevertheless, cutting is a useful technique and one which continues alongside burning. Currently the aim is to cut or burn 300 acres of heather on a 12-year rotation, this deliberately leaves a fair amount unmanaged, because old heather has a particular value, notably for lichens and invertebrates.

The purpose of cutting and burning is to stimulate new growth. In the case of young heather plants this is readily achieved, as they soon sprout again. By contrast, plants more than 12 or 15 years old fail to do so, and regeneration of the heather depends on the successful germination of seedlings. This happens more quickly where the heather has been burned rather than cut because a good clean burn (though easier to wish for than to achieve) clears the litter, bares the ground and creates good conditions for germination.

Red Grouse

One of the species favoured by heather burning is the Red Grouse which persists in small numbers on The Stiperstones. It has real nature conservation importance as a signature bird of heather-clad hills. The Stiperstones and The Long Mynd are now its only breeding sites in Shropshire, and these two hills are southerly outliers of its range in England.[3] Grouse like short heather for feeding (heather shoots make up some 90% of their diet), and longer heather for cover and nest sites. They are said to be reluctant to feed more than about 15 yards from cover, which means that cuts and burns should be no more than 30 yards wide. On The Stiperstones, cuts with sinuous shapes are preferred to

Shropshire Red Grouse

Male on The Stiperstones, photo courtesy of Christopher Sutcliffe; female on The Long Mynd, photo John Hawkins/flpa-images.co.uk

Heather burning

In this case near to Habberley Rock in December 1989. Photo Tom Wall.

Rejuvenation

Young Common Heather plants two years after burning. The flowers in the foreground are on re-growth from rootstock, whereas the small non-flowering plants in the centre are new seedlings. On the right are Bilberry plants, some with an orange tinge to their leaves. In the background are the yellowing stems of Wavy Hair-grass, a common but ephemeral early colonist. Photo August 2013, Gisèle Wall.

straight-sided ones, and they are made following the contours rather than up and down the slopes. Although the result looks very odd from the air, viewed from the ground this pattern of management fits well with the landscape and it creates lots of 'edge', a transitional zone considered to be of particular value to wildlife.

A decline in Grouse numbers was evident by the 1930s and it continued up until the 1990s, by which time there were so few birds left that shooting ceased. With perhaps just 5-10 pairs hanging on, the extinction of Red Grouse on The Stiperstones seemed a real possibility. The NCC did not hold the sporting (ie shooting) rights, which had been retained by the previous landowner, but there was no suggestion that the population had been 'shot out' by his sporting tenants. Clearly, however, the birds had not prospered under their guardianship.

Requests made on a number of occasions by the NCC and its successor body, English Nature, for the opportunity to purchase the sporting rights had never

Heather and grassland management

Sinuous strips cut out of uniform stands of Common Heather show up strongly in this aerial photograph taken at the north end of the hill in July 1996. The more amorphous shapes mark where heather has been burnt some years previously. In both cases, Bilberry, showing pale green, is typically an early beneficiary. The rectangular grasslands of Blakemoorflat appear in the foreground and those of Blakemoorgate at top left. Small 'clearance cairns' of stone removed years ago from the fields can be seen at the bottom edge of the former. The colonisation of the heathland by young trees is evident in the bottom left corner and dark patches of heather creep back into the fields which are, in local parlance, 'going back to the hill'. Here lime has been applied in recent years with the objective of reversing the trend. Photo courtesy of Clwyd-Powys Archaeological Trust (ref CPAT 96-C-1017).

been agreed to, but in the 1990s a series of short-term leases were granted to English Nature. This ensured a moratorium on Grouse shooting while the recommendations of leading experts as to how to increase numbers were put in hand.[4] These were that Foxes and Carrion Crows, the main predators of Red Grouse, needed to be controlled in order to improve breeding success. English Nature adopted and persisted with this policy for a number of years, in the face of significant local opposition, and although the really rigorous control that might have led to a significant increase in Grouse numbers proved impractical, there was a small increase in the breeding population and this may have been the result of the measures that had been taken.

After 10 years the owner of the sporting rights declined to negotiate either a further renewal of lease, or a sale to English Nature, and instead sold the rights to another private individual. This new sporting rights owner stepped up the predator control for a while, with the intention of reinstating shooting, and a further modest increase in the population to some 20-25 pairs may have been the consequence. Sadly however this improvement was not sustained and the population slipped back to in the order of 10-12 pairs before rallying again with good numbers of young birds fledging in 2013, possibly as a result of an enhanced commitment to predator control. Natural England (successor to English Nature) continues to work with the owner of the sporting rights in order to achieve a level of heathland management and predator control which will hopefully in time lift the population to a more secure level.

Two headaches

Management work carried out with the support of the Commoners includes the control of Bracken, a native species, but one with much less value as wildlife habitat than the dwarf-shrub heathland that it tends to displace. It is a very successful plant, and something of a headache, as it can be invasive and is very difficult to keep in check. Cutting the plant repeatedly can significantly weaken it, but also weakens the heather amongst which it grows, and the most effective method of control is by the application of Asulam, a herbicide which, whilst it kills all fern species, not just Bracken, normally has little effect on other plants apart from members of the dock family. On large, rough, or steep areas, helicopter application is the only practical technique, and a remarkably economical one; knapsack sprayers are used where smaller areas are treated. In both cases other fern species are safeguarded wherever possible. But it is not the intention to eliminate Bracken – even if that were feasible – particularly because Whinchat, a bird in sharp decline, favours some areas of Bracken, notably where these occur in conjunction with wet ground and heathland.

The Heather Beetle is another 'headache species'. Always present, the numbers of this small, brownish beetle reach plague proportions from time to time, and have done so more frequently it seems in recent years, possibly because the deposition of nitrogen through aerial pollution has enriched their feed. The tiny larvae (smaller than a grain of rice) feed almost exclusively on heather, damaging the plant's foliage, which turns foxy-red, and then, as the damaged

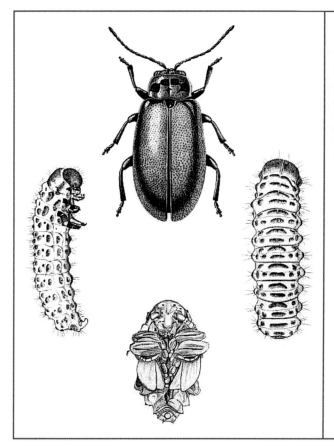

The Heather Beetle

This illustration from *The Grouse in Health and in Disease* (1911) shows the adult, two views of the larva, and at bottom, the pupa seen from below. The beetle, larva and pupa are all less than a quarter of an inch in length.

leaves die off, a depressing grey. The larvae can be so numerous that they destroy hundreds of acres of previously healthy foliage, but all the heathland manager can do is watch and wait. In theory, insecticide could be applied, or infected areas burned, but neither is acceptable: the application of insecticide would kill many other insect species, including the predators and parasitoids that might otherwise act as biological controls; and burning of the affected areas would have to be done in June or July, a time when birds are nesting and fire control is highly problematic. But, all being well, after two or three years, the numbers of the various predators, parasitoids and pathogens of the Heather Beetle build up to levels which make for effective biological control, the beetle population then crashes, and eventually the heather recovers.[5]

One nightmare

So much for headaches, September 2011 brought a potential nightmare when, during routine monitoring undertaken by the Food and Environment Research Agency, *Phytophthora pseudosyringae* was found on a patch of Bilberry (Whinberry) at the south end of the hill.[6] It had been found on Cannock Chase in Staffordshire in January 2009, where it has since killed extensive areas of Bilberry, and it has subsequently been identified in Derbyshire too. The various species of *Phytophthora* are soil or water-borne fungus-like pathogens which can kill a variety of trees and shrubs; they include *Phytophthora infestans* better known as Potato Blight. The symptoms of *Phytophthora pseudosyringae* on Bilberry include wilting, black bands on the plant's stems and discolouration of its foliage.

Initially, on The Stiperstones, the area in which infestation was detected appeared relatively small and it was 'sprayed-out' using herbicide. Subsequently however, infected Bilberry plants were found all along the ridge, and the application of herbicide over such an extensive area was unthinkable. In the hope of containing the infestation visitors were asked to follow bio-security measures, in particular cleaning their boots on entry and exit. It subsequently became clear however that The Long Mynd was infected too, indeed it may well have been infected prior to The Stiperstones. Given the extent of local infection and the amount and diversity of access, particularly across the extensive and widely-used area of The Long Mynd, effective bio-security measures became impractical.

Currently there is no practical way of controlling *Phytophthora pseudosyringae*. It can only be hoped that there may be some measure of natural resistance and that it doesn't spread to all parts of the hill. A further hope is that it will not 'cross over' to the closely related Cowberry, or indeed other species. An Interdepartmental Board has been established to oversee a programme aimed at containing and eradicating this and other *Phytophthora*; it needs to work fast.

Restoration

Back to purple: the Emperor Moth

When, in 1914-16, she lived at Pontesbury and walked the Shropshire Hills, Mary Webb would have approached The Stiperstones from its north end, near Lordshill. From there she could have walked for six miles through a virtually continuous cover of heathland right along the ridge and on to Black Rhadley Hill and Heath Mynd, north of Bishop's Castle. The heathland would have occupied a broad swathe across the hill, running well down its flanks and grading into gorse and herb-rich grassland, bog and flush, hay meadows and holly brakes. This was Bill Francis's 'boundless heath'.

This situation persisted without dramatic change until the 1950s, but by the 1990s the heathland had been fragmented and narrowed. Forestry, as witnessed by Miss Merry, had engulfed areas around The Rock and Nipstone. Meanwhile, agriculture had pushed its way up the hillsides, draining, cultivating and fertilising, and a combination of agriculture and forestry had completely breached the heath between Cranberry and Nipstone Rocks. It was to these losses that English Nature responded in 1995 with a restoration strategy which developed into the project known as *Back to purple: conserving and restoring The Stiperstones.*

Before, during and after the conifers (well, almost)

Top: The view looking northeast from Black Rhadley Hill in June 1960 prior to the planting of conifers. The first tor stands adjacent to Rock Farm, the second is The Rock and, on the far horizon, the final tor visible is the Devil's Chair. The only conifer plantation is Big Wood lying on the flank of the hill just right of centre. Photo A P Wallace. *Middle*: The same view in June 2002 showing the crops of conifers which had been planted in the 1960s/70s. *Bottom*: The same view in May 2005. Most of the conifers have gone, but an intrusive belt persists.

Middle and bottom photos courtesy of Paul Glendell/Natural England.

The principal objective of the project is to 're-establish the ridge of The Stiperstones as a broad and virtually continuous run of lightly grazed heathland, stretching from Heath Mynd in the south to The Hollies in the north'. The objective is expressed through the notion of a caterpillar of the Emperor Moth, which feeds on heather, being able to accomplish the long march from end to end of The Stiperstones crawling from one heather plant to the next without (apart from three minor road crossings) ever touching the ground.

Thanks to a grant from the Heritage Lottery Fund, work started in 1998 on realising this objective through a project run jointly by English Nature, Shropshire Wildlife Trust and the Forestry Commission; further funding came from the European Union and, through Tarmac, from Landfill Tax Credits. The first phase concentrated on clearing the Gatten Plantation, which lies on the east side of The Stiperstones below Cranberry and Manstone Rocks, and removing conifers surrounding Nipstone Rock. At the Gatten Plantation 70 acres of conifers were cleared followed by a further 32 acres at Nipstone.

Powerful bales

Shropshire Wildlife Trust staff at Nipstone Rock atop a stack of bales of branchwood prior to their transport to Shotton Power Station, February 2007. Back row: Carl Pickup, John Hughes; next row: Chris Powell, Viv Geen, Helen Gilmour, John Powell; next row: Colin Preston (seated), Sarah Gibson, Liz Etheridge (seated), Helen Trotman, Sara Bellis, Jan McKelvey; front: Mike Winter (seated).

Following felling, the timber was extracted and sold; but then the real work began, with huge volumes of branchwood to be cleared and burned. Following more recent felling, branchwood has been baled for use as a fuel at Shotton Power Station, Deeside, in Flintshire. Consideration was given to the removal of the conifer stumps, but this would have greatly disturbed soil profiles, been very costly and created a major disposal problem.

When it comes to re-creating heathland it is fortunate that heather produces an abundance of seed; it has been estimated that a mature heather canopy can produce between 188,000 and 350,000 seeds per square metre per year.[7] By no means will all of these almost microscopic seeds survive, but studies have revealed large, if variable, banks of germinable seed in the plant litter and surface soil. At The Stiperstones, trials carried out by the Institute of Terrestrial Ecology for *Back to purple*, gave estimates of 1,840 to 15,560 germinable seeds per square metre. A proportion of seeds will survive a long time in the seed bank, indeed viable seeds of heather have been found under 60 year old conifer plantations.[8] The trees felled at the Gatten Plantation and Nipstone Rock were younger than this, so good results could be expected. But there were complicating factors, such as the quantity of needle litter, the long history of conifers at the Gatten (a first conifer crop is thought to have been planted here as long ago as 1850), and the disturbance to soils and seed banks because of forestry ploughing prior to tree planting. Consequently a 'belt and braces' approach was followed in places: some areas were scarified to disturb the needle litter, let light in and stimulate germination, and in other areas seed harvested from elsewhere on The Stiperstones was sown.

Scarification on the flatter ground at Nipstone was done with a tracked excavator, but at the Gatten Plantation a horse-drawn harrow was tried. Here, on steep, ploughed and stump-ridden terrain, a horse could go where an excavator or a tractor would soon be 'stumped'. But conventional agricultural harrows snagged on the stumps, or simply bounced over the undulating terrain, so, in a throw-back to what must have been Neolithic man's harrow, we tried a Hawthorn bush. It must be one of the oldest agricultural tools, yet it was still being used locally within living memory, as Clifford Hampson (born 1942) recalls: 'If we wanted to chain-harrow anything, Granddad [Neddy Davies of Blakemoorgate] would cut down a hawthorn bush and put it on a chain behind the horse – that's how he would chain-harrow'.[9]

The bush we used at the Gatten Plantation had all the necessary flexibility, angularity and scratchiness, and it followed the contours well, but it proved insufficiently durable, so a metal version was designed. This was no look-alike, but it shared the essential properties of the original, to which it added durability. It was christened the 'Heathland Rehabilitation Horse Harrow' (or HRH Harrow for short). It excited some considerable interest and HRH the Prince of Wales asked to see it on a subsequent visit to Powys Castle.[10]

By contrast, modern technology, in the form of a helicopter, is invaluable when applying the tiny seeds. The seeds are mixed in water and sprayed out through booms slung beneath the helicopter, using what is basically the same kit as for Bracken spraying. Forty acres were seeded at the Gatten. Just 20 lbs of heather seed was needed, equivalent to spreading nine standard (2.2lb/1kg) bags of sugar over 23 football pitches, yet the seed is so small that an estimated 100 million seeds were spread at a rate of 600-700 per square metre. At Nipstone Rock approximately 17 acres were seeded, and here Bilberry, Cowberry and Crowberry seed were mixed in with the heather. Additionally, thousands of heather and Bilberry plants were grown from cuttings taken on the site, and these have been trowelled in by volunteers.

Hawthorn harrow

Ella and Doug Joiner harrowing with a Hawthorn bush at the Gatten Plantation, January 1999. This photo had star billing in *The Times*, framed by the Court Circular and the listing of society weddings. Photo courtesy of Richard Stanton.

HRH and the HRHH

Prince Charles with the Heathland Rehabilitation Horse Harrow (see inset), Doug Joiner and Ella at Powys Castle, 1999. Photos courtesy of John Bacon/English Nature.

Results are by no means uniform, and some of the areas where heather has re-established most successfully have been neither harrowed nor seeded! But within three years of the trees being felled, carpets of flowering heather could be found over extensive areas. Each year sees further progress, but grazing is needed to keep tree and gorse growth in check, push back brambles and control grasses. At the former Gatten Plantation, Natural England is grazing stock of its own. Here there are Exmoor ponies and Hebridean sheep, a combination of browsing animals which, it is hoped, will prove successful in keeping back the woody vegetation.

Gatten Plantation three years after felling

Common Heather flowering between conifer stumps, summer 2001. Photo courtesy of Ben Osborne.

Heathland browsers at Gatten Plantation

Exmoor ponies. Photo courtesy of Paul Glendell/Natural England.

Hebridean ewe. Photo Gisèle Wall.

Farming and Wildlife: the Curlew and Mountain Pansy

So, by 1982, through a combination of local and national initiative, the best known parts of The Stiperstones, including Cranberry Rock, Manstone Rock and the Devil's Chair, had been safeguarded from afforestation or other major change, and had become a National Nature Reserve. And, since 1998, as outlined above, progress has been made in reversing the afforestation of parts of the ridge. But the wildlife interest of the area is by no means restricted to the heathland, and, as explained in the preceding chapter, the wildlife habitats of the surrounding area have been much diminished since the 1950s.

The loss of wildlife like the Mountain Pansy, Curlew, Lapwing and Snipe convinced the *Back to purple* partnership that in addition to heathland re-creation there was a pressing need to stem wildlife losses in surrounding habitats. They sought and gained the ready support of the Rural Development Service (part of the Department for Environment Food and Rural Affairs) and their predecessors, who, in an effort to hold the line, negotiated what were then known as Environmentally Sensitive Area agreements with many local farmers.[11] These agreements, now superseded by Entry and Higher Level Stewardship, were designed to put a break on further agricultural intensification. They were a step in the right direction but in practice did nothing to restore what had been lost.

In addressing issues of wildlife conservation and restoration on farmland in the valley between The Long Mynd and The Stiperstones (sometimes referred to as 'LongStones'), a major boost has been the work of the Upper Onny Wildlife Group established through 'Down to Earth', an element of 'Blue Remembered Hills', a Heritage Lottery Fund 'Area Partnership' project. The Group is surveying a range of wildlife species in the area, most notably Curlew, Lapwing and Mountain Pansy, and is working for their conservation. It is to be hoped that their efforts will be supported through a new project: the *Stiperstones and Corndon Hill Country Landscape Partnership Scheme*, funded by the Lottery and launched in November 2013.

The prescriptions for Curlew, Lapwing and Snipe conservation are well known and not particularly demanding, and there is an urgent need to bring farmers, gamekeeping interests and nature conservationists together to agree on areas where they can be applied. The appropriate remuneration and compensation would have to be put in place in order to offset any loss of agricultural output, but this would be an admirable investment of Stewardship funding. The fields below the National Nature Reserve car park at The Knolls would be a good place to start, restoring something of the 'rushy roughs', the Curlew ground of which H W Timperley wrote in the 1940s.

Prescriptions for Mountain Pansy conservation are being developed through the work of Ian Trueman and Eleanor Cohn of the University of Wolverhampton. Ian was one of the joint authors of the *Ecological Flora of the Shropshire Region*; they sagely observed back in 1985 that 'it is easy to see how ploughing for the improvement of hill grassland destroys this living museum [of Mountain

Pansy and other grassland plants], but it is much harder to determine precisely what form of management is best for maintaining it'. Working on fields at Blakemoorgate and Blakemoorflat that are examples of this living museum, but which are, in local parlance, 'going back to the hill', Ian and Eleanor are monitoring very assiduously the effects of a series of lime applications.[12] These began in 2006, but it is still too early for them 'to determine precisely' what liming and associated management is needed. In time, however, their work should help to address not just the issues of conserving this habitat, but also of getting its restoration underway too.

Brook Vessons and The Hollies safeguarded

Meanwhile, this strand of *Back to purple* received a boost through the acquisition by Shropshire Wildlife Trust of two new nature reserves encompassing farmland lying on the edge of the hill. With the support of the Heritage Lottery Fund, the Tubney Charitable Trust, English Nature (and subsequently Natural England) and thanks to the generosity of individual donors, the Wildlife Trust purchased Brook Vessons (45 acres) in 2001, and much of The Hollies (91 acres) in 2008.

The Hollies

A drawing commissioned by Shropshire Wildlife Trust for their nature reserve sign. Reproduced courtesy of the artist, Bob Guy.

Brook Vessons is a miniature of the Shropshire Hills, its landscapes preserved in a pocket handkerchief nature reserve. Here there are fragments of common land, rough grazing, woodland, wet pasture and heathland. Across them green lanes bordered by old walls and outgrown hedges creep to ruined cottages. There are 'champion trees' here too, and close-by, at The Hollies, a grove of hundreds of ancient former pollards that have fed livestock and, at Christmas, decorated front rooms over generations and centuries. As stated in Chapter 7, this is a most remarkable relict, a 'hollin', a survivor of a once widespread feature of the uplands, one of those places farmed in the past for their winter browse, which have now almost all been erased. The reserve safeguards some of the oldest Hollies in the country, and, to add to their distinction, many are crowned by Rowan trees. Seeded serendipitously into the tops of the Holly trunks by visiting thrushes, these now overtop their hosts.

Reversing 'the final devastation'

When Miss Merry surrendered her tenancy (see Chapter 9), her landlord declined to re-let Rock Cottage. On a visit in 1979, she bemoaned its neglected state but speculated that it might stand for another 200 years. However, in 1984 Bill Francis described it as 'a wreck', and within a few years it had been knocked flat by its owner. This act may never be reversed, but what Miss Merry called 'the final devastation', the planting of the conifers all round her cottage, has proved to be an interlude, not an ending.

In the 1990s, plantations at and surrounding the former Rock Cottage were acquired by the Linley Estate, and in 2004/05 Justin Coldwell of Linley Hall, nephew and heir of Sir Jasper and Lady More (see Chapter 6), embraced the spirit of *Back to purple* by felling 75 acres of conifers, leaving the land open for heathland to recolonise, which it has. This was the young Bill Francis's back-yard, the site of Miss Merry's former retreat, the very ground she saw planted in 1969. 'The final devastation' is being reversed.

And in 2005, the adjacent ground at Nipstone Rock, from which conifers had been removed in 1999, became a Shropshire Wildlife Trust reserve. The Trust also purchased an adjacent stand of conifers running to 30 acres known as 'Big Wood' lying on the eastern flank of the site. These trees were subsequently felled, with 19 acres earmarked for restoration as heathland and 11 acres on the lower slopes re-planted with broadleaves. The Trust runs Hill Radnor sheep on its ground while the Linley Estate grazes Hebrideans at The Rock.

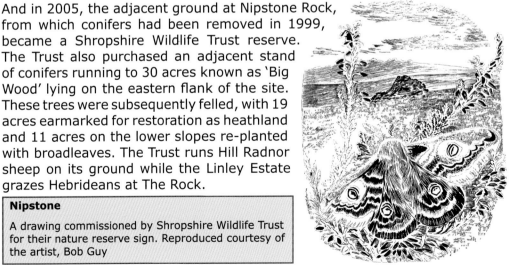

Nipstone

A drawing commissioned by Shropshire Wildlife Trust for their nature reserve sign. Reproduced courtesy of the artist, Bob Guy

The Rock before and after felling

Two views of The Rock from the south east. The first in June 2002 showing an extensive spread of conifers; the second in May 2005 after some, but not all, had been felled. Miss Merry's Rock Cottage stood beneath the tor just to the right of centre. Rock Farm, the home of Bill Francis lies behind the tor on the left. Photos courtesy of Paul Glendell/Natural England.

More remains to be done to realise the principal objective of *Back to purple*, making possible the long march of the ambulatory Emperor Moth caterpillar over a continuous band of heather from Heath Mynd to The Hollies. In particular, conifers and grassland divorce Nipstone from Cranberry Rock, cutting adrift the southern half of The Stiperstones, while at a smaller scale a conifer stand between Black Rhadley and The Rock forms both an ecological barrier and a screen across the finest rock scenery of the entire ridge, an outcrop 'so riven and shattered', wrote Walter White in 1860, 'that you might fancy it the target against which the giants had practised their rock throwing'. Finally, ecological and visual connectivity indicate the restoration of a heathland corridor at the southern end of the ridge between the vigorous heathland of Heath Mynd and the relict heathland of Cefn Gunthly. Here, and, in part, between Nipstone and Cranberry Rocks, heathland has been replaced by grassland. Whilst techniques

Scenery above Rock Farm

This image by the Rev J Parker, from Murchison's *Siluria* (1854), shows the tor above Rock Farm, which lies further to the right. To the left, the River West Onny snakes through the Linley Estate. Behind the tor lies one of the finest boulder fields of the entire ridge.

have been developed for reversion of grassland back to heathland, they have yet to be applied on The Stiperstones. I hope that one day soon they will be.

But much has been achieved so far, and the felling of the trees at Rock Cottage has revealed anew a wonderful rocky skyline and the splendid chaos of the adjacent boulder field. Miss Merry described 'masses of heather all around'. The heather is coming back and with it another step has been taken in restoring the 'boundless heath' of the Singular Stiperstones on which the young Bill Francis wandered.

Once upon a hill

Although the 'final devastation' is being reversed, Miss Merry's cottage, which she thought would stand for 200 or more years, is never likely to be re-built. It is just one of many such remote dwellings that were abandoned in the twentieth century and are now all but gone. In the words of Bill Francis in his 'Lyric to the Stiperstones by one of its sons':

> 'In times long past stood many a lowly cott
> Where happy miners tilled their tiny plot;
> All that remains – a crumbling heap of stones
> And creeping nature claims again its own.'

Or, in the words of Moyra Stewart Wyllie: 'Shells of tumbled habitation' ... 'Grey stones nursing the last warm dregs of summer'.[13]

Blakemoorgate, at the opposite end of the hill to Miss Merry's Rock Cottage, was the last of the isolated little groups of upland habitations to be abandoned. Here a small community had for many years worked their small-holdings and grazed the adjacent heath, and their last representatives, Bob and Fanny Cook at No 1 Blakemoorgate, and their neighbour Edwin (Neddy) Davies at No 2, finally left in the mid 1950s.

Once vacated, properties in such exposed locations soon deteriorate and tend to be pillaged for re-usable materials. Today 'a crumbling heap of stones' is the only reminder of virtually all of them. But Nos 1 and 2 at Blakemoorgate are the exceptions. Some ongoing maintenance had kept No 1 more or less wind and water-tight, but by 2010 No 2 was all but down. In that year however, Natural England finally secured funding from English Heritage, the European Union (through LEADER), the Heritage Lottery Fund and the Onny Valley Book Project, for the restoration of both cottages, work which was completed in 2011.

It is assumed that these homes started life as 'squatters' cottages', hovels thrown together in a day by miners from Snailbeach intent on claiming shelter and land within walking distance of the mine. As such they dovetail admirably with the industrial heritage of Snailbeach which is conserved and interpreted by the ever-industrious volunteers of the Shropshire Mines Trust.

Funding for the restoration of the cottages was secured through successful bids for an over-arching project called *Once upon a hill: the lost communities of The Stiperstones*. The restoration of the cottages was an important strand of the project, another was the recording of oral reminiscences, which, along with census and other historical information, were published in 2011 in a book also called *Once Upon a Hill*.[14] It relates the hey-day and decline of settlements all around the hill, and readers who have persevered thus far will know that along with its sister volume, *Never on a Sunday*, it has been at the heart of *The Singular Stiperstones*. Conserving, restoring, honouring and recording The Stiperstones, its history, heritage, landscape and wildlife is the purpose of *Once upon a hill*, as it is of *Back to purple*, and will be too of the *Stiperstones and Corndon Hill Country Landscape Partnership Scheme*.

The Cook family at Blakemoorgate

This photo, dating probably from the late 1930s, shows Bob Cook (1886-1962), his wife, Fanny (1886-1973) and their children Gordon (1919-1999) and Irene (Rene) (1920-1987). Is Gordon holding a kitten?

Reproduced courtesy of the Cook family.

Bob Cook

This photo is thought to date from about 1952, it was taken at Blakemoorgate; opinions differ as to the identity of the visitor. Reproduced courtesy of the Cook family.

Edwin Davies

Edwin (Neddy) Davies (1882-1971) is seen here in about 1964 astride his pony, Peggy. Reproduced courtesy of his grandson, Clifford Hampson.

Violet Davies

Violet (1910-1992) was the eldest of Edwin Davies's three children; this photo was taken when she was 21. The family lived at Eastridge, but following the death of Edwin's wife, Emily, they moved to Blakemoorgate. Reproduced courtesy of her son, Clifford Hampson.

Bob and Fanny Cook's Cottage, No 1 Blakemoorgate

This painting is understood to be the work of a wartime evacuee; the artist's signature appears to be F Greaves. Note the thatch on the outbuildings to the left and right and the roof linking the latter to the cottage. The painting is reproduced courtesy of Bob and Fanny's grandson, Tony Cook.

Left: the cottage in 1986; photo Tom Wall.

Right: the cottage in April 2008; photo courtesy of Gordon Dickins.

The cottage in 2013, following restoration work in 2010/2011. Note the subterranean 'root store' to the left of the cottage, a feature common to many dwellings on The Stiperstones. Photo Gisèle Wall.

Edwin Davies's Cottage, No 2 Blakemoorgate

The cottage in 1986. Photo Tom Wall.

In 2006. Photo Gisèle Wall.

In 2013, following rebuilding in 2010/2011. Photo Gisèle Wall.

Tailpiece: towards a singular future

Sir Roderick Murchison's observation about the singularity of The Stiperstones relates just to its physical geography - its geology as modified by natural processes. Hopefully I have shown that this singularity extends to a whole range of aspects – mining, transport, lore and legend, literature, reminiscence, human history, wildlife and conservation. All of this singularity flows from the fundamentals of the site's geology together with its physical structure and soils. Without the geology, there would have been no mining, therefore no railway, no ropeway, and an impoverished human history. Without the physical structure, the layers of lore and legend would be lacking, the literature wanting. Without the site's elevation and soils the wildlife would be less distinctive and would not have been enriched in the same way by mining and smallholding. This whole diverse mix, interleaved and intertwined, has led to a singular bookshelf of travelogue, memoir, literature and reminiscence.

However this multiple singularity comes with no guarantee of perpetuity. It has been threatened and eroded and continues to be so. We only begin to conserve once we see loss occurring, and sometimes we allow debilitating losses to accumulate. A loss may however be a spur to conserve what remains. So the destruction of the Halvans Engine House was a spur to the conservation of the fast-crumbling relics of the Snailbeach Mine, while the afforestation and reclamation of large parts of the southern end of The Stiperstones led to the frustration of further such plans and the subsequent declaration of the National Nature Reserve.

But much has, and continues to be, lost. Think for example of the headframes and shafts of the mines, Mountain Pansies and Curlews, locomotives and their tracks, Cuckoos and Whinchats. Little may be possible locally to turn the tide for the last two, and thoughts of restoring tracks and locos are surely pipe-dreams, but conservation of the principal features of the mines, and access to them, is being constantly improved. Meanwhile, the alert has been sounded for Pansies, Curlews and other wildlife and there is now the chance to ensure their survival and increase.

The hope for the future of The Stiperstones lies not just in the recognition and honouring of its singularity, but through the vigilant safeguard of this quality and the tenacious and energetic clawing back of those elements that have been lost. Such is the purpose of the many restoration projects at the mines, of *Back to purple*, *Once upon a hill* and of *Stiperstones and Corndon Hill Country*.

In the words of Emily Griffiths: 'This heritage preserve we must/ For all posterity'. I can only hope that, through highlighting this heritage, *The Singular Stiperstones* will contribute towards its preservation.

Notes and sources

'The hill': an introduction

Notes

1   The figure currently given on Ordnance Survey maps is 536 metres (1,759 feet) above sea level; an edition of 1974 gives 537 metres (1,762 feet) and an edition of 1947 a mere 1,731 feet (528 metres). Note that, in 1947, precedence was accorded to the imperial measure, illustrating how, when drawing on a wide temporal range of sources, a mix of imperial and metric measurements inevitably arises. Imperial is used by most of those who are quoted, and comes to me most naturally in what I have written, but where others have used metric (as here) I have followed their lead.

2   For notes on Ellis Peters and The Stiperstones, see Chapter 6. It seems however that the Devil has not always enjoyed the naming rights for this tor. In a map of 1840 held in Shropshire Archives (ref D3651/F/S/3), the name 'Devil's Chair' is not used, instead the tors to east and west of the ridge-path are referred to collectively as 'Great Rocks'.

3   Wolfestone appears on the map and related documents referred to in the previous note.

4   Camden's Latin text was translated by Philemon Holland, but there are inconsistencies in the modern versions of this translation. The one used here is from an edition by D F Sutton, University of California, 2004.

5   Each July since 1981 'Music at Leasowes Bank' has arranged a series of concerts celebrating an eclectic range of predominantly English music. In the early days concerts were held in the former farmhouse; subsequently, expanding audiences have squeezed into a stone barn, around which a bat patrols as night falls. Inspired perhaps by 'Music at Leasowes Bank', 'Farmer Phil's Music Festival' was founded a mile or so to the south at Near Gatten Farm; here a miniature Glastonbury erupts each August. The year 2013 marked Farmer Phil's 15th festival and the 33rd – but sadly the last – at Leasowes Bank. The 1980s rock band 'Half Man Half Biscuit' have never, it seems, played at Farmer Phil's Festival, but their 2011 album '90 Bisodol (Crimond)', includes the track 'Descent of The Stiperstones'. The hill gets no more than a namecheck however, as the lyricist takes us straight to Bunners of Montgomery in search of a jar of Swarfega!

6   Clark Tracey is a percussionist, son of pianist Stan Tracey, 'the godfather of British jazz'; the other members of the Quintet who performed at Leasowes Bank were Steve Melling (piano), Guy Barker (trumpet), Jamie Talbot (tenor saxophone) and Alec Dankworth (double bass); Alec is son of John Dankworth and Cleo Laine, two other major figures in British jazz. The Quintet recorded *Stiperstones* (Steam SJ115) and subsequently took it on a tour supported by the British Council which included a number of venues in the Far East. Clark Tracey brought *Stiperstones* to the Leasowes Bank Festival again (in 2006) and in 2008 to the Mary Webb School, Pontesbury, when it was performed as part of a celebration of the twenty-fifth anniversary of the declaration of The Stiperstones National Nature Reserve.

7   Coles (1998), pp 11-12.

8   Interestingly, the names Perkins Bach and Mytton Bach appear in documentation of 1847 (Foxall 1984).

Sources

Allott A 2011

Bradley A G 1905

Coles G M 1998

Foxall H D G 1984

Fraser A 1983

Gelling M 2000

Lawrence D H 1925

Mais S P B 1939

Merry J 1979

Morgan R 1997

Morton G H 1869

Murchison R I 1839

Perrin J 2003

Peters E 1999

Saville M 1944

Timperley H W 1947

Weale M 1935

Webb M 1916

Chapter 1 'The singular Stiperstones': geology and landscape

Notes

1 Michael Rosenbaum and Peter Toghill point out in correspondence that Arthur Aikin published his findings on the geology of the area before Murchison, to whom he made available his notebooks; the Rev James Yates also wrote about the area before Murchison's first visit.

2 Ross (2000).

3 Peter Toghill lives in Church Stretton. A university lecturer, he was formerly a geologist with the British Geological Survey and the Natural History Museum. He is the author of *Geology of Britain* (2000) as well as *Geology of Shropshire* (1990 and 2006), various guides and numerous papers. In 2001 he was awarded the Geological Society of London's R K Worth Prize for the promotion of the public understanding of geology.

4 Whilst acknowledging that the 'Silurian kingdom' was centred on South Wales, Murchison argued that its limits probably extended north and east to the banks of the Severn. However, Sinclair & Fenn (1999) point out that Murchison benefited from the practical support, patronage and hospitality of 'the border squires', not least the Lewises of Harpton Court on the Radnorshire-Herefordshire border, who owned a farm and farmhouse built of the local limestone. The farm was, and still is, called 'Siluria', leading to speculation that this was at the origin of Murchison's naming of the geological period.

5 Shropshire Archives D3651/F/S/3/10; the statement was taken as evidence in a boundary dispute. It is unclear as to precisely what was whitewashed, but the wording may indicate that it was not what is now referred to as the Devil's Chair but the two un-named tors which lie to its southeast; all three are visible from Attingham Hall. I am indebted to James Lawson for drawing my attention to this curiosity.

6 The story of Thomas Edwards is an interesting one. His father, Samuel, died in 1875 at the age of 46 in an accident at Snailbeach Mine (Brown 2005). Thomas was 16 at the time, and it is said that his pay was immediately raised from that of a boy to that of a man, so that he could support his mother and his five sisters. Later in life, when Thomas moved to the Paddock House, he made his late father's house over to the Methodist Circuit for use as a meeting house. Thomas's daughter Mabel (1897-1985) married George Lewis (1894-1985); one of their two children, Clifford (1923-2004), of Welsh Row and The Old Post Office, Pennerley, is mentioned on a number of occasions in this book. The information given here was gathered by Clifford and passed on by his widow, Verna.

7 Brown (1971).

8 Clark (1994).

9 *The Golden Arrow* (1916).

10 This photo shows the effects of fire. The two tors are predominantly grey because the stone is covered with a film of lichens, but to their left the stone glistens white where fires have burned away this film revealing the true colour of the stone. Richard Clark found isolated masses of peat up to about 60cm thick on parts of the tors and at other locations too. He thought that they were 'residuals of a once-extensive peat cover'; presumably, over the years, this had been burned away by fires. On 9 April 1941 'incendiary bombs [had] rained down along the length of The Stiperstones' (*Never on a Sunday*) when, for unknown reasons, the area was 'attacked' by German bombers; widespread hill fires are said to have resulted. Some of the peat cover may have been burned off at this time, and there is certainly much rocky ground evident in this photo of 1955. However, Frank Pinches (born 1939), tells me that as a child, after the War, he rode in a pony and trap along the highest part of the ridge, something that is inconceivable today due to all the exposed stone. It may be, therefore, that it was the major

fire of the hot, dry, summer of 1976 which burned off the remaining peat from the track along the spine of the hill. Since then the stretch from Cranberry Rock to beyond the Devil's Chair has been rocky throughout. Years ago I drove it in a Land Rover in order to see whether, in an emergency, it was drivable. I got through, but only just.

11   Although nowadays referred to as 'barite', the name 'barytes' is employed throughout this book as this was the word used during the mining period.

Sources

Allott A 2011

Brown I J 2005

Brown M J F 1971

Clark R 1994

Collie M & Diemer J 1995

Dean W T 1967

Dictionary of National Biography

Earp J R & Hains B A 1971

Francis P, Price J & Yapp K 2000

Fraser A 1983

Goudie A S & Piggott N R 1981

Lapworth C 1887

Morton G H 1869

Murchison R I 1835

Murchison R I 1839

Murchison R I 1854

Piggott N R 1977

Rosenbaum M 1996

Ross J 2000

Saville M & O'Hanlon M 1998

Sinclair J B & Fenn R W D 1999

Toghill P 1992

Toghill P 2006

Timperley H W 1947

Weale M 1935

Webb M 1916

Whittard W F 1966

Whittard W F (compiled by W T Dean) 1979

Chapter 2 'Wold ancient mines': miners and mining

Notes

1   The *Memoir* was edited by W Benson of Hertford. Benson was related to the Gilpins of Pulverbatch and it was through them that he came to know Samuel Hughes. The Reverend William Gilpin (1757-1848), rector of Pulverbatch for 42 years, was the son of the Reverend William Gilpin (1724-1804), celebrated exponent of 'the picturesque' in landscape appreciation. The pious lives of the younger Gilpin's children and those of their relatives and acquaintances, including Samuel Hughes, are related in *More Than Notion* by J H Alexander (1964). The Bodleian Libraries' copy of the *Memoir* has the shelfmark (OC) 200 i. 62 (13).

2   Coles (1978) suggests that Mary Webb's 'the Clays' was Pennerley. It seems to me that Snailbeach fits Webb's description of Nancy Corra's surroundings rather better.

3   This is one of two short stories by Mary Webb published in 1923 under the title 'Glimpses of Old Shropshire', first in the *Transactions of the Caradoc and Severn Valley Field Club* and subsequently in the *Shrewsbury Chronicle*; the other story is entitled 'Shrewsbury's Abbey Fair'. She also wrote a poem entitled 'Viroconium'.

4   The full name was Viroconium Cornoviorum, 'the settlement of Virico of the Cornovii tribe'.

5   Shaw (2009).

6   This assumption is drawn from White (2000) who points to the discovery of slave-gang chains found in the gold mines worked by the Romans at Dolaucothi, Wales.

7   Hugh Hannaford reports finding possible 'bole' sites at The Hollies, above Snailbeach, during his 'walk-over' archaeology survey (Hannaford 2006).

8   An earlier authority (Whittick 1932) states that the Shropshire pigs had been 'de-silvered', ie their silver content had been extracted, and that the palm-branch symbol may well have indicated that the lead had undergone this process.

9   This building, which dates from the mid-nineteenth century, was used as a barracks where men who lived some distance away stayed during the week; it also served as a place where the miners changed before and after their shift. Today it is used by the Shropshire Mines Trust to house artefacts and a display, and is regularly opened to visitors.

10 The shrine may have been made elsewhere and brought to Wroxeter, or made at Wroxeter from recycled lead objects from a variety of sources. It is also conceivable that it was made on site from lead brought from The Stiperstones, but the fourth century date attributed to it (Lloyd-Morgan 2000), post-dates significantly the pigs of lead, which are the only clear evidence of mining by the Romans at The Stiperstones.

11 'A 'Forest' is land on which the king (or some other magnate) has the right to keep deer. This is the original sense of the word: to the medievals a Forest was a place of deer, not a place of trees' (Oliver Rackham (1986) *The History of the Countryside*). About a third of the 142 royal and private Forests, including The Stiperstones, were chiefly moorland.

12 James Lawson (unpublished).

13 Shaw (2009).

14 Here, and subsequently, this text follows the lead of Shaw (2009) when attributing a lower or upper case 'c' to 'company'. Shaw applies a lower case 'c' to enterprises which pre-date the Companies Acts of the mid nineteenth century, because prior to this 'company' had no legal significance. He reserves 'Company' with a capital 'C' for joint stock companies, where the word does have legal significance.

15 From Brown (1993).

16 Information on mine employment is from Shaw (2009).

17 The Earl of Tankerville also owned 'The Crown'; the Marquess of Bath owned 'The Cross Guns' and Lord Rowton 'The Miners' Arms'. This and other information comes from the 'Return of Licensed Houses' for 1901 and an exhibition about the pubs and inns of southwest Shropshire put together in 2006 by David and Janet Preshous, on behalf of the South-West Shropshire Historical and Archaeological Society, for Bishop's Castle's Michaelmas Fair.

18 John Sproson continues to manage the adjacent Stores. He is something of a legend in his own lifetime, celebrated for his maverick behaviour and his individuality as a retailer (his shop is described on the family website as a 'bizarre bazaar'). He keeps his two racehorses adjacent to the Inn, and when beyond pensionable age, trotted around with them in his wake, and rode and fell from them on the hazardous terrain of The Stiperstones; he still rides in amateur races at Ludlow. An earlier celebrity resident was William Humphrey (1882-1963) whose wife, Esther, ran the Inn in the 1930s and '40s. He was a renowned dog breeder, particularly of the famous Llewellin Setters, and a falconer, whose mews included 'Lady Ben Nevis', a Golden Eagle, which he flew on The Long Mynd and elsewhere. This was courtesy of Max Wenner of Batchcott Hall who owned The Long Mynd at the time. William Humphrey inherited The Long Mynd when, in 1937, Wenner died mysteriously in a fall from an aeroplane. George Evans (see Chapter 3) worked for some time as chauffeur to Max Wenner.

19 Quoted by Brown (1995).

20 Seeking to tie novelists' descriptions to specific locations can be pointless, as they will often be amalgams, translocations or largely imaginary. However, as indicated here, a good case can be made for nominating 'Tin House' as Stephen Southernwood's cottage and placing Mary Webb's 'Lostwithin' hamlet and mine in Perkins Beach, rather than at The Bog, as is usually suggested.

21 Anon (1898).

22 Old Shaft is also known as George's Shaft – the engineman for 21 years at the time of the disaster was George Williams.

23 This recalls a humorous observation by Emily Griffiths about another chapel inscription. Describing the old Chapel House in Perkins Beach she mentions a large inscription at the back of the congregation, facing the preacher; she says that it was 'always a joke locally', reading, as it did: 'Prepare to meet thy God'. Emily gave the land on which a new chapel was later to be built, performing the opening ceremony in 1993.

24 It was Thomas Thynne (1765-1837), the Second Marquess of Bath, who is said to have declined to provide land for a chapel for the Baptists. However, in 1875, John Alexander Thynne (1831-1896), the Fourth Marquess, granted a lease of land on which the Methodist Chapel at Snailbeach was built, and this despite the Marquess apparently being a devout Anglo-Catholic. The involvement of mine captains as trustees may have been an astute move by the Methodists, and Enoch Parry (see note 27), Chief Agent of the New Central Snailbeach Mining Company, and a staunch Methodist, was one of three named as holders of the lease.

25 The Chapel had been rebuilt and enlarged in 1873 with a seating capacity of 350. Today the congregation meets in the former 'Ore House' (where crushed lead was formerly stored) at Snailbeach, but the Chapel itself is still used for informal monthly prayer meetings. Much of the information about the Chapel is drawn from a note by Blake Dalton in newsletter 38 of the Shropshire Mines Trust, Spring 2006

26 According to Margaret Corfield (1961), the Earl was accompanied by his wife, their two sons, his mother-in-law and a small retinue of servants; they were accommodated at Prospect House, Snailbeach. Margaret Corfield, who would have been about 19 at the time, reports that the Earl had large quantities of venison brought down from his Chillingham Castle Estate.

This was distributed to his Stiperstones tenants but it failed to meet with unanimous approval. Margaret Corfield contributed a number of articles to the *Shropshire Magazine* in the 1950s and '60s, some of which are referred to in the pages that follow. One of her daughters, Emily Griffiths, is quoted above (see note 23), and will be, on many other occasions, throughout this book.

27 Enoch Parry's story is a particularly interesting one; it is related by Andy Cuckson (2004). He left the mines on health grounds in 1881 and set up 'Central Stores' at Crowsnest, a shop which, though it finally closed in 1953, still figures prominently in the memories of older residents and is included in reminiscences quoted in this book.

28 Lerry (1952). In addition to writing about Henry Dennis, George G Lerry (1883-1971) editor of the *Wrexham Leader*, published books and articles on Denbighshire collieries, Welsh railways, Welsh football and the Archbishop of Wales.

29 Allbutt & Brook (1969).

30 Lerry (1952).

31 Pearce (2008).

32 Brown (2005).

33 Biographical details for Alfred Hewitt are drawn from Brown (1997).

34 Ivor Brown believes that the pump will have been named after a major shareholder, but if so, her surname has yet to be determined.

35 Shaw (2009).

36 By the 1870s it became cheaper to use better quality coal brought by rail to Minsterley rather than inferior coal from Pontesbury (Andy Cuckson, personal communication).

37 Shropshire Archives, referenced SA mi 6750. 'Signal rapper': by reference to the term as used in other mining areas it appears that this was a device used to signal to the engineman that men or materials were ready to be raised or lowered up or down the shaft.

38 Shaw (2009).

39 Brown (1990); Shaw (2009); Brown (2005).

40 Brown (2001).

41 Evans (1997/98).

42 The band continued up until about 1937. Following a long hiatus it was re-formed in 1972; it is now known as 'Stiperstones Brass' (Evans 1997/98).

43 Brook (1976).

44 Authorities differ as to the duration of activities at Snailbeach. The dates given here are from Pearce (2008). According to Shaw (2009), underground working at Snailbeach had ceased by 1950, but the working of the tip for calcite continued into the 1980s.

45 This statement was first used by the Shropshire Caving and Mining Club in the representations made to the County Council in 1979; it has subsequently been endorsed by other authorities.

Sources

Adams D, Brown I J & Lake K 2008

Alexander J H 1964

Allbutt M & Brook F 1969

Anon 1898

Benson W (ed) 1878

Brook F 1976

Brook F & Allbutt M 1973

Brown I J 1976

Brown I J 1990

Brown I J 1993

Brown I J 1995

Brown I J 1997

Brown I J 2001

Brown I J 2005b

Brown I J 2005c

Coles G M 1978

Corfield M 1961

Cuckson A 2004

Evans G circa 1994

Evans P 1997/8

Francis P (no date)

Francis P, Price J & Yapp K 2000

Hannaford H R 2006

Hooson W 1747

Lerry G G 1952

Lloyd-Morgan G 2000

More J 1978

Morton G H 1869

Murchison R I 1839

Pearce A (ed) 1995

Pearce A (ed) 1997

Pearce A (ed) 2008

Reid Chappell W 1930

Saville M 1949

Shaw M 2007

Shaw M 2009

Shropshire Mines Trust Newsletters

Silouan P-M 2011a

Silouan P-M 2011b

Silouan P-M 2013

Smith B 1922

Weale M 1935

Webb M 1916

Webb M 1917

Webb M 1977

White R 2000

Wright T 1872

Chapter 3 'Tushing and lugging': transport by road, rail and you name it

Notes

1 Roneo was one of the most popular makes of mimeograph or stencil duplicator machines, a cheap form of printing in which ink was forced through the perforations made by the keys of a type-writer in a wax stencil.

2 Forty-five instalments were published in the *Snailbeach District News* but *A Voice from the Hills* is in 40 instalments.

3 Potter's Pit was a small lead mine. It is said to owe its name to the purity of its ore which was suitable for use in pottery glazes (Shaw 2009).

4 The 'Ventor' Mine was in Perkins Beach. In official documents it was called the 'Venture' or 'New Venture' Mine but the local pronunciation is 'Ventor' or 'Ventnor'.

5 'The Devil's Chair car park' is the one at The Knolls serving the National Nature Reserve.

6 According to a number of authorities the actual gauge used, as opposed to proposed, was 2 ft 3¾ inches.

7 'Belmont' and 'Fernhill' were respectively the names of the residences of Colonel Heaton Lovett and John Henkin Lovett, both of them directors of the SDR (Tonks 1974). According to the Shropshire Mines Trust they were descendants of Thomas Lovett one of the founders, in 1783, of the Snailbeach company (see Chapter 2). In the 1950 edition of his account Eric Tonks gives Henniker as John Lovett's second name.

8 Cuckson (2001) states that there is no known date for the photograph but observes that the locomotive looks fairly new, which would suggest a date in the 1880s. Although Cuckson attributes the photo to Albert Hewitt he subsequently (in correspondence) shed doubt on the attribution and it cannot now be verified. Brown (2001) believes it was taken in about 1918, however, according to Tonks (1974) 'Fernhill' was scrapped either in 1906 or during the First World War.

9 This and other supporting information comes from Andy Cuckson's researches which contradict Eric Tonks's claim of a decline during the war years.

10 Colonel Stephens' father was a member of the Pre-Raphaelite Brotherhood and he named his son after another member, the artist Holman Hunt, the boy's godfather.

11 'Stephens became an expert in the provisions of the Light Railways Act of 1896. The legislation was intended to open up rural areas not served by the main line railways by relaxing construction and safety standards in return for restricted speeds (usually a maximum of 25 mph)' (Colonel Stephens Society 2011).

12 Tractor haulage is well documented. The tractor ran with two wheels between the rails and two outside. This was possible because, whilst the SDR operated on narrow gauge track, the Act of 1873, under which the railway was established, required that the earthworks on which the track was laid should be wide enough to accommodate standard gauge track.

13 The mystery is compounded by Eric Tonks naming 'Fitter-Driver Gatford' in his 'Acknowledgements', indicating, surely, that he had had personal contact with him.

14 I am indebted to Ivor Brown for this and many other pieces of documentary evidence (Brown 2001).

15 According to the web site for 'Batchcote Hall', Max Wenner was of Swiss and Austrian descent. He was born into a family of wealthy Manchester industrialists. Said to have Nazi connections, he made frequent flights between England and Germany, on the last of which, in 1937, he fell to his death.

16 This was the original 'charabanc', a word adopted from the French 'char-à-banc'; a 'char' is a wagon or cart, and a 'banc' is a bench, ie a wagon with benches.

Sources

Austin A 2008

Baker A C 2001

Brook F & Allbutt M 1973

Brown I J 2001

Corfield M 1961

Cuckson A 2001

Evans G circa 1994

Francis P, Price J & Yapp K 2000

Hannaford H R 2006

Jones I M 2009

Lawrence D H 1925

Morgan J S 1999

Pearce A (ed) 2008

Redwood C 1981

Saville M 1944

Saville M 1949

Shaw M 2009

Strange P 1989

The Colonel Stephens Museum

Colonel Stephens Society 2011

Tonks E S 1950, 1974

Tudor G (ed) circa 2000

Weaver R 1977

Webb M 1917

Chapter 4 'Diafol Mountain': lore and legend

Notes

1   Katherine M Briggs (1978) in an essay on the history of the Folklore Society introducing a volume marking the Society's centenary.

2   A 'shechinah' is 'a radiant light symbolizing God's presence' (*Oxford English Dictionary*). Mary Webb's 'grey shechinah' would seem to be a sombre pall symbolizing the presence of the Devil! The notion of a weather-shrouded Chair being tenanted by Beelzebub is taken up by Emily Griffiths who, in addition to reminiscing knowledgeably about The Stiperstones, produced a collection of verse including 'The Devil's Chair Legend':

> 'So now, when fog obscures the light
> Or thunder-clouds hang, black as night
> With bated breath folks say "He's there,
> The Devil's sitting in his chair".'

Another local poet, Brenda Shaw (1917-1975) , uses 'broad Shropshire' to give expression to the same notion in her poem 'The Devil's Chair':

> 'When thunder claps re echo
> Locals are thought to say,
> Each sagely nodding head to head,
> "Ee be a wum today".' [He be at home today]

3   Charlotte Burne states 'or 1854' but the Crimean War started in 1853.

4   Charlotte Burne notes that she 'never succeeded in getting a second version of this curious story', nor could she trace the original teller. Jennifer Westwood (1985) suggests that 'we might well be chary of accepting at face value some of the features of her tale, which includes details of Saxon costume which sound as if they have been added on [by others] for "authenticity"'. Charlotte Burne notes that 'the name given to Edric's wife, the "Lady Godda" curiously coincides with that of Frau Gauden or Gode', the German huntress whose declaration 'The chase is better than Heaven' condemned her to follow it to eternity. Jennifer Westwood is reluctant to accept that the name Lady Godda is derived from English tradition and speculates that it may have been added in by someone familiar with Jacob Grimm's account of Frau Gauden published in 1835.

5   Hughes (1977).

6   This is evident from Mrs Marston's show exhibits which include: '1906, plums; 1908, gooseberries; 1909, cherries, sugarless'.

7   For a detailed discussion see Armstrong (1970).

8   Context and call make clear that Mary Webb is referring to Wigeon, yet in her *Shropshire Word Book* (1879) Georgina Jackson states that the name 'Magpie Widgeon' is used for a very different duck, the Goosander. The latter's flight call is a croak not a whistle.

9   Outdoor services known as 'camp meetings' were very popular occasions, drawing worshippers from all round the hill.

10 Mulroy (no date).

11 This comes from an article published in the *Shrewsbury Chronicle* of 8 June 2000.

12 Rolt (1910-1974) was a historian of engineering, a professional author of more than 30 books, and devotee of vintage cars, canal boats, narrow gauge railways and industrial archaeology.

He played a major part in the rescue of the Talyllyn Railway. At a later date (the 1960s) rails removed from the defunct Snailbeach District Railway saw further service on the Talyllyn.

13   Mary Webb's words for this song are:

> 'We have sought it, we have sought the golden arrow!
> (Bright the sally-willows sway)
> Two and two by paths low and narrow,
> Arm in crook along the mountain way.
> Break o' frost and break o' day!
> Some were sobbing through the gloom
> When we found it, when we found the golden arrow –
> Wand of willow in the secret cwm.'

W Reid Chappell states that Mary Webb wrote the words having heard a rendering of 'a semi-revivalist hymn popular in these parts, "God be with you till we meet again",' and that the words of the 'Golden Arrow Song' fit the tune perfectly.

14   Andy Cuckson advises that it is referred to as 'Mutton Dingle' on Henry Dennis's survey of 1872 for the Snailbeach District Railway.

15   The age of the document from which this quotation is drawn is unclear but it appears to date from the second half of the seventeenth century (Shropshire Archives 1037//2/21). Clearly if this is the case, the date 1745 would have been inscribed later.

16   This account is drawn largely from Nicholas (1990).

17   See Somerville C (2008) *Britain and Ireland's Best Wild Places*.

18   From an account by Frances Williams of 'Music at Leasowes Bank'.

Sources

Armstrong E A 1970

Ashman G & Bennett G 2000

Bennett G 2001

Briggs K M 1978

Burne C S 1883, 1885, 1886

Coles G M 1978

Corfield M 1955

Dictionary of National Biography

Foxton H D G 1984

Francis P (no date)

Francis P (ed) 1992

Francis P, Price J & Yapp K 2000

Griffiths E 1990

Hands M J 2012

Hughes J 1977

Jackson G F 1879-81

Lawrence D H 1925

Map W 1923

Mulroy B (no date)

Nicholas J D 1990

'Nimrod' 1837

Palmer R 2004

Peters E 1992

Reid Chappell W R 1930

Ridge R 1937

Rolt L T C 1994

Shaw B 2012

Simpson J 2003

Sustins N 2008

Tonge S 2007

Weale M 1935

Webb M 1916

Webb M 1917

Webb M 1924

Webb M 1929

Westwood J 1985

Williams W H 1967

Wright T 1862

Chapter 5 'Natural magic': the novels and nature of Mary Webb

Notes

1   From the Introduction to *Gone to Earth* in the *Collected Works of Mary Webb* published by Jonathan Cape in 1928. John Buchan (1875-1940) was a writer and politician; he is best known for his novel *The Thirty-Nine Steps* (1915).

2   W Reid Chappell (1930) provides a photo (reproduced here) which appears to be of 'Tin House', though it shows no tin! He refers to it as the home of Deborah Arden and Stephen Southernwood, though their fictional cottage would have been closer to the Devil's Chair.

3   Whilst Lostwithin is generally considered to be the Bog Mine, the New Venture Mine in Perkins Beach seems to me a better candidate. Other locations have been suggested including both Snailbeach Mine and Cothercott Mine which lies to the east of The Stiperstones.

4   Philip French in the *The Observer*, 7 August 2005.

5   The production, by the Shared Experience Theatre Company, toured various southern theatres in Spring 2004.

6   From the review by Susannah Clapp in *The Observer*, 16 May 2004.

7   'Hollywood Comes to Shropshire. The Making of Mary Webb's *Gone to Earth*', QV Productions, 1998.

8   The Lordshill Project began in 2005 and aimed to record the memories of those who took part in or watched the filming, as well as providing background information; the two CDs were released in 2006, further material is archived.

9   This analysis was done for a lecture given by the author in 1995 to the Summer School of the Mary Webb Society.

10 The 'pencilled chickens' are the Whimbrel chicks with pencil-like markings on their plumage.

11 A fair assumption, because not only was Mary Webb a student of nature, but also, according to W Reid Chappell (1930), H E Forrest was 'a great friend' of hers.

12 The nearest breeding location is in northern Scotland.

13 For Mary Webb the two bird names become interchangeable. In *The Golden Arrow* the cries of both Curlew and Whimbrel are likened to the sound of broken glass. The 'elfin peals' of the Whimbrel in *Seven for a Secret* are echoed by the 'elfin music' of the Curlews in *The Golden Arrow*. And in her poem 'On the Wild Hill' (Webb 1987) she refers to 'pencilled Curlew chickens', thereby duplicating the description of 'Whimbrel chickens' from *Seven for a Secret*.

Sources

Coles G M 1978	Hardy T 1878	Thomson D 1993
Coles G M 1990	Hardy T 1891	Wall T 2003
Edmundson H 2004	Powell M 1992	Webb M 1916
Forrest H E 1899	Reid Chappell W 1930	Webb M 1917
Francis P, Price J & Yapp K 2000	Saville M 1943	Webb M 1922
Gibbons S 1932	Sharrock J T R 1976	Webb M 1987

Chapter 6   'The aboriginal hill': literature and tourism

Notes

1   Some authorities give 1885 as the year of his birth.

2   Additional material comes from David Ellis's third volume of 'The Cambridge Biography' of Lawrence (1998). I have drawn too on the introduction by Mara Kalnins to a 1995 edition of Lawrence's posthumously published *Apocalypse*, and on Carter's own writings.

3   Clark (1998) gives 'The Deanery' as Carter's home in Pontesbury, but according to Ellis (1998) he was living at 'The Rectory', while Francis (2003) says he was at 'The Manor House'. Peter Francis has explained to me that the confusion arises from the parish of Pontesbury having been divided at one time into three 'Portions', 'Rectories' or 'Prebends', each with its own Rector, each of whom had his own dwelling, these being named 'The Deanery', the 'Manor House' and 'The Old Rectory'.

4   Carter (1932).

5   Lawrence named it Kiowa Ranch after the Indian tribe which had once camped in the area.

6   Lawrence appears confused in matters of geology (the rock is Stiperstones Quartzite not granite) and territoriality (does English blood really run in Welsh veins?!).

7   Mara Kalnins in her introduction to the Penguin edition of *Apocalypse* (1995).

8   It was however published as an essay in *The London Mercury* of July 1930. *The Dragon of Revelation* was later revised and reissued as *Symbols of Revelation* (1934). See Mara Kalnins for this and other information on the complicated history of *Apocalypse*, of Carter's work and of his association with Lawrence. She notes *inter alia* that the immediate fruits of their early contacts had been essays by Lawrence entitled 'On Being Religious' and 'On Human Destiny', published in the *Adelphi* magazine in February and March 1924. She adds that their discussion of the dragon emblem in Revelation clearly influenced Lawrence who made it the central symbol of his novel *The Plumed Serpent*.

9   In the case of L S Lowry the connection is too tenuous for inclusion in the body of the text, but it is perhaps worth recording here that his biographer, Shelley Rohde, states that Harold Timperley commissioned Lowry, who had illustrated Timperley's *A Cotswold Book*, to provide illustrations for a new title 'The Shropshire Book'; this would have been in 1942. All but two of the illustrations were complete (they were drawn from photographs) when the publishers said they wanted photographs instead. It is not known what happened to the completed drawings, but Claire Stewart, Curator of the L S Lowry Collection at The Lowry, Salford, advises me that a pencil drawing entitled 'From the Stiperstones' and dated 1942 is mentioned in auction catalogues, most recently in 1981, but no image of the work is known to her. Oddly, the book subsequently published in 1947 by Timperley was entitled *The Shropshire Hills*, and was illustrated not by photographs, but with drawings by Albert T Pile FRSA (1882-1981) a gifted but little-known artist; they include one distant and rather featureless view of The Stiperstones. Timperley's book is discussed at a later point in this chapter.

10   Rowland Hilder was later to state 'My life had taken a decisive turn, meanwhile, when Jonathan Cape commissioned me to illustrate a special edition of *Precious Bane*, that enormously popular novel by Mary Webb, in 1928' (Hilder 1987). Wren Howard of Jonathan Cape arranged for Hilder to stay for several weeks in Mary Webb's former home, Spring Cottage at Lyth Hill (Lewis 1978). It was a seminal time: 'The experience of working as an artist in the depths of an English winter opened my eyes to an aspect of landscape painting which, so far as I could see, no English painter had tackled before. It was an opportunity to look at landscape that appealed to my draughtsman's eye – showing the bare bones of winter – and to set off, at last, on the road to becoming a painter' (Hilder 1987). And it is for his paintings of the English countryside in winter – 'Hilderscapes' – that he became renowned.

11 *Precious Bane* is generally acknowledged to be the finest of Mary Webb's novels; it has been adapted for television and the theatre. It is set amongst the Shropshire meres, but Felena, one of its minor characters, comes from the Shropshire Hills.

12 The novel on which she was working was *Armour Wherein He Trusted*; it remained incomplete at her death in October 1927. What survives is however a fragment complete in itself; it was published in 1929. The novel is centred on 'Polrebec', which is Castle Pulverbatch, three miles to the northeast of The Stiperstones.

13 *The Flower of Light* (1978).

14 For further information about Magdalene Weale see 'A Biographical Report on Magdalene M Weale' by Mark O'Hanlon (2010) www.MagdaleneWeale.co.uk

15 'Nimrod' was the pen name of the sporting writer Charles James Apperley (1777-1843) author of *Memoirs of the Life of the late John Mytton* (1837); see Chapter 4.

16 Garlands placed on the coffins of young girls who had died unmarried – especially if they were engaged to be married at the time of their death – and then displayed in the church; the custom is said to have died out at the end of the eighteenth century.

17 However, in a later article, Jim Perrin says that having first read Mary Webb in his youth he still re-reads her with pleasure. Perrin was born in Manchester, he was a leading British rock-climber of the 1960s and '70s and today writes on mountaineering and environmental topics.

18 The road to Basra was followed in 1991 by Iraqi troops retreating from Kuwait during the Gulf War. They were harried and bombed by coalition forces and presumably Perrin is referring to the shocking images of soldiers' corpses that subsequently appeared in the media.

19 See 'Publishing History' by John Allsup in the 2006 edition of *Seven White Gates* published by Girls Gone By Publishers, Bath.

20 Nor do I recall a visit made to the River Teme near Leintwardine, setting for Saville's *The Secret of the Gorge* (1958). The site was later to become Downton Gorge National Nature Reserve of which, like The Stiperstones, I was extremely fortunate to become the first Warden in 1986.

21 From the introduction to *The Silent Hills of Shropshire* which was written by Malcolm Saville in 1978. He produced a synopsis, wrote parts of all seven chapters, but completed only the Introduction and the first chapter before his death in 1982. The book was eventually completed and published in 1998 by Mark O'Hanlon, a co-founder, in 1994, of the Malcolm Saville Society. In 2001, Mark's biography of Malcolm Saville entitled *Beyond the Lone Pine* was published; this followed on from his *The Complete Lone Pine* (1996), a literary gazetteer and exploration of Lone Pine fiction and Lone Pine country.

22 Pauline Fisk lives in Shropshire and is the author of 11 children's books of which *Midnight Blue* was the first; it won the Smarties Book Prize 1990.

23 I owe the information and reflections in this paragraph to Peter Francis.

24 Ida Gandy was the author of eight books (autobiography, family history, history and children's stories) and ten plays (Gandy 1989, Redd 2012).

25 The official account of this visit was published in the *Salopian and West Midland Journal* in 1877 and reproduced in *Below!* (2001.3) thanks to Ivor J Brown. It puts a more positive spin on the weather conditions than the report that Alice shared with her diary. She records that her group was 'enveloped in mist'. By contrast, the published account is lyrical: 'The view was magnificent, the somewhat stormy sky, with gleams of sunshine, giving great charm and variety to the scene, while the refreshing breeze made the toilsome ascent less fatiguing than in hot sunshine'.

26   The 'Log Book' of Thos J(?) Poole. Shropshire Archives, referenced SA mi 6750.

27   Much of the information in this section is drawn from Ivor Brown's series on 'Nineteenth century visitors to the South West Shropshire Mines' in *Below!*.

28   Jasper More was conservative MP for Ludlow; he was knighted on his retirement from politics in 1979. Julian Critchley, a fellow Conservative MP, described him as 'the last of the Tory party's "library squires", a tall cultured man with the most exquisite manners' (Critchley & Paterson no date). Jasper More, with the help of his wife, Clare, did much to restore the flagging fortunes of his long-established Shropshire family and their estate and residence at Linley. The demise and restoration of his family's affairs is told with much charm and humour in *A Tale of Two Houses*, these being Linley Hall, Shropshire and Westport House in County Mayo, the seat of his mother's family, the Brownes, Marquesses of Sligo.

29   Haffey (1999).

30   To cater for less able walkers and wheel-chair users, English Nature established an 'All-ability Trail' leading from the car park at The Knolls. The trail was opened in 2002; it formed part of the *Back to purple* project.

31   In 2013 there were 489 participants of which 381 completed the course within 24 hours. The fastest time to date is 7 hours 51 minutes recorded by Andrew Davies in 2007.

32   In 2013, 357 registered for the start and 262 completed the course within an hour.

33   Taylor *et al* (2005).

34   National Trust (2005).

35   The obituary was published on 11 November 1987.

Sources

Byford-Jones W 1937

Brown I J 2001b

Brown I J 2001c

Brown I J 2002

Brown I J 2003

Brown I J 2005

Carter F 1926

Carter F 1931

Carter F 1932

Clark R G 1998

Coles G M 1978

Coles G M 1990

Critchley J & Paterson D (no date)

Dickins G 1987

Dictionary of National Biography

Ellis D 1998

Evans P 2002

Fisk P 1990

Francis P 2003

Francis P, Price J & Yapp K 2000

Gandy C 1989

Gandy I 1970

Haffey D 1999

Hilder R 1987

Horton S 1937

Horton S 1938

Lawrence D H 1925

Lawrence D H 1931

Lawrence D H 1995

Lewis J 1978

Lewis M 2003

More J 1978

National Trust 2005

O'Hanlon M 1996

O'Hanlon M 2001

Perrin J 1986

Perrin J 2003

Peters E 1964

Peters E 1999

Pither R G 2003

Redd D 2012

Reid Chappell W 1930

Rohde S 1999

Saville M 1944

Saville M 1949

Saville M 1953

Saville M 1962

Saville M & O'Hanlon M 1998

Taylor K, Anderson P, Taylor R, Longden K & Fisher P 2005

Timperley H W 1947

Trumper D 2001

Waite V 1970

Weale M 1935

White W 1860

Wood J 1944

Chapter 7 'The natural web': habitats and wildlife

Notes

1   The Field Studies Council is an educational charity providing opportunities for people of all ages to discover and understand the natural environment; it has 17 centres, 14 of which, including Preston Montford, are residential.

2   The Shropshire Conservation Trust is now known as the Shropshire Wildlife Trust.

3   Wynne (1986).

4   'Coincidence maps' plot the number of species occurring within a given recording unit from a selection known to be favoured by particular ecological conditions. One use for the technique is the highlighting of 'species-rich' examples of particular habitat types, an important tool in prioritising nature conservation effort.

5   Sinker (1962).

6   For this brief biography of Charles Sinker I have drawn on obituaries written by Philip Oswald, Ian Trueman and John Packham, together with information kindly supplied by his family and friends.

7   Gimingham (1972).

8   Rodwell (1991-2000). The plant communities listed here are prefaced by 'H', indicating heathland; 'MG', indicating mesotrophic grassland ie grassland growing on soils which are moderately well endowed with plant nutrients; 'U', upland and 'W', woodland.

9   Other spellings include Whimberry, Winberry and Wimberry, the last two being the main ones given by Georgina Jackson (see Chapter 4) in her *Shropshire Word-Book* of 1879; she maintains that 'Winberry is a contraction of Wine-berry, an old name for the fruit'. Mary Webb favoured Wimberry and this spelling is retained in quotations from her work. Amongst names used elsewhere in Britain are Whortleberry, Blaeberry, Whorts, Hurts and Urts.

10   Local botanist Kate Thorne found it in three places in 2002 (Lockton & Whild 2005).

11   Pedley (2009).

12   At a later date, when in conversation with Delaine Haynes, a nature reserve volunteer, Emily Griffiths used another vernacular name, referring to a time when there were 'yards of Buckshorn' in Perkins Beach. Georgina Jackson (see Chapter 4) cites the name 'Knives and Forks' in her *Shropshire Word-Book* of 1879, and also 'Lambs'-Tails' which is descriptive of the cylindrical appearance of the stems.

13   David Hatfield was on the National Nature Reserve staff for many years.

14   Latin names for the three species are, respectively, *Lycopodium clavatum*, *Diphasiastrum alpinum* and *Huperzia selago*. Historical information about clubmosses is drawn from the *Ecological Flora*; recent records are reported in Lockton & Whild (2005 & 2012).

15   Newton (1992 & 2009).

16   Atherton, Bosanquet & Lawley (eds) (2010); Mark Lawley lives in Ludlow and has contributed many Stiperstones bryophyte records.

17   The Latin names for these species are respectively *Scapania scandica*, *Andreaea rothii*, *Racomitrium sudeticum* and *Ptychomitrium polyphyllum*.

18 The Latin names for these species are respectively *Sphagnum capillifolium, S denticulatum* and *S flexuosum.*

19 Latin names for the species of fungi mentioned in this and the preceding paragraph are, respectively, *Hygrocybe coccinea, H ceracea, H conica, H reidii, Clavaria argillacea, Cystoderma amianthinum, Psilocybe semilanceata, Naohidemyces vacciniorum* and *Exobasidium vaccinii.*

20 The darkness of heather-clad hills in winter presumably provides the explanation for the frequency in the Marches of the name 'Black Hill' or 'Black Mountain'. One can conjecture that Blakemoorgate, at the northern end of The Stiperstones was, at one time known as Black Moor Gate, but we know for certain that it has been called Bleakmore Gate (Foxall 1984).

21 In *Fern Ticket to the Magic Forest of The Wrekin* (2004), George Evans of Wellington provides a more oblique reference: 'Fern ticket is an ancient joke that's worth renewing. Any couple seen slipping out of the Forest Glen during a dance, heading for the woods, were asked by friends, "Have you got a fern ticket?" '.

22 *Lutea* = yellow; however, some populations, notably in the Pennines, are purple or purple and yellow, and, although on The Stiperstones part-purple flowers have been seen in the past and still sometimes occur, nowadays at least, the flowers are almost all just yellow.

23 This comment is drawn from speculation by Charles Sinker in the *Ecological Flora* (p 101) that calcite from the spoil-heaps may have been used as a soil improver.

24 This passage comes from Chapter 6 of the *Ecological Flora* (p 101) which was jointly authored by Charles Sinker, Ian Trueman and John Packham, but Ian Trueman confirms that it was Charles Sinker who wrote the passage in question; he was the only one of the authors of the *Flora* whose personal knowledge of Shropshire botany went back to the 1940s.

25 Many a student botanist is indebted to Charles Sinker for his 'A lateral key to common grasses', and for his co-authoring of 'British Water Plants'. He was also an expert on willows and their hybrids and, with A L D Bebbington, devised 'A lateral key to Salix species and hybrids', though this does not appear to have been published (Oswald 2011). His many Stiperstones records include those of both a hybrid willow *Salix x multinervis* and a hybrid grass *Festulolium loliaceum* (Whild & Lockton 2009).

26 Trueman & Millett (2003).

27 This is the same Cliff Lewis who is referred to in the chapters on mining and transport. The first published record of Scottish Laburnum appears to be that of John and Kate Thorne (Shropshire Botanical Society 2002).

28 The wood of Laburnum is particularly beautiful, with the heartwood, described by Mabey (1996) as 'purple-chocolate' in colour, contrasting with the 'pale yellow' of the outer wood, making it sought after in the making of ornamental furniture. But there is no significant tradition of furniture-making in the locality, nor of the making of musical instruments, which is another use to which the wood is said to have been put.

29 In his *Flora of Cardiganshire* Arthur Chater states that in the southwest of that county there are 'probably some hundreds of pure Laburnum hedges'; he believes they were planted for decorative effect. He wonders how toxic it actually is to livestock, and states that he has seen 'horses, sheep, cattle and goats eating shoots in both flower and fruit'. Philip Oswald kindly drew my attention to this reference.

30 In her *Shropshire Word Book*, Georgina Jackson (see Chapter 4), gives the name 'Seyny-tree' (without a 't') for Laburnum and states that 'the leaves are thought to resemble *senna*-leaves, whence the name, *seyny-tree*'. Senna, like Laburnum, belongs to the pea family, and similarities include the seed pods, leaves and flowers; some of the numerous species have medicinal and culinary uses.

31 Brenda Shaw (1917-1975) lived in Curlew country: brought up at the Gravels Post Office she subsequently dwelt at Ritton Place, near The Bog. Her collection of *Shropshire Poems* was published posthumously by her nephew Wynford Wyke and his family.

32 Rothamsted Experimental Station in Hertfordshire has been co-ordinating a national network of moth light-traps of standard design since 1968. This has enabled the generation of national population trends for individual species.

33 Boardman (2007).

34 Kelly (1999); Whild (2002).

Sources

Atherton I, Bosanquet S & Lawley M (eds) 2010

Boardman P 2007

Boardman P (ed) 2010

Chater A O 2010

Cheeseborough I 2007

Evans G 2004

Foxall H D G 1984

Francis P, Price J & Yapp K 2000

Gimingham C H 1972

Jackman E (no date)

Jackson G F 1879-1881

Kelly M 1999

Legg C 1995

Lockton A 2002

Lockton A & Whild S 2005

Lockton A & Whild S 2012

Mabey R 1996

Marren P 2012

Newton M E 1992

Newton M E 2009

Oswald P H 1985

Oswald P H 2011

Packham J & Trueman I 2010

Pearce A (ed) 2008

Pedley I 2009

Peterken G F 1967

Peterken G F & Lloyd P S 1967

Phillips R 2006

Poynton D 1995a

Poynton D 1995b

Price J, Yapp K, Francis P, Jones C & Wall T 2011

Radley J 1961

Rodwell J S (ed) 1991-2000

Shaw B 2012

Shropshire Botanical Society 2002

Shropshire Ornithological Society 1992

Sinker C A 1962

Sinker C A (ed) 1987

Sinker C A, Packham J R, Trueman I C, Oswald P H, Perring F H & Prestwood W V 1985

Smith L 2009

Smith L 2013

Spray M 1981

Trueman I C 2010

Trueman I & Millett P 2003

Wall T 1991

Webb M 1916

Webb M 1917

Webb M 1922

Whild S 2002

Whild S & Lockton A 2009

Wynne G 1986

Chapter 8 'Picking our clothes off the hill': heathland harvests

Notes

1   The Fieldfare is a Blackbird-sized thrush which nests in northern Europe, wintering further south, including in Shropshire.

2   This is the Gilbert Hotchkiss who figures, as a child, in the family photograph on page 90.

3   A 'burthin' is an armful.

4   Hannaford (2006).

Sources

Berry A Q, Gale F, Daniels J L & Allmark B 1996

Bringéus N-A 2001

Evans G circa 1994

Francis P, Price J & Yapp K 2000

Hannaford H R 2006

Jones I M 2009

Price J, Yapp K, Francis P, Jones C & Wall T 2011

Radley J 1961

Sinker C A, Packham J R, Trueman I C, Oswald P H, Perring F H & Prestwood W V 1985

Snailbeach WI 2003

Spray M 1981

Trehane J 2004

Wall T 1992

Webb M 1916

Webb M 1917

Whild S & Lockton A 2009

Chapter 9   'A boundless heath': paradise, devastation and preservation

Notes

1   'Hasty Pudding was made hanging a pot of skimmed milk over the fire and mixing into it a cupful or so of plain flour (often home grown) and a little salt. Nourishing and filling. But I hardly imagine today's children giving it a welcome as we did. Kettle Broth was also a filling meal. Here we had bread broken into a basin, a few chopped chives, a lump of bacon fat or beef dripping (both plentiful in those days) and hot water poured over the lot. Kettle Broth. Well, sneer if you may, but still better than the diet of the workhouse where so many of my parents' generation ended their pitiful lives.' From Bill Francis's diary entry for 26 September 1988.

2   Hannaford (2006).

3   Watson (2002).

4   Chitty (1968).

5   Wall (1908).

6   Hannaford (2006).

7   Pannett (forthcoming). Between the two main blocks of open land lie the areas still identified today as the parish wards of Upper and Nether Heath suggesting that heathland had once dominated a huge tract of land.

8   Miss Merry visited the original Rigmoreoak which lies above Pennerley, immediately adjacent to the open hill. When, in 2004, Natural England established a base on The Stiperstones much further down the slope, I foolishly named it 'Rigmoreoak' too, showing no regard for place-name history and inevitably causing confusion as to which location was meant when the name was used.

9   This was the era of 78 revolutions per minute rather than the 33 of the later 'long playing records'. There would have been less than five minutes of music on each side of a disc, so many discs would have been required for a complete recording of *Messiah*.

10   The three eldest children had been born in the cottage at Rigmoreoak, its location chosen partly, presumably, because of the proximity of water. Apparently this was piped into the house – a significant luxury at the time.

11   Nurse Hand lived at Snailbeach in what is still known locally as the Nurse's Bungalow.

12   Biographical details are taken from her sister Dorothy's *A Merry Family Omnibus* (1974). Dorothy also published *The History of Minsterley* (1976).

13   Price comparisons across time are complex, but the equivalent of a 1948 leasehold cost of £3 would now be in the range of a mere £90 to £380 depending on the terms of tenancy (these figures are for 2011 and come from measuringworth.com).

14   The subsequent planting of conifers stifled the 'masses of heather' which Miss Merry described as dominating the surroundings, the Red Grouse disappeared with the heather, while Curlews are increasingly scarce and Snipe, Lapwing (Peewit) and Nightjar no longer breed in the vicinity. However, both Raven and Buzzard are now frequent.

15   Shaw (2011).

16 Hilda Murrell (1906-1984) had a deep love for the countryside, especially that of the Marches and Wales. Extracts from her nature diaries were edited by Charles Sinker and published in 1987. Her mysterious murder had been a national news story.

17 Walker *et al* (1983).

18 Shropshire Wildlife Trust (1989). The report refers to the loss of 'Prime Site' grassland as equating to 74 miles of football pitches laid end to end, but this appears to be a miscalculation.

19 I gathered the information in this paragraph during a discussion with Ken Stott on 9 November 2009.

20 The Lapwing Act of 1926 prohibited egg collection, so presumably Ted Tuer's employer was the beneficiary of some form of local exemption.

21 From Chapter 51 of *The Golden Arrow* in which Mary Webb compares the 'fir trees' unfavourably with the 'breathless May freshness' of Larch (also a conifer, albeit a deciduous one).

22 The proposal is outlined in a letter of 27/1/67 from the BBC to Shropshire County Council of which there is a copy in Natural England files. Apparently the television mast on The Wrekin is a mere 171 feet tall, so perhaps in that location the mast did not need to be as tall, or the proposal was scaled down.

23 Nature reserves managed directly by Britain's official nature conservation bodies (in England this is now Natural England), or with their formal approval, are 'declared' to be National Nature Reserves; they exist to protect and manage some of the most important wildlife habitats and geological formations in the country.

24 Twenty-five years on, in 2007, the celebration of the anniversary of the opening of the National Nature Reserve included a gathering of some of the primary school children who had been present in 1982. And a new cohort of children, this time from the Mary Webb (secondary) School in Pontesbury, were given the opportunity of working with jazz composer and performer Clark Tracey, in putting together a concert of original music backed by video footage shot by school parent, Ben Osborne, Shell Wildlife Photographer of the Year 2007. Clark then led his quintet in performing *Stiperstones*, the jazz suite which he and pianist Steve Melling had been commissioned to write and perform in 1987 by 'Music at Leasowes Bank' (see Introduction).

25 The quotation comes from Bellamy's foreword to Riley 1991.

Sources

Bellamy D 1991

Bennett K D 1988

Birks H J B 1988

Chitty L F 1968

Evans P 2011

Francis P (ed) 1992

Hannaford H R 2006

Merry D T 1974

Merry J 1979

Pannett D J, Thomas D & Ward R G 1973

Pannett D J (forthcoming)

Shaw B 2011

Shropshire Wildlife Trust 1989

Walker C, Paskell C, Hunter D, Porley R & Phillips G 1983

Wall J C 1908

Watson M 2002

Chapter 10   'Back to (and beyond) purple': conservation and restoration

Notes

1   From *Stiperstones and Thereabouts* (1990). A collection of 40 poems; Shropshire Archives C83 v.f. LS26876.

2   Environmental Stewardship is a government-funded agri-environment scheme that is designed to deliver good environmental management in return for which farmers receive payments. The part of the scheme known as Higher Level Stewardship relates to potentially more demanding requirements and provides higher payments through agreements tailored to local circumstances.

3   Red Grouse once occurred on several hills in Shropshire, but by the 1990s The Stiperstones (including Heath Mynd), The Long Mynd and Brown Clee were the only surviving locations. It is not thought that they breed any longer on Brown Clee. Red Grouse occur sparsely but quite widely in Wales, and the small Black Mountains population of South Wales just creeps over into the upland sliver that lies within Herefordshire but these may be regarded as Welsh rather than English birds. They also occur on Dartmoor and Exmoor but were introduced to both in the twentieth century (Wesley 1988).

4   Various reports were commissioned from the Game Conservancy and the Wildlife Conservation Research Unit, University of Oxford.

5   The most comprehensive review of current knowledge of the Heather Beetle's biology, occurrence and control in the UK is provided by Rosenburgh & Marrs (2010).

6   I am indebted to Simon Cooter, Senior Reserve Manager at The Stiperstones National Nature Reserve, for briefing me in relation to *Phytophthora*.

7   Pywell *et al* (1997).

8   Pywell *et al* (1997).

9   A 'chain-harrow' is a standard agricultural harrow designed to scarify the ground and create a good seed bed. It consists of a 'carpet' of inter-linked chains from which a series of short spikes project; it is towed by horse or tractor.

10   Results from use of the harrow at The Stiperstones have been inconclusive and more trials would be needed to develop this technique into a reliable one.

11   In October 2006 the Rural Development Service and the major part of the Countryside Agency joined with English Nature to form Natural England.

12   Trueman & Cohn (2006).

13   From 'The Stiperstones' written in 2006, along with others by the Border Poets, as a contribution to 'The Lordshill Project' (see 'Revisiting and remembering 'Gone to Earth' in Chapter 5).

14   Other elements of *Once upon a hill* included the conservation of upland grassland, the restoration of stone walls and hedges and the development of self-guided trails from mine sites onto the hill under the title *From mine-shaft to fire-side*.

Sources

English Nature 1995

Francis P (ed) 1992

Francis P, Price J & Yapp K 2000

Griffiths E 1990

Leslie A S (ed) 1911

Merry J 1979

Price J, Yapp K, Francis P, Jones C & Wall T 2011

Pywell R, Pakeman R, Walker K, Manchester S & Barratt D 1997

Rosenburgh A & Marrs R 2010

Sinker C A, Packham J R, Trueman I C, Oswald P H, Perring F H & Prestwood W V 1985

Trueman I C & Cohn E V J 2006

Wall T 1992

Wall T & Clayton C 2008

Webb M 1916

Wesley N A 1988

White W 1860

Bibliography

Adams D, Brown I J & Lake K 2008 Obituaries of Ken Lock. *Below!* 2008.3: 1-2

Alexander J H 1964 *More than Notion*. Fauconberg Press, London. Reprinted, most recently in 1999, by Zoar Publications, Ossett

Allbutt M & Brook F 1969 The Snailbeach Mining Company 1767 to 1911. *Memoirs, Northern Cavern and Mine Research Society*

Allott A 2011 *The Marches.* HarperCollins, London

Anon 1898 *A Short History of Perkins Beach Mine*. Manuscript in Shropshire Archives referenced 4743/45

Armstrong E A 1970 *The Folklore of Birds. An Enquiry into the Origin and Distribution of some Magico-Religious Traditions.* Dover, New York

Ashman G & Bennett G 2000 Charlotte Sophia Burne: Shropshire folklorist, first woman president of the Folklore Society, and first woman editor of 'Folklore'. Part 1: A life and appreciation. *Folklore* 111: 1-21

Atherton I, Bosanquet S & Lawley M (eds) 2010 *Mosses and Liverworts of Britain and Ireland – a field guide.* British Bryological Society

Austin A 2008 Tom Gatford and the Snailbeach Railway. *The Colonel* 92: 8-10

Baker A C 2001 Dennis at Snailbeach. *Industrial Railway Record* 164: 467-470

Bellamy D 1991 Foreword to: Riley A M *A Natural History of the Butterflies and Moths of Shropshire*. Swan Hill Press, Shrewsbury

Bennett G 2001 Charlotte Sophia Burne: Shropshire folklorist, first woman president of the Folklore Society, and first woman editor of 'Folklore'. Part 2: Update and preliminary bibliography. *Folklore* 112: 95-106

Bennett K D 1988 A provisional map of forest types for the British Isles 5000 years ago. *Journal of Quaternary Science* 4: 141-144

Benson W (ed) 1878 *Memoir of the late Samuel Hughes, a Shropshire Miner. With some of his hymns, spiritual songs, and letters.* Hertford

Berry A Q, Gale F, Daniels J L & Allmark B 1996 *Fenn's and Whixall Mosses.* Clwyd County Council, Mold

Birks H J B 1988 Long-term ecological change in the uplands. *In*: Usher M B & Thompson D B A (eds) *Ecological Change in the Uplands*. Blackwell, Oxford

Boardman P 2007 *A provisional account and atlas of the craneflies of Shropshire*. Privately published

Boardman P (ed) 2010 *The Invertebrate Fauna of The Stiperstones area.* Field Studies Council and Natural England

Bradley A G 1905 *In the March and Borderland of Wales*. Constable, London

Briggs K M 1978 The folklore society and its beginnings. *In*: Porter J R & Russell W M S (eds) *Animals in folklore*. Brewer, Ipswich

Bringéus N-A 2001 *Man, Food and Milieu: a Swedish approach to food ethnology*. Tuckwell Press, East Linton

Brook F & Allbutt M 1973 *The Shropshire Lead Mines*. Moorland Publishing, Stafford

Brook F 1976 The Snailbeach Lead Mine, a Company History. *Shropshire Caving and Mining Club Annual Journal*

Brown I J 1976 *The Mines of Shropshire*. Moorland Publishing, Stafford

Brown I J 1990 Burgam: Shropshire's last working metal mine 1957-1963. *Bulletin of the Peak District Mines Historical Society* 11 (2): 80-84

Brown I J 1993 *Snailbeach Lead Mine, near Minsterley, Shropshire. A short history of some of the surface remains*. Shropshire Caving and Mining Club, Telford

Brown I J 1995 Miners' housing in the Shropshire hills. *Shropshire Caving and Mining Club Annual Journal* 3: 46-48

Brown I J 1997 Alfred Hewitt of Snailbeach, lead mine worker 1878-1974. *Below!* 97.3: 4-5

Brown I J 2001a *West Shropshire Mining Fields*. Tempus Publishing, Stroud

Brown I J 2001b Nineteenth century visitors to the South West Shropshire Mines, No 1. *Below!* 2001.3: 6

Brown I J 2001c Nineteenth century visitors to the South West Shropshire Mines, No 2. *Below!* 2001.4: 8

Brown I J 2002 Nineteenth century visitors to the South West Shropshire Mines, No 3. *Below!* 2002.1: 4

Brown I J 2003 Nineteenth century visitors to the South West Shropshire Mines, No 8. *Below!* 2003.2: 17

Brown I J 2005a Nineteenth century visitors to the South West Shropshire Mines. *Below!* 2005.2: 5

Brown I J 2005b *A list of fatal accidents in Shropshire Mines from 1850-1979*. Shropshire Caving and Mining Club, Account no 24

Brown I J 2005c Clifford Lewis 1923-2004. *Below!* 2005.1: 8-9

Brown M J F 1971 *Glacial geomorphology of Montgomeryshire and West Shropshire*. PhD thesis, University of London

Burne C S 1883, 1885, 1886 *Shropshire folk-lore: a sheaf of gleanings edited by Charlotte Sophia Burne from the collections of Georgina F Jackson*. In three parts. Trübner, London

Byford-Jones W 1937 *The Shropshire Haunts of Mary Webb*. Wilding, Shrewsbury

Carter F 1926 *The Dragon of the Alchemists*. Elkin Mathews, London

Carter F 1931 *The Dragon of Revelation*. Harmsworth, London

Carter F 1932 *D H Lawrence and the Body Mystical*. Archer, London

Chater A O 2010 *Flora of Cardiganshire*. Privately published, Aberystwyth

Cheeseborough I 2007 *Dragonfly Survey of The Stiperstones, 2006 and 2007*. Report to Natural England

Chitty L F 1968 Recorder's Report on Archaeology. *Transactions of the Caradoc & Severn Valley Field Club for the years 1961-67* 16: 43-84

Clark R 1994 Tors, rock platforms and debris slopes at Stiperstones, Shropshire, England. *Field Studies* 8: 451-472

Clark R G 1998 *Frederick Carter ARE. A study of his etchings*. Apocalypse Press, Guildford

Coles G M 1978 *The Flower of Light: a biography of Mary Webb*. Duckworth, London (second edition 1998, Headland, Wirral)

Coles G M 1990 *Mary Webb*. Seren, Bridgend

Collie M & Diemer J 1995 Murchison in Moray, a geologist on home ground. *Transactions of the American Philosophical Society*: 85 (3)

Colonel Stephens Society 2011 *Colonel Stephens: some fascinating facts*

Corfield M 1955a Some superstitions associated with the Stiperstones district. *Shropshire Magazine* January: 26-27

Corfield M 1955b The Devil's Chair, famous Shropshire Landmark. *Shropshire Magazine* February: 22-23

Corfield M 1961 Lord Tankerville's Stay in Stiperstones. Perilous journey through the Boat Level. *Shropshire Magazine* January: 21-22.

Critchley J & Paterson D (no date) *Border Lands, Shropshire and the Welsh Marches.* Peak Publishing, London

Cuckson A 2001 'Fernhill' – The Snailbeach Barclay. *Industrial Railway Record* 164: 463-466

Cuckson A 2004 The Parrys and Central Stores. *Shropshire Caving and Mining Club Journal* 9: 13-18

Dean W T 1967 Relationships of the Shelve trilobite faunas. *In*: Whittard W F 1966 The Ordovician trilobites of the Shelve Inlier, West Shropshire. *Palaeontographical Society (Monograph)* 9: 308-320

Dickins G 1987 *An illustrated literary guide to Shropshire*. Shropshire Libraries, Shrewsbury

Dictionary of National Biography

Earp J R & Hains B A 1971 *The Welsh Borderland* (Third edition). British Regional Geology. HMSO London

Edmundson H 2004 *Gone to Earth. Based on the novel by Mary Webb*. Nick Hern Books, London

Ellis D 1998 *D H Lawrence: dying game, 1922-1930*. Cambridge University Press

English Nature 1995 *The Stiperstones Upland: a conservation and restoration strategy*. English Nature, Shrewsbury

Evans G circa 1994 *A Voice from the Hills*. Privately published, Minsterley

Evans G 2004 *Fern Ticket to the Magic Forest of The Wrekin*. Wellington Civic Society

Evans Pat 1997/8 A brief history of brass bands in the Snailbeach District. *Stiperstones Brass Newsletter* December 1997 and January 1998

Evans Pat 2002 *Poetic Landscapes*. Tankerville Gallery, Pennerley

Evans Paul 2011 The Living Edge. *In*: National Trust *The Living Edge. A wanderer's guide to Wenlock Edge*. National Trust, Church Stretton

Fisk P 1990 *Midnight Blue.* Lion, Oxford

Forrest H E 1899 *The Fauna of Shropshire*. Wilding, Shrewsbury

Foxall H D G 1984 *Field name maps for Worthen Parish*. Shropshire Archives

Francis P (ed) 1992 *Hasty Pudding and Kettle Broth. Extracts from the diaries of Bill Francis of Minsterley*. Francis & Francis, Snailbeach

Francis P (no date)a *The Stiperstones Lead Mines*. Riddles of the Past

Francis P (no date)b *The Story of Wild Edric*. Riddles of the Past

Francis P 2003 Revelations in Pontesbury. *Snailbeach District News* 193: July

Francis P, Price J & Yapp K 2000 *Never on a Sunday. Memories of the Stiperstones mining communities*. Scenesetters, Bucknell

Fraser A 1983 On The Stiperstones. *In*: *Poet's England – 14. Shropshire*, 1994 (compiled by N Griffiths & J Waddington-Feather). Brentham Press, St Albans

Gandy C 1989 Biographical Introduction to a new edition of Gandy I 1970 *An Idler on the Shropshire Borders*. Sutton Publishing, Gloucester

Gandy I 1970 *An Idler on the Shropshire Borders*. Wilding, Shrewsbury

Gelling M 2000 Place names. *In*: Leonard J, Preshous D, Roberts M, Smyth J & Train C (eds) *The Gale of Life*. Logaston Press, Almeley

Gibbons S 1932 *Cold Comfort Farm*

Gimingham C H 1972 *Ecology of Heathlands*. Chapman & Hall, London

Goudie A S & Piggott N R 1981 Quartzite tors, stone stripes and slopes at The Stiperstones, Shropshire, England. *Biuletyn Periglacjalny* 28: 47-56

Griffiths E 1990 *Stiperstones and Thereabouts*. Privately published

Haffey D 1999 *The Stiperstones: visitors, residents and conservation*. 'Background Studies', a report to English Nature by Countrywise

Hands M J 2012 *The Broken Shield.* Austin & Macauley, London

Hannaford H R 2006 *The Stiperstones Hills Archaeological Survey: a report for land management purposes*. Shropshire County Council Archaeology Service Report Number 238-3

Hardy T 1878 *The Return of the Native*

Hardy T 1891 *Tess of the D'Urbervilles*

Hilder R 1987 *Rowland Hilder Country. An artist's memoir*. The Herbert Press, London

Hooson W 1747 *The miner's dictionary. Explaining not only the terms used by miners but also containing the theory and practice of that most useful art of mineing, more especially of lead-mines. Being observations made by the author from more than forty years practice*

Horton S 1937 *Rainbow Farm*. Epworth Press, London

Horton S 1938 *The Chapel on the Hill*. Epworth Press, London

Hughes J 1977 *Shropshire folklore, ghosts and witchcraft*. Westmid Supplies, Shrewsbury

Jackman E (no date) *Mary Webb and the Natural History of her Countryside.* Privately published

Jackson G F 1879-1881 *Shropshire word-book, a glossary of archaic and provincial words, etc., used in the county*. Trübner, London

Jones I M 2009 *Stiperstones Child. The childhood recollections of life in Pennerley in the 1920s.* Privately published

Kelly M 1999 *Metal resistance in trees and their potential for the remediation of metal-contaminated land*. BSc dissertation, Coventry University

Lapworth C 1887 The Ordovician rocks of Shropshire. *Report of the British Association for the Advancement of Science* 56 C: 661-663

Lawrence D H 1925 *St Mawr*. Secker, London

Lawrence D H 1931 *Apocalypse*. Heinemann, London

Lawrence D H 1995 *Apocalypse and the writings on Revelation*. Edited, with an introduction and notes by Mara Kalnins. Penguin Books, London

Legg C 1995 Heathland dynamics: a matter of scale. *In*: Thompson D B A, Hester A J & Usher M B *Heaths and Moorland: cultural landscapes*. HMSO, Edinburgh

Lerry G G 1952 Henry Dennis: a Cornish captain of Welsh industry. *Denbighshire Historical Society Transactions* 1: 33-45

Leslie A S (ed) 1911 *The Grouse in Health and Disease.* Smith, Elder & Co, London

Lewis J 1978 *Rowland Hilder, painter and illustrator*. Barrie & Jenkins, London

Lewis M 2003 *Edith Pargeter – Ellis Peters*. Seren, Bridgend

Lloyd-Morgan G 2000 The Venus shrine. *In*: Ellis P (ed) *The Roman Baths and Macellum at Wroxeter. Excavations by Graham Webster 1955-85.* English Heritage Archaeological Report 9

Lockton A 2002 Rare Plants. *Shropshire Botanical Society Newsletter* 7: 4-7

Lockton A & Whild S 2005 *Rare Plants of Shropshire*. Third edition. Shropshire Botanical Society, Montford Bridge

Lockton A & Whild S 2012 Recording report: all about clubmosses. *Shropshire Botanical Society Newsletter* Spring 2012: 7-8

Mabey R 1996 *Flora Britannica*. Sinclair-Stevenson, London

Mais S P B 1939 *Highways and Byways in the Welsh Marches*. Macmillan, London

Map W *De Nugis Curialium* translated (1923) by M R James. Honourable Society of Cymmrodorion, London

Marren P 2012 *Mushrooms*. British Wildlife Publishing, Gillingham

Merry D T 1974 *A Merry Family Omnibus*. Privately published

Merry J 1979 *The Rock: reminiscences to share with those who enjoy the Stiperstones*. Onny Press, Church Stretton

More J 1978 *A Tale of Two Houses*. More, Shrewsbury

Morgan J S 1999 *The Colonel Stephens' Railways: a view from the past*. Allan Publishing, Shepperton

Morgan R 1997 *Welsh Place-Names in Shropshire*. Morgan, Cardiff

Morton G H 1869 The geology and mineral veins of the country round Shelve, Shropshire. *Proceedings of the Liverpool Geological Society 1868-9*

Mulroy B (no date) *Carving by Candlelight. A history of Holy Trinity Church, Middleton*. Reproduced from *Country Quest Magazine*

Murchison R I 1835 On the Silurian System of Rocks. *London and Edinburgh Philosophical Magazine* 7: 46-52

Murchison R I 1839 *The Silurian System founded on geological researches in the counties of Salop, Hereford, Radnor, Caermarthen, Brecon, Pembroke, Monmouth, Gloucester, Worcester, and Stafford; with descriptions of the coal-fields and overlying formations*. Murray, London

Murchison R I 1854 *Siluria*. Murray, London

National Trust 2005 *Open Countryside. Report of the Access Review Working Party*

Newton M E 1992 *The Stiperstones and The Hollies SSSI: Bryophyte Survey*. Report to English Nature

Newton M E 2009 *The Stiperstones and The Hollies SAC: Bryophyte Survey*. Report to Natural England

Nicholas J D 1990 The Old Haunted Hogstow Hall. *Shropshire Magazine* January: 22-23

'Nimrod' 1837 *Memoirs of the life of the late John Mytton, Esq of Halston, Shropshire, formerly M.P. for Shrewsbury, High Sheriff for the counties of Salop and Merioneth, and Major of the North Shropshire Yeomanry Cavalry; with notices of his hunting, shooting, driving, racing, eccentric and extravagant exploits*. Methuen, London

O'Hanlon M 1996 *The Complete Lone Pine*. O'Hanlon, Worcester

O'Hanlon M 2001 *Beyond the Lone Pine Club. A Biography of Malcolm Saville*. O'Hanlon, Worcester

Oswald P H 1985 History of botanical recording. *In*: Sinker C A *et al Ecological Flora of the Shropshire Region*. Shropshire Trust for Nature Conservation, Shrewsbury

Oswald P H 2011 Charles Adrian Sinker OBE MA FIBiol (1931-2010). *BSBI Yearbook*: 82-86 (with additions)

Packham J & Trueman I 2010 Charles Sinker OBE (1931-2010). *Bulletin of the British Ecological Society* 41: 36-37

Palmer R 2004 *The Folklore of Shropshire*. Logaston Press, Almeley

Pannett D J (forthcoming) Commons of the Stiperstones Mining District. *Transactions of the Shropshire Archaeological and Historical Society*. Typescript seen courtesy of the author

Pannett D J, Thomas D & Ward R G 1973 Farm patterns in the Stiperstones mining district: I. Field method and historical analysis. *Field Studies* 3: 763-782

Pearce A (ed) 1995 *Mining in Shropshire*. Shropshire Books, Shrewsbury

Pearce A (ed) 1997 *Metal Mines of Shropshire*. Shropshire Caving and Mining Club, Account no 22

Pearce A (ed) 2008 *Snailbeach Lead Mine*. Shropshire Mines Trust

Pedley I 2009 *The Lichen Communities of The Stiperstones NNR and The Hollies*. Report to Natural England

Perrin J 1986 *On and Off the Rocks*: *Selected Essays 1968-1985*. Gollancz, London

Perrin J 2003 Stone Circle, Sickle Moon. *The Great Outdoors*, March 2003

Peterken G F & Lloyd P S 1967 Biological flora of the British Isles: *Ilex aquifolium*. *Journal of Ecology* 55: 841-858

Peterken G F 1967 The Hollies, Stiperstones. *Shropshire Conservation Trust Bulletin* XI: 12-13

Peters E 1964 *Flight of a Witch.* Collins, London

Peters E 1999 *Ellis Peters' Shropshire*. Sutton Publishing, Stroud

Phillips R 2006 *Mushrooms*. Macmillan, London

Piggott N R 1977 Witches' stones on Shropshire crags. *Geographical Magazine* 49: 772-775

Pither R G 2003 *Guide to St George's Church, Pontesbury*

Powell M 1992 *Million-Dollar Movie*. Heinemann, London

Poynton D 1995a *Olethreutes mygindiana* – new to Shropshire. *Entomologist's Record* 106: 73-74

Poynton D 1995b *Olethreutes mygindiana* in South Shropshire and its suspected parasitoid *Glypta gracilis* – new to Britain. *Entomologist's Record* 107: 307-309

Price J, Yapp K, Francis P, Jones C & Wall T 2011 *Once Upon a Hill. The lost communities of the Stiperstones*. Scenesetters, Welshpool, on behalf of Natural England

Pywell R, Pakeman R, Walker K, Manchester S & Barratt D 1997 *Habitat Restoration Study: The Stiperstones*. Institute of Terrestrial Ecology for English Nature

Radley J 1961 Holly as a winter feed. *Agricultural History Review* 9: 89-92

Redd D 2012 *Ida Gandy (1885-1977) Rural Author and Playwright*. Geiriau Gardd Aderyn, Haverfordwest

Redwood C 1981 *The Weston, Clevedon and Portishead Railway*. Sequoia Publishing, Weston-super-Mare

Reid Chappell W 1930 *The Shropshire of Mary Webb*. Palmer, London

Ridge R 1937 *Shropshire Highland Folk Tales*. Shrewsbury Chronicle

Rodwell J S (ed) 1991-2000 *British Plant Communities*. Cambridge University Press

Rohde S 1999 *L S Lowry, a biography*. Third edition. The Lowry Press, Salford

Rolt L T C 1994 *Sleep No More. Railway, Canal and other stories of the Supernatural*. Sutton Publishing, Stroud

Rosenbaum M 1996 Stone runs in the Falkland Islands. *Geology Today*, July-August: 151-154

Rosenburgh A & Marrs R 2010 *The Heather Beetle: a review. Report to the Heather Trust*. University of Liverpool

Ross J 2000 Letters of Dr Henry Graves Bull to Thomas Blashill 1864 to 1885. *Transactions of the Woolhope Naturalists' Field Club* 50: 82-89

Saville M & O'Hanlon M 1998 *The Silent Hills of Shropshire*. O'Hanlon, Worcester

Saville M 1943 *Mystery at Witchend.* Newnes, London

Saville M 1944 *Seven White Gates*. Newnes, London

Saville M 1949 *Lone Pine Five*. Newnes, London

Saville M 1953 *The Neglected Mountain.* Newnes, London

Saville M 1962 *Not Scarlet But Gold.* Newnes, London

Sharrock J T R 1976 *The Atlas of Breeding Birds in Britain and Ireland*. British Trust for Ornithology, Tring

Shaw B 2011 *Shropshire Poems. Walk With Me through the enchanted Stiperstones Hills.* Privately published

Shaw M 2007 The Shropshire barytes industry. *In*: Poyner D, Browning A, Lake K (eds) *NAMHO conference proceedings, 2006*. Shropshire Caving and Mining Club

Shaw M 2009 *The Lead, Copper and Barytes Mines of Shropshire*. Logaston Press, Almeley

Shropshire Botanical Society 2002 First County Records. *Shropshire Botanical Society Newsletter* 7: 3

Shropshire Mines Trust Newsletters

Shropshire Ornithological Society 1992 *An atlas of the breeding birds of Shropshire*. Shropshire Ornithological Society, Shrewsbury

Shropshire Wildlife Trust 1989 *Losing Ground in Shropshire.* Shropshire Wildlife Trust, Shrewsbury

Simpson J 2003 *Folklore of the Welsh Border*. Tempus, Stroud

Silouan, Priest-Monk 2011a *Wisdom Songs*. Theotokos Press

Silouan, Priest-Monk 2011b *Wisdom and Wonder*. Theotokos Press

Silouan, Priest-Monk 2013 *Wisdom, Prophecy and Prayer*. Theotokos Press

Sinclair J B & Fenn R W D 1999 Geology and the Border Squires. *The Radnorshire Society Transactions* 69: 143-172

Sinker C A (ed) 1987 *Hilda Murrell's Nature Diaries 1961-1983*. Collins, London

Sinker C A 1962 The north Shropshire meres and mosses, a background for ecologists. *Field Studies* 1 (4): 101-138

Sinker C A, Packham J R, Trueman I C, Oswald P H, Perring F H & Prestwood W V 1985 *Ecological Flora of the Shropshire Region*. Shropshire Trust for Nature Conservation, Shrewsbury

Smith B 1922 Lead and zinc ores in the pre-carboniferous rocks of west Shropshire and north Wales. *Memoirs of the Geological Survey*. HMSO, London

Smith L 2009 *The Birds of The Stiperstones: Breeding Bird Survey Report 2004-07*. Unpublished report to Natural England

Smith L 2013 The Stiperstones Breeding Bird Survey 2004-2007. *The Shropshire Bird Report 2007*: 9-13

Snailbeach WI 2003 *Wednesday … was baking day*. Scenesetters, Bucknell

Spray M 1981 Holly as fodder in England. *Agricultural History Review* 29: 97-110

Strange P 1989 *The Weston, Clevedon and Portishead Railway: a pictorial record.* Twelveheads Press, Truro

Sustins N 2008 *Wild Edric. A narrative poem.* Marchland Books, Wentnor

Taylor K, Anderson P, Taylor R, Longden K & Fisher P 2005 *Dogs, access and nature conservation.* English Nature Research Report No 649. Peterborough

The Colonel Stephens Museum *A short history of the Snailbeach District Railways* www. hfstephens-museum.org.uk Accessed 5/11/12

Thomson D 1993 *Showman. The life of David O Selznick*. André Deutsch, London

Timperley H W 1947 *Shropshire Hills*. Dent, London

Toghill P 1992 The Shelveian event, a late Ordovician tectonic episode in Southern Britain (Eastern Avalonia). *Proceedings of the Geologists' Association* 103: 31-35

Toghill P 2006 *Geology of Shropshire*. Second edition. The Crowood Press, Marlborough

Tonge S 2007 *Shropshire Ghost Stories*. Sutton Publishing, Stroud

Tonks E S 1950, 1974 *The Snailbeach District Railways*. Privately published, 1950; revised in 1974 when published by The Industrial Railway Society. The Society re-printed the 1974 version in 2007 with brief notes and a statement of minor corrections

Trehane J 2004 *Blueberries, Cranberries and other Vacciniums*. Timber Press, Cambridge

Trueman I C & Millett P 2003 Creating wild-flower meadows by strewing green hay. *British Wildlife* 15: 37-44

Trueman I C & Cohn E V J 2006 *A study of management for Mountain Pansy* Viola lutea *at The Stiperstones NNR, Shropshire*. A report to Natural England by the University of Wolverhampton

Trueman I C 2010 Charles Adrian Sinker OBE. *Shropshire Wildlife Trust Magazine* Spring: 8

Tudor G (ed) circa 2000 *Shropshire's Century Speaks*. Shropshire Books, Shrewsbury

Trumper D 2001 *Britain in Old Photographs. South Shropshire.* Sutton Publishing, Stroud

Waite V 1970 *Shropshire Hill Country*. Dent, London

Walker C, Paskell C, Hunter D, Porley R & Phillips G 1983 *Habitat Loss in the Stiperstones Area 1979-1982*. Shropshire Trust for Nature Conservation, Occasional Paper no 2

Wall J C 1908 Ancient Earthworks. *In*: Page W (ed) *The Victoria County History of Shropshire*. Vol 1. Constable, London

Wall T & Clayton C 2008 *The Stiperstones NNR Management Plan, 2008-2013*

Wall T 1991 Managing veteran holly trees – a preliminary note. *In*: Read H J *Pollard and Veteran Tree Management*. Corporation of London, London

Wall T 1992 The Red Grouse in Shropshire. *Shropshire Naturalist* 1 (2): 18-23

Wall T 2003 Shropshire Ravens on a roll. *British Wildlife* February: 160-166

Watson M 2002 *Shropshire, an archaeological guide*. Shropshire Books, Shrewsbury

Weale M 1935 *Through the Highlands of Shropshire on Horseback*. Heath Cranton, London

Weaver R 1977 More about Snailbeach. *Industrial Railway Record* 70: 13-17

Webb M 1916 *The Golden Arrow*. Constable, London

Webb M 1917 *Gone to Earth*. Constable, London

Webb M 1922 *Seven for a Secret*. Hutchinson, London

Webb M 1924 *Precious Bane*. Cape, London

Webb M 1929 *Armour Wherein He Trusted*. Cape, London

Webb M 1977 *Collected Prose and Poems* (ed G M Coles). Wildings, Shrewsbury

Webb M 1987 *Selected Poems* (ed G M Coles). Second edition. Headland, West Kirby

Wesley N A 1988 *Red Grouse*. *In*: Sitters H P (ed) *Tetrad Atlas of the Breeding Birds of Devon*

Westwood J 1985 *Albion. A Guide to Legendary Britain*. Granada, London

Whild S 2002 The vegetation of the Stiperstones mines. *Shropshire Botanical Society Newsletter* 6: 9-10

Whild S & Lockton A 2009 *The Flora of The Stiperstones*. The University of Birmingham & the Shropshire Botanical Society

White R 2000 The Roman Lead Workings at Linley. *In*: Leonard J, Preshous D, Roberts M, Smyth J & Train C (eds) *The Gale of Life. Two thousand years in south-west Shropshire*. Logaston Press, Almeley

White W 1860 *All round the Wrekin*. Chapman & Hall, London

Whittard W F 1966 The Ordovician trilobites of the Shelve Inlier, West Shropshire. *Palaeontographical Society (Monograph)* 8: 265-306

Whittard W F (compiled by W T Dean) 1979 An account of the Ordovician rocks of the Shelve Inlier in west Salop and part of north Powys. *Bulletin of the British Museum Natural History (Geology)* 33: 1-69

Williams W H 1967 The Eve of St Thomas. *Shropshire Magazine* January: 34-35

Wood J 1944 *Quietest Under the Sun*. Museum Press, London

Wright T 1862 On the local legends of Shropshire. *Collectanea Archaeologica* 1: 50-66

Wright T 1872 *Uriconium: a historical account of the ancient Roman city*. Longmans, Green & Co, London

Wynne G 1986 Review of the *Ecological Flora of the Shropshire Region*. *Watsonia* 16: 102-103

Index

H